ORGANISED POLITICS, LAW AND PRACTICE

This is the first comprehensive guide to the rules of organised political activity in Britain and the standards of conduct expected of those involved in it.

Organised politics involves not only political parties (their members, leaders, officials, and elected representatives in local and national governments) but also trade unions, charities, lobbyists and others. This book codifies the statutory and case law regulating their activity, including much not addressed elsewhere.

It provides detailed and practical guidance on establishing and operating political parties, the rights of party members and powers of committees, electing party leaders, selecting candidates, party discipline, controlling political factions, holding meetings, political campaigning by charities and trade unions, lobbying, Parliamentary conduct and standards, and other matters.

This accessible guide is designed for those needing to ensure that political office-holders act lawfully, for those who want to hold them to account, for lawyers, politicians (eg MPs, peers, local councillors, mayors, and electoral candidates) ordinary party members and others involved in political activity, and for students and everyone interested in how politics works.

Organised Politics, Law and Practice

Tom Gillie

•HART•
OXFORD • LONDON • NEW YORK • NEW DELHI • SYDNEY

HART PUBLISHING

Bloomsbury Publishing Plc

Kemp House, Chawley Park, Cumnor Hill, Oxford, OX2 9PH, UK

1385 Broadway, New York, NY 10018, USA

29 Earlsfort Terrace, Dublin 2, Ireland

HART PUBLISHING, the Hart/Stag logo, BLOOMSBURY and the Diana logo are trademarks of Bloomsbury Publishing Plc

First published in Great Britain 2024

A catalogue record for this book is available from the British Library.

A catalogue record for this book is available from the Library of Congress.

Library of Congress Control Number: 2024940208

ISBN: PB: 978-1-50996-915-9
HB: 978-1-50996-911-1
ePDF: 978-1-50996-913-5
ePub: 978-1-50996-912-8

Typeset by Compuscript Ltd, Shannon

To my parents and to John

PREFACE

There has been no text to which people may turn to discover the rules governing political parties' internal affairs, the conduct of their members, and political activity of other organisations. This book aims to fill that gap.

It is intended to complement many admirable works already available about politics and about the law; and I have generally avoided duplicating what can be found there, for example, in *Schofield's Election Law* and *Parker's Law and Conduct of Elections*, which serve those who wish to know about the rules of public elections. The contents pages provide a detailed overview of what is covered here. The focus is on Britain, but important differences between Northern Ireland and the rest of the United Kingdom are pointed out where necessary.

I have written this book against a backdrop of unusually acrimonious, and well publicised, divisions within the main political parties. Those divisions have generated complaints of unlawfulness to the courts and intervention by statutory regulators.

Political parties are crucial intermediaries between the public and the state; their good governance is important generally for democracy. A thread running through the book relates to the balance that must be struck between political expediency on one hand, and, on the other, transparency, fairness, equality, and good faith. I hope that the chapters which follow contribute, at least in some small way, to a better understanding of how political activity should be conducted.

I would like to thank those who commented on various drafts of the text, including Karon Monaghan KC and Dr Richard Thompson. Thanks are also due to my practice team at Matrix Chambers and to my editors at Hart Publishing.

Tom Gillie
23 April 2024

CONTENTS

1

The Right to Organise

I. Introduction

1.1 Political parties are special. Among all the private bodies in the UK (clubs, trade unions, companies, partnerships, religious institutions etc) they alone have the ability to assume control of the legislature and government. The members of political parties therefore have an important and responsible position in society; they choose candidates for Parliament and local government, select party leaders, and may become MPs. In short, political parties are fundamental to the UK's system of democracy. This chapter is about the rules and laws that protect their existence and people's rights to be members of them. Those protections underpin many of the rights of political organisation examined elsewhere in this book.

1.2 There are three significant areas of legal recognition set out in this chapter. We begin with the recognition afforded by Parliament to the parliamentary wings of political parties. The parliamentary parties are, in one sense, the most basic element of political organisation. By organising their members in Parliament, parties are able directly to control (or at least to influence) majorities in the House of Commons and the House of Lords, change national legislation and exercise control over who becomes the Prime Minister. Nonetheless, the rules of Parliament largely ignore the fact and status of political parties; though some statutory provisions recognise that the positions of Prime Minister, the Leader of the Opposition and their respective Chief Whips are linked fundamentally to the parliamentary parties. The second part of this chapter addresses the recognition of political parties under the UK's constitution. The constitution is not expressed in a single written document. Much of it comprises well known legal principles developed since the seventeenth century; a period of several hundred years in which political parties have been active and dominant. Unsurprisingly, given that context, basic constitutional legal principles allow for the maintenance of political parties, even if the constitution does not expressly guarantee their existence.

1.3 The third part of this chapter explains how Article 11 of the European Convention on Human Rights (ECHR), the right to freedom of association, protects the rights of parties and their members. The ECHR is a charter of fundamental rights established by the Council of Europe (which is older than, and separate from, the European Union). Article 11 has direct legal effect in the UK via the Human Rights Act 1998. The right to freedom of association enumerated by Article 11 is a fundamental one. It articulates the clearest legal protection of political parties' rights to carry on political activity in concert with members. It protects the rights of parties to compete in elections without undue interference from the state and without oppression or coercion, allows parties to decide their own membership and to operate autonomously from government; and protects the right of individuals to undertake political activity within parties and also to refuse to be a member of a party. These protections are the bedrock of modern parliamentary democracy and everybody in the political sphere should be familiar with them.

II. Political Parties' Status in Parliament

1.4 Modern political parties developed within Parliament, especially within the House of Commons, to support religious and landowning interests and, later, the interests of the working class, and other interests. The Conservative Party and the Liberal Party were born from factions among MPs and Members of the Lords; their extra-parliamentary parties emerged later.[1] The Labour Party and the smaller parties founded themselves outside Parliament. For almost a century, however, the Labour Party's fundamental aim has been to maintain a political organisation in Parliament representing labour.[2] Smaller parties typically strive to return MPs to the Commons even if they have other

[1] Political parties began in Great Britain with loose political associations of MPs in Parliament. Those groups started with no extra-parliamentary elements or organisation. It was not until after the Reform Acts of the mid-nineteenth century that political associations across the country at large really got going – principally to support political groupings in Parliament and to register electors on the new electoral rolls. The emergence of political party organisations outside Parliament is, therefore, a relatively recent phenomenon in the long history of parliamentary democracy. The Labour Party only introduced uniform constituency Labour Parties in 1918. A collection of Conservative working men's clubs and other associations emerged in the 1870s and formed the National Union of Conservative and Constitutional Associations, though it was not until the late nineteenth century that the Conservative Party established constituency organisations predicated on uniform models and rules. The other extant parliamentary parties established themselves with standard constituency and regional party structures later, in the twentieth century.

[2] 'Its purpose is to organise and maintain in Parliament and in the country a political Labour Party': *Labour Party Rule Book* (as amended from time to time), Ch 1, cl I.2.

political ambitions in local or regional government. In modern times Parliament and political parties have developed a symbiotic relationship. The operation of parliamentary democracy today relies on political parties to supply the electorate with a choice of candidates to be MPs. The main parties depend on amassing sufficient numbers of MPs and Members of the Lords to control majorities in both Houses to pass legislation and change the law. The parties rely on obtaining sufficient sympathetic MPs so that their leaders may command the support of the Commons and assume the office of Prime Minister (or to support a larger party's attempts to do so, as the case may be).

1.5 The presence of the parliamentary parties within the House of Commons, and their respective party machinery, is largely disregarded by the Commons' standing orders.[3] There is statutory recognition of the fact and necessity of the Official Opposition in both the Commons and the Lords, including by the provision of financial assistance to it (Short money[4]). Legislation recognises and defines the offices of Leader of the Opposition and the Opposition Chief Whip so that those people may be paid salaries. The statutory definition of the Leader of the Opposition implies some recognition of the parliamentary parties: the Leader of the Opposition is the leader of 'the party in opposition to Her Majesty's Government having the greatest numerical strength in the House of Commons'.[5] Jurisprudence has recognised explicitly the importance of parliamentary political parties: it is by acting as part of a political party that MPs are able to engage in coherent and effective political activity and the maintenance of a parliamentary majority (though not necessarily a majority held exclusively by their own party[6]); and it is by acting as part of a political party that they are open to being held accountable to the electorate.[7]

1.6 The structure and rules of each parliamentary party are dictated by political parties' own internal constitutions, which are governed by the law of contract (see Chapter 2 on the establishment of parties). The rules governing the rights and duties of a party's MPs or peers in respect of each other are a private contractual matter for each political party; they have nothing to do with the rules and standing orders of Parliament.[8] Two points common to all parliamentary parties are their management by party whips, who are also MPs or peers, and the parliamentary party's oversight by party-political

[3] *Erskine May: Parliamentary Practice*, 25th edn (LexisNexis, 2019) Pt 1, Ch 4, para 4.5.

[4] Short money (named after Edward Short, who proposed the funding) is the name given to funding to support opposition political parties in the Commons. It has three elements: funding to assist opposition parties to carry out their parliamentary business; funding for the opposition parties' travel and associated expenses; and funding for the running costs of the Leader of the Opposition's office. Similar funding is provided to the Opposition in the Lords, referred to as 'Cranborne money'. For an explanation of the operation of the Short money scheme see R Kelly, 'Short Money' (House of Commons Library, 8 June 2023).

[5] Ministerial and other Salaries Act 1975, s 2(1); see also Minsters of the Crown Act 1937.

[6] ie the support of a shared majority in coalition, as with the National Government of 1931–1940, the wartime government 1940–1945 and the Conservative Party–Liberal Democrat coalition of 2010–2015; or a confidence and supply arrangement by a smaller party in favour of a larger one, eg the Lib-Lab Pact of the late 1970s and the DUP's confidence and supply agreement with the Conservative Party in 2017, when the DUP agreed to support the government on all motions of confidence; and on the Queen's Speech, the budget, finance bills, money bills, supply and appropriation legislation and estimates.

[7] *McClean v First Secretary of State* [2017] EWHC 3174 (Admin), [2018] 1 Costs LO 37 at para 30 per Sales LJ.

[8] See Ch 2 for the constitution and rules of political parties.

committees comprised of MPs and peers.[9] The effect of that common management structure is that the activities of each parliamentary party are governed by itself autonomously and not substantially by the remainder of the party existing outside Parliament. The managerial autonomy of parliamentary parties is necessary to ensure that MPs' freedom of action in Parliament is not fettered or limited by the external party organisation, an outside body.[10]

III. Protection under the Constitution

1.7 The principles of the UK's constitution do not expressly protect the position of political parties.[11] Nonetheless, the following constitutional principles are consistent with the basic proposition that people should be free to organise within political parties, as well as to challenge the executive by participating in public elections through party political activity.

1.8 The first principle encapsulates a fundamental idea of political freedom: Parliament should be free in its election, free in its advice; and its members, once elected, serve the whole realm.[12] That ancient freedom is the constitutional foundation that has permitted the emergence and maintenance of a representative party system in Britain.

1.9 Second, Parliament is the nexus of the political system and it uniquely controls rights of political participation generally, and of political parties specifically. The right to participate in the democratic regime has for centuries been derived from statute. Statutory obligations govern parties' activities in public elections[13] and permit trade unions and other organisations to fund political parties. Parliament has provided for a legally enforceable charter of fundamental rights, including the right of political parties to enjoy freedoms of association and expression without unnecessary state interference, by passing the Human Rights Act 1998. The Supreme Court has recognised that it is not the common law but Parliament that delineates the boundaries of political participation. To adopt the words of Baroness Hale: 'expansion of the franchise, from the great Reform Act of 1832 onwards, has been the creation of Parliament'.[14] As Lord Hodge put it in an

[9] See Ch 7 for the operation of the party whip and the relationship between the parliamentary party and a political party's wider organisation.

[10] House of Commons Resolution of 15 July 1947, amended on 6 November 1995 and 14 May 2002: Conduct of Members: 'It is inconsistent with the dignity of the House, with the duty of a Member to his constituents, and with the maintenance of the privilege of freedom of speech, for any Member of this House to enter into any contractual agreement with an outside body, controlling or limiting the Member's complete independence and freedom of action in Parliament or stipulating that he shall act in any way as the representative of such outside body in regard to any matters to be transacted in Parliament'.

[11] It is interesting to note, for example, that the main legislation governing the conduct of elections (ie the Representation of the People Act 1983) has evolved from mid-Victorian statutes and does not recognise the role political parties play in public elections. It was not until the year 2000 that the government enacted legislation that expressly acknowledged and regulated the role played by political parties themselves in election campaign spending (ie the Political Parties, Elections and Referendums Act 2000).

[12] *Osborne v Amalgamated Society of Railway Servants (No 1)* [1910] AC 87 at 112 per Lord Shaw.

[13] ie the Political Parties, Elections and Referendums Act 2000 and subsidiary regulations.

[14] *Moohan v Lord Advocate* [2014] UKSC 67, [2015] AC 901 at para 56 per Lady Hale.

important case about prisoners' voting rights, Parliament 'controls the modalities of the expression of democracy'.[15] Only Parliament, therefore, has the power to impede the creation and maintenance of the parliamentary parties.

1.10 The third principle is that political parties are the primary unit of political organisation and collective expression in Britain's representative system of government. Thus, 'party politics is the lifeblood of representative democracy'.[16] That recognition mirrors the principles developed by the European Court of Human Rights in respect of the ECHR: parties have an essential role in a democratic regime.[17] The common law and Convention law are closely aligned in this respect, which is unsurprising given that judges seek to apply the common law consistently with the ECHR where possible; and especially where the common law is uncertain, unclear or incomplete.[18]

1.11 Fourth, human rights, the rule of law and democracy are interlinked. The common law recognises this as the liberal democratic tradition in which Parliament legislates. The common law recognises the fundamental rights necessary for any political party to coalesce and to function. Acts of Parliament should not be seen in a vacuum: Parliament has 'legislated for a liberal democracy founded on particular constitutional principles and traditions'.[19] So, to take the establishment of the devolved legislatures by way of example, 'Parliament cannot have been taken to have intended to establish a body which was free to abrogate fundamental rights or to violate the rule of law'.[20] Democracy is a concept which the common law has sought to protect by the incremental development of a system of safeguarding fundamental rights. The protection of human rights, democracy and the rule of law are interwoven and all part of the domestic legal system.[21] Within this fabric of the rule of law the common law has long recognised the right to freedom of speech and freedom of assembly: 'the right of free speech is one which it is for the public interest that individuals should possess, and, indeed, that they should exercise without impediment, so long as no wrongful act is done';[22] and there is an 'undoubted right of Englishmen to assemble together for the purpose of deliberating upon public grievances'; to quote the famous jurist Lord Denning, 'our history is full of warnings against suppression of these rights'.[23]

1.12 The political neutrality of the sovereign is an additional important principle. It is not necessary to deal further with this self-explanatory concept here, save to note that

[15] ibid per Lord Hodge at para 34.

[16] *Cruddas v Calvert* [2015] EWCA Civ 171, [2015] EMLR 16 at para 18.

[17] eg *Socialist Party v Turkey* (1999) 27 EHRR 51; *Republican Party of Russia v Russia* (2015) 61 EHRR 20.

[18] 'If, and to the extent that, development of the common law is called for, such development should ordinarily be in harmony with the United Kingdom's international obligations and not antithetical to them': *A v Secretary of State for the Home Department (No 2)* [2005] UKHL 71, [2006] 2 AC 221 at para 27 per Lord Bingham.

[19] *AXA General Insurance Ltd and Others v HM Advocate* [2011] UKSC 46, [2012] 1 AC 868.

[20] ibid at para 153 per Lord Reed.

[21] *Moohan* [2015] AC 901 at para 86 per Lord Kerr.

[22] *Bonnard v Perryman* [1891] 2 Ch 269 per Lord Coleridge CJ.

[23] *Hubbard and Others v Pitt and Others* [1976] QB 142 per Lord Denning MR at 178. See also *Hirst and Agu v Chief Constable of West Yorkshire* (1987) 85 Cr App R 143 at 151 per Otton J.

it is a vital feature of the constitutional settlement that the monarch cannot be seen to favour one political party above another.[24]

1.13 In giving effect to the legal principles set out above, the courts have a responsibility to uphold the values and principles of the constitution. The courts determine the legal limits on government power and decide whether an exercise of power has overstepped those limits.[25] The constitutional principles developed by the common law are not confined only to the protection of individual rights but also include principles about the conduct of public bodies and the relationship between them.[26]

1.14 In theory, the courts could declare as unconstitutional legislation that sought heavily to restrict, or ban, the right of rival political parties to compete in public elections and to challenge the government. That is theoretically so because the courts have a responsibility to declare legislation unlawful if that legislation were passed abusively to entrench a government's position by curtailing the franchise or by a similar device.[27] The importance of that responsibility finds clear expression in a judgment of Baroness Hale determining prisoners' rights to the franchise: 'If there is a Constitution, or a Bill of Rights, or even a Human Rights Act, which guarantees equal treatment in the enjoyment of its fundamental rights, including the right to vote, it would be the task of the courts, as guardians of those rights, to declare the unjustified exclusion unconstitutional'.[28] Nonetheless, only in extreme circumstances would a court declare legislation validly passed by Parliament to be unconstitutional.[29]

IV. Protections under the European Convention on Human Rights

A. The Right to Freedom of Association

1.15 Political parties and individuals alike enjoy the right to associate freely without unjustified state interference. The right is guaranteed by Article 11 ECHR, which secures freedom of association with others, as well as the right to freedom of peaceful assembly. The right may be limited where it is necessary to do so in a democratic society to respond to various social needs. Article 11 provides:

> 1. Everyone has the right to freedom of peaceful assembly and to freedom of association with others, including the right to form and to join trade unions for the protection of his interests.

[24] *R (Evans) v Attorney General* [2015] UKSC 21, [2015] AC 1787 at para 181 per Lord Wilson.
[25] *R (on the application of Miller) v Prime Minister* [2019] UKSC 41, [2020] AC 373.
[26] ibid at paras 39–40 per Lady Hale.
[27] *Moohan* [2015] AC 901 at para 35 per Lord Hodge. Note, though, that the ability of the courts to strike down legislation is a matter that has been explored in the abstract and which, unsurprisingly therefore, has not been settled conclusively.
[28] *R (Chester) v Secretary of State for Justice and Another* [2013] UKSC 63, [2014] AC 271 at paras 88–90 per Lady Hale.
[29] *AXA General Insurance Ltd and Others v HM Advocate* [2011] UKSC 46 at 49 per Lord Hope.

2. No restrictions shall be placed on the exercise of these rights other than such as are prescribed by law and are necessary in a democratic society in the interests of national security or public safety, for the prevention of disorder or crime, for the protection of health or morals or for the protection of the rights and freedoms of others. This Article shall not prevent the imposition of lawful restrictions on the exercise of these rights by members of the armed forces, of the police or of the administration of the State.

1.16 In practice, the right to freedom of association is closely related to the right to freedom of expression under Article 10 of the ECHR, which is also a qualified right. For a political party it is not just the right to associate with those of a similar political persuasion that matters, but also the right to express the party's political programme and for its members to engage in political speech. Both freedoms, alongside the other rights in the Convention, have direct effect in UK law via the Human Rights Act 1998. The Human Rights Act is no ordinary law: it is a legally enforceable charter of human rights, securing for everyone within the UK's jurisdiction the fundamental freedoms that are enshrined in the European Convention on Human Rights and entrenched by the UK's ratification of the Convention.[30] The Human Rights Act 1998 achieves this by various mechanisms. First, it requires courts to interpret primary and secondary legislation compatibly with the rights guaranteed by the ECHR, so far as it is possible to do so.[31] Second, it permits courts to declare that legislation is incompatible with the Convention. Although such declarations are incapable of striking down a statute, they should encourage the government and Parliament to reconsider and to amend legislation that is incompatible with the Convention.[32] Third, the Act requires courts, along with all other public authorities, to act compatibly with Convention rights.[33] This means that courts must give effect to Convention rights so far as it is possible to do so when they apply the common law, determine legal disputes or grant legal remedies. Fourth, the Act requires a government minister in charge of a Bill in Parliament to make a statement certifying that, in her opinion, the Bill is compatible with the Convention rights before the Bill's second reading; if it is not, then she must positively state that the government wishes Parliament to press ahead with the passage of the Bill nonetheless.[34]

B. Application of Article 11 to Political Parties

1.17 Political parties themselves, as well as the individuals who comprise them, enjoy the right to freedom of association. It is important that they do: the European Court of Human Rights has repeatedly emphasised that democracy depends on the right to freedom of association; and one of the most important parts of the right is that individuals should be able to form a collective entity to act in their common interest.[35] The manner

[30] A Lester et al, *Human Rights Law & Practice*, 3rd edn (LexisNexis, 2009) para 2.05.

[31] Human Rights Act 1998, s 3.

[32] ibid s 4.

[33] ibid s 6.

[34] ibid s 19.

[35] The fact that political parties' activities form part of a collective exercise of freedom of expression in itself entitles them to enjoy the protection of Arts 10 and 11: *United Communist Party of Turkey v Turkey* (1998) 26 EHRR 121 at paras 42 and 43.

in which national legislation enshrines this freedom, as well as its practical application by the state, reveals the condition of a country's democracy.[36] Freedom of association is one of the basic conditions for a democratic society's progress.[37] There is no doubt that political parties come within the scope of Article 11: they are a form of association essential to the proper functioning of democracy,[38] and democracy is the only system of government compatible with the ECHR.

1.18 Political parties' capacity to implement public policies on assuming power differentiates them from other types of organisations which undertake activities in the political arena.[39] States have an obligation to hold free and fair elections that will ensure the free expression of the opinion of the people in the choice of the legislature.[40] The European Court of Human Rights has held that any such free expression is inconceivable without the participation of a plurality of political parties that represent the different shades of opinion found within the population. Thus, political parties make an irreplaceable contribution to the political debate that lies at the heart of the concept of a democratic society.[41] The protections afforded to political parties by Article 11, seen through the lens of Article 10, are therefore broad and important. It is precisely because political parties are essential to the functioning of democracy that any measure taken against them affects democracy itself.[42] The protection of Article 11 lasts for the entirety of a party's life.[43]

C. Parties' Rights under Article 11

1.19 The right to freedom of association guarantees the internal organisational autonomy of political parties. A party has the right to draw up its own rules, administer its own affairs, decide who should be granted or retain membership and to determine how to organise its party conferences,[44] free from unjustified state interference.[45] The right to freedom of expression entitles a party member to express her opinions on internal party matters generally; and the right of freedom of association entitles her to influence the policies and actions of the party (see, for example, the analogous case of *Unison v Kelly* concerning union members' rights).[46] The first modern domestic case to examine the extent of political party members' rights under Article 11 in detail concerned a challenge to the Green Party in the county court in 2024. In that case, the court framed the right of party members more widely than in *Unison v Kelly*, taking Articles 9, 10 and 11 of the ECHR together. The county court decided that

[36] *Republican Party of Russia v Russia* (2015) 61 EHRR 20 at para 75.
[37] *Sidiropoulos v Greece* (1999) 27 EHRR 633 at para 48.
[38] *United Communist Party of Turkey v Turkey* (1998) 26 EHRR 121 at para 25.
[39] *Republican Party of Russia v Russia* (2015) 61 EHRR 20 at para 106; *Ouranio Toxo v Greece* (2007) 45 EHRR 277 at paras 27 and 28; *Refah Partisi v Turkey* (2003) 37 EHRR 1 at para 87.
[40] ECHR, Art 3 of the First Protocol.
[41] *United Communist Party of Turkey v Turkey* (1998) 26 EHRR 121 at para 44.
[42] *Republican Party of Russia v Russia* (2015) 61 EHRR 20 at para 78.
[43] *United Communist Party of Turkey v Turkey* (1998) 26 EHRR 121 at para 33.
[44] *Republican Party of Russia v Russia* (2015) 61 EHRR 20 at para 88.
[45] *Cheall v UK* (1985) 8 EHRR 74.
[46] *Unison v Kelly* [2012] IRLR 442 (EAT) at para 44. It also includes the right of associations, as well as individuals, to free speech: Clayton and Tomlinson, *The Law of Human Rights* (Oxford University Press, 2009) para 16.96.

the Convention not only guarantees political party members the right to advocate or oppose particular policies or positions, but also to criticise other party members who act inconsistently with such policies and positions, even using language which political opponents might find offensive; and to advocate and organise within the party to promote members who support shared policies and positions and against members who do not.[47] The court's decision is not binding on other courts or tribunals but it is broadly consistent with the treatment of party members' rights in *Unison v Kelly* and by the Equality and Human Rights Commission.

1.20 Article 11 includes a negative aspect: the freedom not to associate with others.[48] The negative right applies to parties as much as it does to individuals, so individuals must not be forced to join a political party[49] and political parties must not be forced to accept members who do not share their fundamental values and objectives.[50]

D. The State's Positive Obligation to Guarantee the Proper Functioning of Political Parties

1.21 States have a positive obligation to secure the effective enjoyment of the right to freedom of association so far as political parties are concerned, not merely a duty not to interfere with them. A crucial element of that positive obligation is to guarantee the proper functioning of a political party even if the party annoys others or pursues lawful ideas or claims that others find offensive or which shock or disturb. It is important that parties are not deterred from openly expressing opinions about controversial issues affecting the electorate by violence or threats of violence. Members of political parties must be permitted to hold meetings without having to fear that their opponents will subject them to physical violence and without the protection of the police authorities and other organs of the state. A party's opponents, of course, have a right under Articles 10 and 11 to demonstrate against it, but that right cannot be used to impede a party's right to freedom of association.[51]

E. Interference by the State

1.22 Freedom of association is not an absolute right, which means that state authorities may restrict it in accordance with the second paragraph of Article 11. That totalitarian

[47] *Ali v Reason* (unreported, 9 February 2024) county court, claim number J00CL858.

[48] *Sorensen v Denmark* (2008) 46 EHRR 29 at para 54.

[49] See ibid and by analogy cases concerning the trade union practice of the 'closed shop', which contravenes Art 11.

[50] See *Cheall v UK* (1985) 8 EHRR 74.

[51] *Ouranio Toxo v Greece* (2007) 45 EHRR 277 (ECtHR) at para 30. That case involved a political party in Greece that promoted the rights of Macedonians. The party put a sign outside its offices in Macedonian. The Greek police removed the sign. The party put up another sign. That evening, a crowd which included the local mayor and local councillors held a gathering outside the party's offices and shouted threats. The next day the premises were set on fire. The party claimed that it had telephoned the police, who had told them that no officers were available to assist them.

movements have masqueraded under the guise of political parties, prospered under a democratic regime and torn down a democratic state is a matter of recent European history.[52] The state's power to intervene to restrict a party's freedom of association may, in fact, be a significant means to protect the democratic system. A political party must not be allowed to benefit from the rights of freedom of association and expression to subvert the democratic order or to undertake activities designed to destroy the rights and freedoms in the Convention and thus attempt to bring about the destruction of democracy. This means that states have the power under Article 11 to protect their institutions and the rights of individuals in their jurisdiction where a political party's activities, or the intentions it declares explicitly or implicitly in its programme, jeopardise democracy and the fundamental rights of other people.[53]

1.23 Nevertheless, the state's power to curb the activities of political parties must be used sparingly and the exceptions to the right set out in paragraph 2 of Article 11 must be construed strictly. Only convincing and compelling reasons can justify restrictions on the freedom of political parties and states have only a limited margin of appreciation[54] in this area.[55]

F. Dissolution and Proscription of Political Parties

1.24 The dissolution of a political party is a drastic step that requires especially compelling justification. Where the reason relied on is the pressing social need that, otherwise, there is a risk to the state's democratic principles or institutions, courts will concentrate on three factors.[56] Courts may take into account the historical background and the political and social context of a country in its analysis of those factors.[57]

1.25 The first factor is whether there is plausible evidence that the risk to democracy is sufficiently imminent. National authorities have a power of preventative action. The state cannot be required simply to wait until a party has started to take concrete steps to implement a policy incompatible with democracy and fundamental rights. The authorities may act to forestall the execution of such a policy before an attempt is made to implement it, where the presence of a danger to civil liberties or democracy has been established by national courts and detailed scrutiny.[58]

[52] *Refah Partisi v Turkey* (2003) 37 EHRR 1.
[53] *Republican Party of Russia v Russia* (2015) 61 EHRR 20 at para 76; *Refah Partisi v Turkey* (2003) 37 EHRR 1 at para 96.
[54] The term 'margin of appreciation' refers to the space for manoeuvre that the European Court of Human Rights, and associated organs, are willing to grant national authorities in fulfilling their obligations under the ECHR.
[55] *Republican Party of Russia v Russia* (2015) 61 EHRR 20; *Sidiropoulos v Greece* (1999) 27 EHRR 633 at para 48; *Refah Partisi v Turkey* (2003) 37 EHRR 1 at para 96.
[56] *Refah Partisi v Turkey* (2003) 37 EHRR 1 at para 104.
[57] *Ireland v United Kingdom* (1979–80) 2 EHRR 25.
[58] *Refah Partisi v Turkey* (2003) 37 EHRR 1 at paras 103–104.

1.26 The second factor is whether anti-democratic acts, intentions and speeches of a party's leaders and members can be imputed to the party as a whole. A party's political programme may deliberately conceal aims and objectives to do away with democracy and it may in fact have intentions contrary to or different from the ones it formally proclaims. That is why the content of the party's programme must be compared with the actions of the party's leaders and the positions they defend, as well as the party's practical actions.[59] It has been held that the role of party leader or chairman is emblematic. One should perceive remarks on politically sensitive issues by the leader as reflecting the party's views unless the leader declares that this is not the case. Similarly, the European Court of Human Rights has recognised the practical reality of the roles of a party's MPs and elected mayors or government officials: their spoken words are likely to influence voters and are potentially more effective in achieving unlawful ends than abstract words written in a manifesto. Acts and speeches by these people are likely to be imputable to a party unless the party distances itself from them.[60]

1.27 The third factor is whether the acts and speeches imputable to the political party form a whole and give a clear picture of a proposed model of society which is incompatible with the concept of a democratic society. A platform that questions the way in which a state is currently organised, but which does not harm democracy itself, does not justify penalisation or dissolution; the essence of democracy is to allow diverse political programmes to be proposed and debated.[61] A party is entitled to promote a change in the constitutional structures of the state on two conditions: that the means used to achieve the proposed change are legal and democratic; and, second, that the change itself is compatible with fundamental democratic principles. A party will act incompatibly with the Convention, and therefore may not rely on the protections of Article 11, in circumstances where its leaders incite violence; or promote policies that fail to respect democracy, or which are aimed at destroying it, or which flout the rights and freedoms recognised as necessary for a democracy.[62] The name a political party adopts cannot in principle justify a measure as drastic as dissolution, but it may justify a refusal to register the party with that name.[63] (See Chapter 2 for registration of political parties in the UK.)

1.28 There are relatively few examples of a government dissolving or proscribing political parties in the UK, but it has happened. In 1939 the government banned the British Union of Fascists under regulations subordinate to the Emergency Powers Act 1939;[64] a number of people were detained for being members of the BUF.[65] Sinn Fein

[59] ibid at para 101 and *United Communist Party of Turkey v Turkey* (1998) 26 EHRR 121 at para 58.

[60] *Refah Partisi v Turkey* (2003) 37 EHRR 1 at paras 113 and 115. The fact that a party has only recently been founded and has not had an opportunity to undertake much or any political activity is a factor that tends to suggest that penalisation for its conduct would be unjustified: *United Communist Party of Turkey v Turkey* (1998) 26 EHRR 121 at 58.

[61] See *Socialist Party v Turkey* (1999) 27 EHRR 51 at para 47.

[62] *Refah Partisi v Turkey* (2003) 37 EHRR 1 at para 98.

[63] *United Communist Party of Turkey v Turkey* (1998) 26 EHRR 121 at para 54.

[64] Ie The Defence (General) Regulations 1939, SR & O 1939/927.

[65] See for example *R v Secretary of State for Home Affairs, ex p Lees* [1941] KB 72; *R v Secretary of State for Home Affairs, ex p Budd* [1942] KB 14.

was banned under Northern Ireland's Civil Authorities (Special Powers) Act (Northern Ireland) 1922, from the 1950s until the middle of the 1970s. In 1984 the then Secretary of State for Northern Ireland indicated in Parliament that the government would not hesitate to proscribe Provisional Sinn Fein if the circumstances warranted it.[66]

1.29 Various political groups employing violent means or advocating them have been proscribed under the Terrorism Act 2000 (for example, the various paramilitary organisations operating in Northern Ireland).[67] Under section 11 of the Terrorism Act 2000 it is a criminal offence to belong, or to profess to belong, to a proscribed organisation. It is also an offence to support a proscribed organisation or to arrange a meeting to support it or to further its activities.[68] Section 13 of that Act bans a person from wearing clothing or carrying or displaying articles in public so as to arouse a reasonable suspicion that he is a member or supporter of a proscribed organisation. The aim of this latter provision is to ensure that proscribed organisations do not obtain a foothold in the UK through the agency of people in this country; section 13 of the Terrorism Act 2000 is a justified interference with Article 10 of the Convention even though the former is not designed to prevent an immediate threat of violence or disorder.[69]

[66] *Hansard* HC Deb, vol 68, cols 1074–75, 29 November 1984.
[67] ie pursuant to the powers under the Terrorism Act 2000, s 3.
[68] Terrorism Act 2000, s 12.
[69] *Pwr v DPP* [2022] UKSC 2, [2022] 1 WLR 789 at para 77.

2

Establishing a Political Party

I. Introduction

2.1 People who want to be elected to public office under a common banner need to organise as a political party registered with the Electoral Commission. Only political parties can field common candidates, so they are the primary vehicle for organised political activity in Britain. They are by no means the only vehicle. Political pressure can be exerted by trade unions, lobbyists, political clubs and charities. Chapters 8 and 9 address particular rules that affect those secondary groups. A political association that is not registered as a party cannot lawfully stand candidates in its own name; its members must stand as independents – and independent candidates rarely win.

2.2 The law regulates the establishment and organisation of political parties. Anyone who wishes to form a political party and compete in elections must comply with legal rules about the party's constitution, organisational structure and membership. The Political Parties, Elections and Referendums Act 2000 (PPERA 2000) governs the party's financial structure, its officers and how its candidates are referred to on nomination and ballot papers; and those matters are regulated by the Electoral Commission.[1]

2.3 Section II of this chapter explains how people may establish a political party with members, committees, representatives and so forth. The section also addresses the party's constitution, a crucial document that governs the relationship between a party and its members and gives the party legal authority to organise its affairs. Section III sets out how, once established, a political party may obtain legal recognition as such so that it can contest elections lawfully.

II. Establishment

A. Legal Arrangements

2.4 A political party may adopt any legal structure it wishes, but it will plainly want to avoid constituting itself as a body prohibited from undertaking the political activity necessary to fight elections.[2] Another important consideration is whether the party is to be an incorporated or unincorporated body. An incorporated body has a legal personality, ie it is a single legal entity that can enter into legal relations and be sued – or sue – in its own name. Companies are incorporated bodies, and UKIP and Reform UK are examples of parties that are companies.[3] Political parties that decide to establish themselves as companies must follow the rules set out in the Companies Act 2006, and their affairs will be governed by articles of association and statutory directors. Co-operative societies are another example of incorporated bodies, and the Co-operative Party is an incorporated co-operative society registered under the Co-operative and Community Benefit Societies Act 2014 (and subject to a degree of regulation by the Financial Conduct Authority).[4] UKIP, Reform UK and the Co-operative Party, as incorporated bodies, differ in that respect from the larger British political parties.

2.5 The Conservative Party, the Labour Party, the Liberal Democrats and the Scottish National Party are all unincorporated associations. As such they have no legal personality of their own. They are each simply a group of people bound together by a contract. The association is a collective of its members and it has no legal status distinct

[1] Parties' campaign spending and funding are also closely regulated: see R Price and V Sedgley, *Parker's Law and Conduct of Elections* (LexisNexis, looseleaf); B. Posner et al, *Schofield's Election Law* (Sweet & Maxwell, looseleaf), and see Ch 3.VII.

[2] eg a charity or trade union: see Ch 8.

[3] UKIP Constitution, cl 2.2.2. Reform UK is registered as a company with Companies House under the number 11694875.

[4] *Co-operative Party Rule Book*, cl 17.14.

from them. But its members may agree that one or several among them will undertake the activities of the collective on behalf of all (or sometimes particular sections) of the membership, including entering into legal relations and dealing with property. The association may sue or be sued in a representative capacity: ie one member acts as a representative of all the others. Unincorporated associations are subject to relatively little legal regulation of their internal affairs.

2.6 Some unincorporated political parties have subsidiary companies established to hold real property or money. For example, Labour Party Properties Limited deals with the Labour Party's real property assets and the Conservative Party Foundation Limited manages an endowment fund that provides investment income to the Conservative Party. Various subsidiary political organisations that are affiliated to the main parties also exist as companies (for example, the Association of Conservative Clubs or the Socialist Health Association Limited).

B. The Party's Constitution

i. Generally

2.7 Every political party must have a constitution for two reasons. First, the party must have a constitutional instrument to govern its relationship with members, elected representatives and others, and to set out what the party is going to do. The constitution is a multilateral membership contract which binds all the party's constituent parts together (members, local parties, etc).

2.8 Second, a prerequisite for registration with the Electoral Commission is that the party send a copy of its constitution to the Commission along with its application to be on the register of political parties.[5] For those purposes the constitution is the document or documents by which the structure and organisation of the party is determined.[6] The Electoral Commission is not, however, concerned with a party's compliance with its constitution; that is a matter for the courts. In fact a party might depart quite entirely from the rules it provides to the Commission. That happened in the case of Lutfur Rahman and his party, Tower Hamlets First. There, Mr Rahman's 2014 election victory as Mayor of Tower Hamlets was vitiated by his corrupt and illegal practices under electoral law. In passing, the court found that the constitution which Tower Hamlets First had provided to the Electoral Commission in fact formed no part of the running of the party.[7]

2.9 Electoral legislation in Britain and Northern Ireland does not require a political party's constitution to contain any particular rules. This presents a point of difference from those European jurisdictions in which democracy has been more recently established. Germany, Portugal and Spain have detailed requirements for political parties'

[5] PPERA 2000, Sch 4, Pt I, para 5(1)(a).
[6] ibid s 26(9).
[7] See *Erlam v Rahman* [2016] EWHC 111 (Ch), [2016] 2 P & CR DG5.

rules and internal voting systems codified in legislation.[8] Those statutory arrangements mandate a minimum level of democracy in internal decision-making. The UK has no equivalent legislation.

2.10 For the most part, political parties exist as unincorporated associations and there are no statutory requirements that dictate what the contents of their constitutions should include.[9] Where a party exists as an incorporated body, however, the party's constitution should comply with the requirements and parameters mandated for such bodies.[10] Note that the constitution of a political party established as a company is very likely to be set out elsewhere than the company's articles of association. The constitution is likely to be a separate document comprising rules made under the authority of the articles. In other words, the political party's constitutional document (regulating members, candidates, discipline etc) will be a different legal instrument to the *company's* constitution (and the latter is likely to be relevant only so far as it provides for the establishment and maintenance of the company as a legal entity).[11]

2.11 Various parties refer to their respective constitutions as 'the rule book', for this is what the constitution is: the rules that govern the party, its subordinate party units, members and representatives. The constitution is simply, in law, a contract, and it is governed by contract law. Nevertheless, the context in which the contract operates is peculiar: the regulation of political activities in the political arena.

ii. Whom Does the Constitution Bind?

2.12 Where the party is an unincorporated association, the constitution amounts to a multilateral contract between an individual member on one side and the mass of collective membership on the other side.[12] Where the party is incorporated, the constitution amounts to a contract between a member on one side and, on the other, a company rather than a membership collective.[13]

2.13 The primary contractual function of the rules of an unincorporated association is to set out the terms of the contract between an individual member and all the other members *en masse*. This means that the constitution does not create contractual relations and obligations between two individual members that can give rise to a claim for

[8] See, for example, Gesetz über die politischen Parteien (Parteiengesetz), Arts 8–16 (Germany's Political Parties Act). The position in Spain is similar: see Ley Orgánica 6/2002, de 27 de junio, de Partidos Políticos, num. 154, Articulo 3.

[9] But the political party may have subordinate or associated organisations that are incorporated. Of course, those subordinate organisations must comply with the strictures of the legislation that governs them. Such subordinate organisations are not the registered political party but they may be a component part of it.

[10] eg the Companies Act 2006 or, in the case of co-operative societies, the Co-operative and Community Benefit Societies Act 2014, s 14.

[11] eg UKIP, which has a lengthy constitution of rules made under the power afforded by its articles of association.

[12] See *Anderton & Rowland (A Firm) v Rowland* (1999) Times, 5 November (QB); *Nutting v Baldwin* [1995] 1 WLR 201; *Howell v Evans* [2020] EWHC 2303 (QB).

[13] *UKIP v Hardy* [2011] EWCA Civ 1204 para 8.

breach of contract or a claim for damages if broken (except if the rules expressly provide for that eventuality in clear terms).[14] The rules have vertical effect between the party and an individual member, not horizontal effect between different individual members.[15] So, one member cannot sue another member personally for breaking the party's rules. The position in respect of a company's articles is slightly different. It has been held that the contract creates a legal relationship between one member and another member so that one member may sue a director-member personally for a breach of the director-member's obligations. The extent to which that principle holds good between ordinary members of a mass-membership organisation is less clear, however; it is doubtful that the principle will apply in all circumstances.[16]

iii. Ignorance of Rights or Obligations under the Rule

2.14 The constitution is the source of the rights and obligations of members and party officers. The benefits of membership therefore flow from the terms of that contract.[17] A member becomes subject to the contractual effect of the rules when she joins the party. She joins the party on the basis that she will be bound by the rules, if accessible, whether or not she has seen them and even if she is not aware of the rules' particular provisions. A member cannot argue that she has not 'agreed' to be bound by a rule of the party purely because she was, or is, unaware of it or does not agree that it is appropriate.[18]

iv. Implied Rule of Rationality and Good Faith

2.15 The constitution contains contractual terms that are not expressly set out within it. These are 'implied terms', the source of which is the common law.[19] A significant implied term is the obligation on the party or its officers to exercise discretionary powers under the rules rationally, in good faith and without arbitrariness or capriciousness. This obligation is sometimes known as the 'Braganza term' after the Supreme Court case in which it was set out: *Braganza v BP Shipping Ltd*.[20] The Braganza term applies to the exercise of contractual powers generally, not just in the contracts of membership of political parties. An irrational exercise of a contractual power, for these purposes, amounts to conduct or a decision which no reasonable person having the relevant power could have undertaken or reached; or a decision that excludes obviously relevant considerations or takes into account extraneous, irrelevant factors. The precise extent of

[14] *Anderton & Rowland (A Firm) v Rowland* (1999) Times, 5 November (QB); *Howell v Evans* [2020] EWHC 2303 (QB); *UKIP v Hardy* [2011] EWCA Civ 1204.

[15] 'Unless either there is a sufficiently clear expression of that intention in the rule, or it is necessary that it have direct contractual effect between the members in order to give effect to the rule': *Howell v Evans* para 58.

[16] *Rayfield v Hands* [1960] Ch 1, [1958] 2 WLR 851.

[17] *UKIP v Hardy* [2011] EWCA Civ 1204; *Conservative and Unionist Central Office v Burrell* [1982] 1 WLR 522 (CA); *Evangelou v McNicol* [2016] EWCA Civ 817 (re the Labour Party); *Ramsay v Hackett Pain* [2020] EWHC 3655 (Ch) (re the Conservative Party).

[18] *Evangelou v McNicol* [2016] EWCA Civ 817; *Choudhry v Treisman* [2003] EWHC 1203 (Comm); *John v Rees* [1970] Ch 345.

[19] In some circumstances terms are implied by statute but none is relevant here to political party membership contracts.

[20] *Braganza v BP Shipping Ltd* [2015] UKSC 17, [2015] 1 WLR 1661.

the obligation depends on the contract in question. In *Evangelou v McNicol* the Court of Appeal set out that the Braganza term presents a potent limit on the otherwise broad powers of a political party's governing committee.[21] It has been recognised, though, that a binary, factual and objective decision (for example a disciplinary decision following a factual investigation) is to be treated differently from a more subjective, political decision (for example, whether a person should be selected as a party candidate). The latter would require something exceptional to render a political judgement irrational.[22] An implied duty on the part of political bodies to take decisions in good faith and without arbitrariness or capriciousness has been recognised at least since the Victorian era, for example, in the case of *Hopkinson v Marquis of Exeter* (concerning the expulsion of a Conservative Club member who had pledged to vote for various Liberal Party candidates in the 1865 general election).[23]

v. Rules Implied by Custom and Practice

2.16 A party's constitution does not account for every eventuality. Officers have powers that are prescribed by the rules without setting out the way in which the powers should be exercised. Nevertheless, the party may have developed longstanding procedures which are not formally set out in the rules, though well understood by the officers and committees who operate them. In such circumstances a procedure may become part of the rules by implication through custom and practice.[24] For that to happen, the practice must be certain, well-established and unquestioned.[25] If so, the practice will become effective as though actually written in the rules on condition that the authority to take a particular type of action is not excluded by the rules and the implied term would not have the effect of overriding an express term of the rules.[26] The constitutions of political parties and trade unions are in this respect analogous.[27] Examples of terms implied by custom and practice in trade union constitutions include allowing a union to suspend rules relating to its branches where remedial supervision by the regional party was required;[28] and the implication of a rule to preclude a member who would be

[21] *Evangelou v McNicol* [2016] EWCA Civ 817 para 47.

[22] *Rothery v Evans* [2021] EWHC 577 (QB) (re the Labour Party); *Hayes v Pack* [2022] EWHC 2508 (KB) (re the Liberal Democrats).

[23] *Hopkinson v Marquis of Exeter* (1867–68) LR 5 Eq 63. See also *Richardson-Gardner v Fremantle* (1870) 24 LT 81; *Dawkins v Antrobus* (1879) 17 Ch D 615; *Lambert v Addison* (1882) 46 LT 20.

[24] *Heatons Transport (St Helens) Ltd v Transport General Workers Union* [1973] AC 15, [1972] ICR 308 (HL); *Kelly v Musicians Union* [2020] EWCA Civ 736; *Unison v Street* UKEAT/0256/13/LA (appropriate to imply a term allowing the union to suspend rules relating to branches where supervision by the regional party was required); *GMB v Stokes* UKEAT/0769/03/ILB (rule implied to preclude from nomination for the position of Deputy General Secretary a member who would be unable to serve a sufficient time in office because of impending retirement). While there are no reported cases in which the courts have implied into the constitution of a political party a rule by way of custom and practice, the legal principles governing the constitutions of trade unions and political parties are so closely analogous that the courts have reaffirmed the contractual position of each by referring to the cases relating to the other.

[25] *Lewis v Heffer* [1978] 1 WLR 1061; *Choudhry v Treisman* [2003] EWHC 1203 (Comm).

[26] *Heatons Transport (St Helens) Limited v Transport General Workers Union* [1973] AC 15, [1972] ICR 308 (HL); *Taylor v National Union of Mineworkers (Derbyshire Area)* [1985] IRLR 99.

[27] See for example *Kelly v Musicians Union* [2020] EWCA Civ 736 at para 35: 'Our attention was drawn to the decision of this Court in *Evangelou v McNicol* [2016] EWCA Civ 817. Although that case did not concern a trade union, as it concerned the Labour Party, the judgment of Beatson LJ helpfully summarised the relevant principles'.

[28] *Unison v Street* UKEAT/0256/13/LA.

unable to serve a sufficient time in office from nomination for the position of General Secretary.[29] Note that where a constitution contains a prohibition against doing anything contrary to the rules, the rules are not only the express written rules but also those which have to be implied by custom and practice.[30]

vi. Implied Rule to Treat Members Fairly

2.17 The courts have implied into political party constitutions a duty to treat members fairly and an implied power to re-open disciplinary proceedings if justice so requires. These are addressed in more detail in Chapter 6 (selecting candidates) and Chapter 12, Section III (party membership disciplinary procedures).

vii. Changing the Constitution

2.18 The constitutional rules can be altered only in accordance with the constitution and the procedures set out in the rules themselves.[31] For example, the Labour Party and the SNP require amendments to be carried by their respective party Conferences. The Conservative Party requires amendments to be carried by its Constitutional College.[32] Where a company amends its articles it must send to the registrar a copy of the articles as amended no later than 15 days after the amendment takes effect or risk a fine.[33] Registered co-operative and friendly societies must register a constitutional amendment with the Financial Conduct Authority[34] otherwise the amendment will not be valid.[35] In all cases, the party must notify the Electoral Commission of any amendments to its constitution on an annual basis.[36]

III. Registering to Undertake Political Activity

A. The Electoral Commission

i. Role

2.19 The Electoral Commission oversees elections and political finance in the UK. It is a body independent of government, established by the PPERA 2000; it reports directly

[29] *GMB v Stokes* UKEAT/0769/03/ILB.
[30] *Unison v Street* UKEAT/0256/13/LA at para 15.
[31] *Evangelou v McNicol* [2016] EWCA Civ 817; *Kelly v Musicians Union* [2020] EWCA Civ 736.
[32] See the Conservative Party Constitution, Sch 9 for the procedure.
[33] Companies Act 2006, s 26.
[34] The FCA has a regulatory role over co-operative societies, which was increased following the enactment of the Co-operative and Community Benefit Societies and Credit Unions (Investigations) Regulations 2014, SI 2014/574. The stated purpose of those Regulations is to 'create a level playing field with the requirements that companies face and increase confidence in the co-operative and community benefit society form', given the significant number of mutually run businesses, to promote a diverse, healthy and successful mutuals sector: see the Explanatory Memorandum to the Regulations.
[35] Co-operative and Community Benefit Societies Act 2014, s 16.
[36] PPERA 2000, s 32(3).

to Parliament. The Commission also produces guidance and advisory documents on elections and acts as an election observer at polling stations. The Commission regulates several areas of political parties' work:

i. Maintaining registers of political parties. If a political party wants to stand candidates in an election then it must register with the Commission. The party's name, descriptions, emblems etc must all be accepted by the Commission and registered with it for the party to be able to use that information on ballot papers.
ii. Overseeing and examining the financial accounts and records of political parties.
iii. Regulating party 'imprints', that is, the information given by parties identifying them on election leaflets and other election campaigning communications.
iv. Regulating and inspecting records of parties' election campaign expenditure for parliamentary and local elections.
v. Regulating donations to political parties.

2.20 The Commission has investigatory powers which are set out in Schedule 19B to the PPERA 2000. The Commission's powers of investigation include the power to require political parties to disclose documents, to obtain warrants from the court to enter political parties' premises to inspect financial documents in certain limited circumstances, to inspect documents held by political parties and persons associated with them, to apply for a court order to enforce compliance with the Commission's requests, and powers to retain and copy such documents that have been obtained. Document, in this context, includes any book or record (including electronic records). The Commission is not entitled to inspect documents that are protected by legal professional privilege. Persons who refuse to comply with the Commission's lawful requests may commit a criminal offence. The Commission also enjoys various powers of enforcement to ensure political parties comply with the financial regime set out in PPERA 2000.

ii. Appointment of Commissioners

2.21 The Electoral Commission's work is overseen by ten commissioners.[37] The commissioners are appointed by the Crown[38] on an Address from the House of Commons.[39] That is done by a motion being put forward in the Commons with the consent of the Speaker, after consulting on the motion with the leaders of each registered political party having more than two members in the Commons. The Commission should be independent of political parties as much as it is from the government. For that reason, all but four commissioners (the 'nominated commissioners') must be politically independent. Save in the case of nominated commissioners, registered political parties' current members, officers and employees are all ineligible to assume the role of commissioner, as are a party's elected representatives and any person who has been an officer, employee or donor of a political party in the five years preceding his appointment.[40] The four nominated commissioners, however, are political appointments nominated by the

[37] ibid s 1(3). Note that the Act allows for nine or 10 commissioners; there are currently 10.
[38] ibid s 1(4).
[39] ibid s 3.
[40] ibid s 3(4).

leaders of political parties.[41] Those commissioners may be political party members or former political party officers, employees or donors.[42] The leaders of each of the three largest parties in the Commons are entitled to have one nominated person appointed to the commission and the fourth is to be nominated by a further party with at least two MPs.[43] (If two parties have the same number of MPs, their relative size and position in the pecking order will be determined by the total number of votes cast for them at the most recent parliamentary general election.[44])

B. Registering a Political Party

2.22 Having established itself under a constitution, the next step for a party that wishes to carry out election activity is to apply for registration with the Electoral Commission. A party that is not registered cannot nominate or field candidates at a public election.[45]

2.23 The Electoral Commission must maintain two registers of political parties: a register of those intending to contest elections in Great Britain and a separate register of those intending to do so in Northern Ireland.[46] The Commission must be satisfied that a party meets the current requirements for being on a register.[47]

2.24 A party placed on the Great Britain register must be registered in respect of one or more of England, Wales and Scotland. The party's entry on the register must indicate the parts of Great Britain in which it is registered to contest elections and whether it is a minor party.[48] A minor party is one that intends to compete only in (English) parish or (Welsh) community elections.

2.25 A party may register on both the Great Britain and Northern Ireland registers but there are additional administrative consequences of doing so. The party will be registered as two separate parties (one in Great Britain and one in Northern Ireland).[49] The party will also need to organise and administer itself on the basis of that separation to ensure that its financial affairs in Britain are conducted separately from its financial affairs in Northern Ireland.[50]

[41] ibid s 3A.
[42] ibid s 3(4A).
[43] ibid s 3A(3) and (5).
[44] ibid s 3A(7).
[45] ibid s 22. If a party is not on the registers then it is unable to nominate candidates for election in any of the following elections: parliamentary elections, elections to the Scottish Parliament, elections to the National Assembly for Wales, elections to the Northern Ireland Assembly, elections of police and crime commissioners, local government elections in England, Wales and Scotland, or local elections in Northern Ireland: ibid s 22(5). A person does not need to be on the register to stand for election if he does not purport to represent any party, ie he stands under the description of 'Independent' or under no description: ibid s 22(3). (See ibid s 22(4) re parish and community elections.)
[46] ibid s 23(1) and (2).
[47] *R (on the application of English Democrats Party) v Electoral Commission* [2018] EWHC 251 (Admin).
[48] PPERA 2000, s 23(3).
[49] ibid s 23(4).
[50] ibid s 23(5)(a).

i. Financial Scheme

2.26 To register with the Commission a party must, as a preliminary step, devise a financial scheme setting out the arrangements for dealing with its financial affairs concordantly with PPERA 2000. The party must get written approval for the scheme from the Commission.[51] Essentially, this is so that the Commission can pin down the various component parts of a political party that might need to comply with the law regulating donations, spending and other financial transactions in PPERA 2000.[52] As explored in Chapter 3, political parties are organised in different ways; some are federated organisations, others have subsidiary local parties that have a separate existence of their own; and many have various autonomous or affiliated groups catering for young people, women and so on. Some parties, especially small or minor ones, have no organisational division and instead comprise one single body of members. The Commission's oversight and regulation of the financial scheme allows it to determine which component parts of a political party will be held responsible for compliance with financial regulation and when.

2.27 A party should ensure that the structure it sets down in the financial scheme is consistent with the organisational structure set out in its constitution. The scheme must set out whether the party is one single organisation with responsibility for its financial affairs and transactions; or, alternatively, whether the party has a central organisation responsible for the financial affairs of the central party as well as subordinate or affiliated organisations (for example, local area parties) each of which is responsible for its own financial affairs and transactions.[53] PPERA 2000 refers to those subordinate organisations that have financial responsibility as 'accounting units'. None of the following affiliated organisations is capable of being an accounting unit for the purposes of PPERA 2000: trade unions, co-operative societies, friendly societies,[54] any branch of a students' organisation which is wholly or mainly funded from resources provided by a students' union;[55] and a host of political associations and organisations connected to the main parties that support and promote particular interests (eg the Fabian Society, the Conservative Friends of Israel, the National Union of Labour and Socialist Clubs).[56] The effect of this is that, even though those groups may be organisationally affiliated to their respective parties, money given to them shall not be construed as a donation to the political party. Should those groups wish to transfer funds to the political party in question, that financial transaction will count as a donation to a political party and should be regulated as a donation.

[51] ibid s 26(1).
[52] ibid, Explanatory Notes para 77.
[53] ibid s 26(2).
[54] ibid s 26(8).
[55] ibid s 26(8) and the Registered Parties (Non-constituent and Non-affiliated Organisations) Order 2000, SI 2000/3183, Sch 1, Pt II.
[56] See Registered Parties (Non-constituent and Non-affiliated Organisations) Order 2000, SI 2000/3183, Sch 1, Pt I. The full list (at the time of writing) is: Association of Conservative Peers, Association of Loyal Orange Women of Ireland, Black and Asian Society, Christian Socialist Movement, Conservative Animal Welfare Group, Conservative Christian Fellowship, Conservative Disability Group, Conservative Foreign Affairs Forum, Conservative Foreign and Commonwealth Council, Conservative Friends of Israel, Conservative Lawyers, Conservative Medical Society, Conservative National Education Society, Conservative Transport Group, Conservatives at Work, County Grand Lodges of the Loyal Orange Institution of Ireland,

2.28 If the party decides to have both a central organisation and accounting units then the party must identify which organisation is the central party and which organisations are accounting units (the latter will usually be local parties). It must identify those organisations by reference to the different organisations in the party's constitution and give their names (eg 'constituency parties' or Scottish and Welsh parties, student organisations, women's organisations etc).[57]

2.29 A party wishing to be included on both the Great Britain and the Northern Ireland registers will have to provide two financial schemes – one for each part of the party – separately (because the Commission deems there to exist different registered parties in Great Britain and Northern Ireland).[58]

2.30 The scheme should also set out the party's financial year, the person for the time being registered as its treasurer, the quarter dates on which it will make financial and spending reports to the Commission, the role of party officers and set out that it will comply with the various financial regulations imposed by PPERA 2000. The Commission has a model scheme that parties may use or consult, but there is no requirement to use the model scheme (and parties must ensure that if they do, the scheme accurately reflects, or is amended to reflect, the reality of their organisation). It is advisable that the party's registered officers all sign the scheme to show that it has been adopted.[59]

2.31 The Commission may either approve the scheme once it is submitted or notify the party that it must submit a revised scheme, as the Commission thinks fit.[60] If the latter, the Commission is likely to set out which matters the revised scheme should deal with alongside any modifications to the scheme that are needed.

2.32 A party is not bound to keep the financial scheme with which it first registers: it may notify the Commission at any time after registration that it wishes to replace the scheme with another.[61] If a party so desires it must submit the replacement scheme to the Commission for approval. The new scheme will only have effect once the Commission gives its approval in writing.[62]

Fabian Society, Hurst Park Residents Association, Labour Housing Group, Labour Irish Group, National Union of Labour and Socialist Clubs, Poale Zion (ie the Jewish Labour Movement), Socialist Health Association, Socialist Education Association, Socialist Environment and Resources Association, Society of Labour Lawyers, The Association of Conservative Clubs, The Conservative Councillors Association, The Countryside Forum, The 1922 Committee, The Society of Conservative Accountants, The Tory Green Initiative. Also in this category of affiliate for the purposes of the PPERA 2000, s 26(8), are the various corporate bodies listed in PPERA 2000, s 54 and any branch of a students' organisation which is wholly or mainly funded from resources provided by a students' union within the meaning of the Education Act 1994, Pt II. The list requires some updating as some of the organisations listed are no longer active, and other newer extant organisations are not on the list.

[57] PPERA 2000, s 26(3).

[58] ibid s 26(10).

[59] See the Electoral Commission's guidance at www.electoralcommission.org.uk/how-register-your-political-party/your-financial-scheme.

[60] PPERA 2000, s 26(5).

[61] ibid s 26(7).

[62] ibid s 26(7)(c).

ii. The Application for Registration

2.33 Once a party has a constitution and a financial scheme it must send them and the details of the statutory officers it is required to register (leader, treasurer, nominating officer, see Chapter 3 for further detail) to the Commission alongside an application for registration.

2.34 The application for the Great Britain register is made by completing Electoral Commission form RP1 and returning it alongside the requisite fee (which, as of March 2024, is £150). The party must provide its name, the address of its central party headquarters and contact details; the names of its registered officers; and descriptions and emblems to be used on ballot papers. The party must state whether it intends to have accounting units and, if so, state the total number of accounting units. All relevant registered officers of the party must sign a declaration that:[63]

i. the party intends to contest one or more relevant elections in Great Britain (not confined to parish (England) or community (Wales) elections) and is accordingly applying to be registered in one, two or all of the England, Scotland or Wales parts of the Great Britain register;
ii. the party has in place the appropriate mechanisms to comply with the regulations which govern the election and financial activities of political parties; and
iii. the registered officers are authorised to sign on behalf of the party.[64]

2.35 The treasurer must make a declaration about the party's assets and liabilities. He or she must declare whether the total value of either of the party's assets or its liabilities is £500 or less (called the 'assets condition'). If either of the party's assets or liabilities do exceed £500 a record of assets and liabilities must be enclosed by the party.[65] Minor parties do not need to make any declarations about whether the asset condition is met.[66]

2.36 For parties registering on the Northern Ireland register the form RP1 NI should be used instead. The parties must provide the same information and declarations as set out above, save that the first declaration is that the party intends to contest one or more relevant elections in Northern Ireland and is accordingly applying to be registered in the Northern Ireland register.

iii. The Party's Name, Description and Emblems

2.37 The party must register a name. It may also register up to 12 descriptions of itself[67] and three associated emblems[68] to appear on ballot and nominating papers. The

[63] ie the proposed registered leader or nominating officer, the proposed registered treasurer and the proposed campaigns officer (if the party intends to have a campaigns officer): ibid Sch 4, Pt I, para 7(1).
[64] See PPERA 2000, s 28 and Sch 4.
[65] ibid s 28(3B). The financial amount is the correct as of March 2024, but may be susceptible to amendment.
[66] ibid s 28(1)(c), (2)(d) and (3E).
[67] ibid s 28A(1).
[68] ibid s 29(1).

emblems, if accepted, will be registered in black and white.[69] Descriptions can be particularly useful as a means to focus the attention of voters on the party's affinity with a particular place (eg 'Glasgow Labour') or policy (eg 'Conservative Candidate – More Police, Safer Streets'). As one would expect, the party has great latitude to define these things but there are various limitations on how it may refer to itself.[70] The Commission is permitted to remove a description, name or emblem from the register should it contravene one or more of those limitations described below.[71]

a. Language

2.38 The name and descriptions must be in English. They may also be in Welsh or Irish respectively if the party is registering on the Great Britain register in respect of Wales or on the Northern Ireland register.[72] The name may be in a language other than English, Irish and Welsh but only if the party also includes an English translation.

b. Length

2.39 Neither the name nor any proposed description of a party may exceed six words. If the party has indicated that it is registering to stand candidates in Wales then a description may appear in both English and Welsh and each will be subject to the six-word limit.

c. Script

2.40 No script other than the Roman script may be used. Parties should transliterate names etc that use other scripts (eg Greek, Arabic, Hindi and so on).

d. Similarity to Descriptors Used by Another Registered Party

2.41 It is impermissible for the name, descriptions or emblems to be the same as those of a party already registered. Names, descriptions or emblems that would be likely to result in voters confusing the party with another registered party are not allowed either. Two or more registered parties are, however, allowed to stand candidates for election under a joint description. Parties in an electoral alliance may, in that case, apply to register a description for use by a candidate standing in the name of both (or all) parties in the alliance.[73] Candidates who stand for both the Labour Party and the Co-operative Party provide a regular example of this: their joint registered description is 'Labour and Co-operative Party'.

[69] ibid s 29(4).
[70] ibid ss 28(4), 28A(2), 29(2).
[71] *R (on the application of English Democrats Party) v Electoral Commission* [2018] EWHC 251 (Admin), [2018] 4 WLR 54.
[72] PPERA 2000, Sch 4, Pt I, para 2.
[73] ibid s 28B.

e. Obscenity and Offence

2.42 Registration of offensive or obscene names, descriptions or emblems will be refused. The question here is not whether a name, description or emblem is inherently offensive but whether it is offensive in its particular political context. For example: the MP Jo Cox was murdered by a right-wing terrorist shortly before the Brexit referendum. During the attack the terrorist repeatedly uttered the words 'Britain First'. A by-election was held in her former constituency. The Commission was concerned to ensure that the descriptions of candidates on the ballot papers was not offensive in light of Jo Cox's murder. It therefore undertook a review of the registered descriptions of all parties that had indicated an intention to stand in the by-election. The English Democrats Party had already registered the description: 'English Democrats – England Worth Fighting For!'. The Commission decided that the description was offensive in the particular circumstances. It concluded that Jo Cox's murder by a man who repeatedly uttered 'Britain First' meant that voters would likely associate the use of the word 'fighting' by the English Democrats with the use of physical force to defeat an opponent rather than merely campaigning for a cause. The Commission removed the description from the register and the High Court upheld its decision to do so in a subsequent claim for judicial review.[74]

f. Criminal Offence

2.43 A party may not use a name, description or emblem that would be likely to amount to the commission of a criminal offence were it to be published. Names or descriptions that incite racial hatred are therefore forbidden.

g. Misleading

2.44 The proposed name etc will not be registered if it is likely to mislead a voter as to the effect of his vote or if it is likely to contradict or hinder a voter's understanding of directions about how to vote if the name appeared on the ballot paper.

h. Forbidden Words

2.45 Various words to do with royalty, independence and the nation can only be used in specific circumstances (including their use in languages other than English). Otherwise, names, descriptions or emblems that include them will not be registered.

i. **Royal words**: the words or expressions Duke, Duchess, Her Majesty, His Majesty, King, Prince, Princess, Queen, Royal or Royalty may not be used except where they form part of the name of a place, institution or local government area.[75] So a party could not call itself 'The King's Party' but it could call itself 'King's Lynn Party'.

[74] *R (on the application of English Democrats Party) v Electoral Commission* [2018] EWHC 251 (Admin), [2018] 4 WLR 54.

[75] The Registration of Political Parties (Prohibited Words and Expressions) Order 2001, SI 2001/82, Art 2(1), (2)(a) and Sch, Pt I.

This, evidently, is to avoid politicising the monarchy and influencing voters with purported royal authority.

ii. **Terms describing the nation**: None of the words Britain, British, England, English, National, Scotland, Scots, Scottish, United Kingdom, Wales or Welsh may be used unless the relevant word is qualified by another word or expression. Thus, a party could not register its name or description simply as 'England'. The other, qualifying word can be the word 'party' or one of the other national terms in the list (viz the British National Party and the Scottish National Party) or another word. But the qualifying word or expression cannot be the registered name or description already used by another party that is already registered in the part of the UK in which the applicant party is applying to be registered (eg a party could call itself The Scottish Justice Party and register in respect of the Scotland part of the Great Britain register even though there is already a party called The Justice Party registered in the England part of the register).[76]

iii. **Independent and official**: the words 'independent', 'official' and 'unofficial' may only be used if they are qualified by another word or expression that is not: (i) the registered name of another registered party; or (ii) the words 'independent', 'official' or 'unofficial'; or (iii) the word 'party'; or (iv) another registered party's description.[77] Thus, 'The Official Party' is not allowed but 'the Official Monster Raving Loony Party' is; and 'The Independent Party' is forbidden but 'The Tufnell Park Independent Party' would be permissible.

iv. **Denizens**: the words 'residents', 'tenants' or 'ratepayers' may not be used save if they are qualified by the name of a local government or geographical area; so 'Formby Residents Party' would be allowed but 'The Tenants Party' would not.[78]

v. **'None of the above'**: the expression 'none of the above' cannot be used.[79]

iv. Minor Parties

2.46 A minor party must declare in its application that it intends only to contest one or more parish or community elections and that it is applying to be registered in the Great Britain register only.[80] The requirements of registration set out above apply to minor parties; however, minor parties are not caught by the extensive financial regulation in PPERA 2000. Therefore, on registration:

i. minor parties are not required to register a treasurer or campaigns officer;[81] and so there is no requirement that people holding those offices sign the application, nor is the treasurer required to make any declaration;

ii. there is no requirement to adopt a financial scheme for approval by the Commission; and the provisions regulating accounting units do not apply to minor parties.[82]

[76] ibid Art 2(1) and (2)(b), (3) and Sch, Pt II.
[77] ibid Art 2(1) and (2)(c) and Sch, Pt III.
[78] ibid Art 2(1) and (2)(d) and Sch, Pt IV.
[79] ibid Art 2(1) and (2)(e) and Sch, Pt V.
[80] PPERA 2000, s 28(2)(d).
[81] ibid s 34(2)(a).
[82] ibid s 34(2)(b).

3

Operating a Political Party

I. Introduction

3.1 This chapter deals with how political parties are centrally managed and operated. Modern political parties function through four fundamental component parts (with various idiosyncratic variations):

i. the membership, which constitutes the bulk of the main parties;
ii. the governing committees, which rule over the party's day-to-day activities and take administrative decisions on its behalf;
iii. the central party officers, who carry out specific statutory and other functions on behalf of the membership and the committees; and
iv. local parties (which are the subject of Chapter 4).

The party's political direction is usually set by the leadership, who implement it by maintaining influence and control over the governing committees and central officers.

3.2 Jurisprudence has refined the application of general legal principles to the specific context in which political parties exist; and legislation specific to political parties regulates the duties of their national officers in respect of financial matters and the nomination of candidates for election. The paragraphs that follow outline essential elements of the law from a wide field; where relevant, reference is made to secondary sources that deal with particular legal areas in further detail.

II. Members

A. Admission

3.3 A person does not have a right to become a member of a political party. Rights associated with membership derive from the contractual relationship between a person and the political party set out in the party's constitution; a person does not, therefore, have any contractual relationship with the party before she joins it. A prospective party member has no legal grounds to challenge a party's decision to refuse membership to her,[1] unless the decision contravenes the Equality Act 2010 (see Chapter 11 for discrimination against prospective members). A political party has the right to decide to whom it should grant membership,[2] and there is no obligation to admit whoever wishes to join it, for the party depends on its members holding particular values and sharing common goals.[3]

3.4 A prospective member's application for membership is nothing more than an invitation to the party to consider her. At most the application is an invitation to open contractual negotiations. The prospective member will not become a member unless the party actively decides to take her on as a member in accordance with the process set out for doing so in its rules.[4]

B. People Restricted from Full Party Membership

i. Members of the Police

3.5 Members of the police force must not take any active part in politics.[5] Whether that requirement precludes bare membership of a political party is not entirely clear and is likely to depend on the rules and guidance issued by each force.[6] Any activity within a political party by a member of the police force would, however, be forbidden.

[1] See, for example, *Treherne v Amateur Boxing Association of England Limited* [2002] EWCA Civ 381 at para 34 ('Those claims, and the relief that is said to flow from them, cannot succeed unless it can be established that there was an effective contract between WABF and WABA creating or making WABF a member of the defendant'); and *Chamberlain v Boyd* (1883) 11 QBD 407 (CA).

[2] *Cheall v UK* (1985) 8 EHRR 74.

[3] *Associated Society of Locomotive Engineers & Firemen (ASLEF) v United Kingdom* (2007) 45 EHRR 34, [2007] IRLR 361 at para 39: 'where associations are formed by people, who, espousing particular values or ideals, intend to pursue common goals, it would run counter to the very effectiveness of the freedom at stake if they had no control over their membership. By way of example, it is uncontroversial that religious bodies and political parties can generally regulate their membership to include only those who share their beliefs and ideals'.

[4] *Treherne v Amateur Boxing Association of England Limtd* [2002] EWCA Civ 381 at para 36.

[5] Police Regulations 2003, SI 2003/527, reg 6(1) and Sch 1, para 1(2)(a).

[6] See, for example, the disciplining and expulsion of police officers who were revealed to be members of the British National Party when that political party's membership lists were leaked in 2008. The event was reported in *The Guardian*: I Cobain and J Meikle, 'Police scour BNP membership to find officers breaching ban' (*The Guardian*, 19 November 2008).

ii. Members of the Armed Forces

3.6 Service personnel are free to hold political party membership and to attend political party meetings. However, they must not attend political meetings in uniform or if attendance would bring the Service to which they are attached into disrepute. Service personnel must not take any active part in the affairs or organisation of a political party (for example, as a local party branch officer, committee member or delegate), nor are they allowed to participate in political marches or demonstrations.[7] Members of the Armed Forces are disqualified from standing for election to Parliament[8] and permission must be sought (from Head Army Personnel Services Group) to stand for election to local government.[9]

iii. Local Government: Persons Holding Politically Restricted Posts

3.7 Various posts and offices in local government are politically restricted posts,[10] which means that those appointed to them have restrictions on their involvement in political activity. The posts include senior staff of local authorities. A full list is set out in section 2 of the Local Government and Housing Act 1989. Those people in restricted posts are subject to the restrictions set out by the Local Government Officers (Political Restrictions) Regulations 1990, which form part of their terms and conditions of employment.[11]

3.8 The terms and restrictions vary slightly in respect of England, Wales and Scotland; the following restrictions are common to each nation. There is no restriction on holding simple membership of a political party. But it is forbidden for such a person to be an officer of a political party, even at the local party branch level, or a member of any party committee or sub-committee, if the duties of that office or committee membership would be likely to require the person to participate in the general management of the party or branch party or to act on behalf of the party in dealings with anybody else who is not a party member.[12] For example, it would not be possible for a person holding a politically restricted post to be a branch secretary of a local party, as that would entail organising party meetings and liaising with external bodies to arrange meeting venues and so on. It is also forbidden for a person holding a politically restricted post to canvass on behalf of a political party or a party candidate for election,[13] or to act as an election agent or sub-agent of a party candidate.[14] Should a person holding a politically restricted post give notice of resignation because he intends to be a candidate

[7] The Queen's Regulations 2019 (now the King's Regulations), Part 14, para J5.581 and The Reserve Land Forces Regulations, Amendment 8 (2022), para 01.03.601; The King's Regulations for the Royal Air Force, Seventh Edition (2023) para J1012.

[8] But note that reservists and members of the auxiliary forces are not so disqualified: House of Commons Disqualification Act 1975, s 1(1)(b) and (3).

[9] The Queen's Regulations 2019 (now the King's Regulations), Part 14, para J5.587.

[10] Local Government and Housing Act 1989, s 1.

[11] Local Government Officers (Political Restrictions) Regulations 1990, SI 1990/851, reg 3.

[12] ibid Sch 1(4).

[13] ibid Sch 1(5).

[14] ibid Sch 1(3).

for Parliament, his employment terminates immediately, irrespective of any period of notice set out in his employment contract.[15]

iv. Judges

3.9 Salaried judges are effectively prohibited from holding membership of political parties by the requirement that they should be impartial and by the terms and conditions under which they are employed.[16] Judges are disqualified under statute from being political candidates for Parliament or local government. The fact that a judge has held political party membership before his or her appointment as a judge is not something by itself that could give rise to a reasonable allegation of bias.[17]

3.10 'Fee paid' (ie part time) judges are not precluded by statute or other sources from holding membership of political parties. Nevertheless, they are expected to refrain from any political activity which would conflict with their judicial office or be seen to compromise their impartiality,[18] which would be likely to include holding any significant political office within a political party.

v. Civil Servants

3.11 Civil servants are subject to the Civil Service Code, which forms part of their terms and conditions of employment.[19] The Code requires them to avoid acting in a way that is determined by party political considerations, using official resources for a party-political purpose, or allowing their personal political views to determine any advice they give or any actions in the course of their work. The Code also requires them to comply with restrictions laid down on their political activities.[20] Restrictions on political activities are set out in the Civil Service Management Code.[21]

3.12 The effect of those two Codes is that civil servants are not prohibited from holding simple membership of a political party. Some senior civil servants, however, are in a 'politically restricted' category. They are prohibited from taking part in any national political activities and may only take part in local political activities

[15] ibid Sch 1(2).

[16] 'A judge must expect to forgo any kind of political activity': see the *Guide to Judicial Conduct* (Courts and Tribunals Judiciary, July 2023) 14. See also similar principles enumerated in *Guide to Judicial Conduct* (United Kingdom Supreme Court, 2019) at para 3.3.

[17] *Locabail (UK) Ltd v Bayfield Properties Ltd* [2000] QB 451 (CA) at para 25.

[18] *Guide to Judicial Conduct* (Courts and Tribunals Judiciary, July 2023) 15.

[19] Constitutional Reform and Governance Act 2010, s 5(8). Note that, according to the Code, Special Advisors (SPADS), within the meaning of s 15 of that Act, are not bound by the provisions of the Code on objectivity and impartiality.

[20] Civil Service Code (2015). The Code has a statutory basis in the Constitutional Reform and Governance Act 2010, s 5.

[21] Civil Service Management Code (2016). The Civil Service Management Code is issued under the authority of the Constitutional Reform and Governance Act 2010, s 3, under which the Minister for the Civil Service has the power to make regulations and give instructions for the management of the Civil Service, including the power to prescribe the conditions of service of civil servants.

with permission from their managers. Taking part in political activities includes the appointment to any national or local office or committee of a political party (eg secretary of a local branch party or membership of a local or national executive committee), canvassing and speaking in public about political matters.[22] Other civil servants, especially industrial and non-office based staff, are in a 'politically free' category, and should be granted permission to take part in political activity.[23] Civil servants who are not in the politically free category must resign from the Civil Service upon a political party's adoption of them as a prospective parliamentary candidate.[24]

C. Subscription Fees

3.13 The party's constitution will usually require members to pay subscription fees. There is no obligation on a member to do so if the membership contract is silent on the matter. Where the party does require subscription fees to be paid, the subscription is the price the member pays to enjoy the privileges of membership;[25] and the payment of a subscription is a prerequisite for obtaining membership. Thereafter, it is usual for party constitutions to require members to pay subscriptions periodically. Parties' constitutions should include an express rule that a member who fails to pay his subscriptions will cease to be a member; otherwise, a member who defaults on payment of his subscriptions will not automatically cease to be a member.[26] It is common for constitutions to require members to pay their subscriptions even if they are suspended administratively.[27] A political party's membership subscriptions may be exempt from VAT depending on its constitutional arrangements.[28] Once paid, the membership subscriptions form a common fund for the benefit of the party.[29]

D. Ending Membership

3.14 Membership can be brought to an end by several means:

i. **Expulsion**: a party may expel a member for a breach of its rules. Any expulsion must accord with the terms of the rules and the principles of natural justice: see Chapter 12 for the requirements of fairness in the case of expulsion. (Note that a suspension is not tantamount to an expulsion.)
ii. **Resignation**: The position at common law is that a member has a unilateral right to resign from a political party (in common with the position for other types of

[22] Civil Service Management Code (2016), paras 4.4.1 and 4.4.9.
[23] ibid para 4.4.2.
[24] ibid paras 4.4.19–21.
[25] *Re Duty on the Estate of the New University Club* (1887) 18 QBD 720; *Institution of Mechanical Engineers Appellants v Cane (Valuation Officer)* [1961] AC 696, [1960] 3 WLR 978 (HL).
[26] eg *Wycombe Islamic Mission and Mosque Trust Ltd* [2011] EWHC 971 (Ch) para 14.
[27] eg *Dominic Kelly v The Musicians' Union* [2020] EWCA Civ 736.
[28] See the Value Added Tax Act 1994, Sch 9, item 1(e); *Shanklin Conservative and Unionist Club v The Commissioners for Her Majesty's Revenue & Customs* [2016] UKFTT 0135 (TC).
[29] *The Taff Vale Railway Co v The Amalgamated Society of Railway Servants* [1901] AC 426.

association). In the absence of some express rule to the contrary in the party's constitution there is absolutely nothing to stop a member from leaving a party and he does not require the party to accept his resignation to do so. He is not entitled in law, however, to withdraw his resignation once it has been given (he would have to rejoin).[30] A resignation may be written or oral: the resignation will be valid if the member has sufficiently manifested his decision to resign. What amounts to a sufficient manifestation will depend on the surrounding circumstances. Conduct alone may be sufficient to manifest an intention to resign.[31] Where the party's rules set out a contractual procedure to resign then a member must follow that procedure for his resignation to be valid. A member who resigns part way through a period of subscription is not entitled to a refund of his subscriptions unless the rules state otherwise.[32] There is no such thing as a 'constructive expulsion' akin to a constructive dismissal: if a member resigns in response to a breach of contract committed by the party, he cannot rely on his resignation as a form of expulsion.[33]

iii. **Failure to pay membership subscriptions**: A failure to pay membership subscriptions may amount to grounds for expulsion if the party's constitution so provides. Otherwise, a long period in which a member fails to pay subscriptions that he owes may amount to a tacit resignation by conduct that sees his membership lapse. A failure to pay monthly subscriptions for a few months is unlikely to amount to a tacit resignation by conduct but a person who fails over a period of many months to do so may properly be deemed to have resigned.[34]

E. Legal Agency

3.15 Political parties carry out their political business through the activities of their members. Members may be elected or appointed to employed or voluntary positions to undertake particular functions for the party. By assuming these positions members have powers to act on behalf of the party. For example, an employee will have the rights and obligations afforded to her under her employment contract. A party officer or committee member has the duties and powers given to her by the party's rules and any express instructions from superior officers or committees. A company director has the fiduciary duties that appertain to that role. Most members who undertake activity for their parties do so, however, as volunteers. When volunteer members undertake activities on behalf of the party – for example, sitting on committees or arranging party meetings or elections – they act as a legal agent of the party. Legal agency arises from an agreement that one person ('the agent') should act on behalf of another person ('the principal'). A longstanding and essential element of agency is that the agent has the power to affect the principal's relationship with third parties.[35] Third parties may include, for these

[30] *Finch v Oake* [1896] 1 Ch 409 (CA).
[31] *Sick and Funeral Society of St John's Sunday School, Golcar* [1973] Ch 51.
[32] *Finch v Oake* [1896] 1 Ch 409 (CA).
[33] *McGhee v Midlands British Road Services Ltd* [1985] ICR 503.
[34] *Sick and Funeral Society of St John's Sunday School, Golcar* [1973] Ch 51.
[35] See *Bowstead and Raynolds on Agency*, 23rd edn (Sweet & Maxwell, 2024) Ch 1, Art 1, para 1-001; *Chitty on Contracts*, 35th edn, Vol I, Ch 22 'Agency', para 22-001.

purposes, other members of the party. So, a local party chair who organises and chairs a local meeting may act as the party's agent in respect of the landlord from whom the chair hires the meeting venue, as well as in respect of the party's ordinary members who attend the meeting.

3.16 Whether a member is in fact acting as an agent will depend on the functions she is authorised to undertake by the party or its constitution. The general rule is that a member will act as an agent of the party if she is carrying out functions the party has authorised her to undertake and she is doing so honestly in the interests of the party. This is known as 'express authority'. A member may also act as an agent if she has 'implied authority'; that is, while she undertakes tasks that are necessary for, or ordinarily incidental to, her accomplishment of functions she is expressly authorised to do.[36] The following paragraphs set out three broad types of function that members are commonly authorised to undertake in political parties that give rise to an agency relationship.

i. Members in Administrative or Management Positions and Officers

3.17 Members of executive and managing committees, party officers and local councillors will have legal agency for acts done in the course of their authorised functions managing the party. Common scenarios in which agency arises include:

i. officers chairing meetings, running elections and selections, interviewing candidates and corresponding with members on behalf of the local party;
ii. councillors reporting on party business to local party meetings and representing local parties as delegates (for example, to party conferences or party meetings);
iii. complying with the party's financial obligations under the Political Parties, Elections and Referendums Act 2000 (PPERA 2000); collecting membership subscriptions and so on.

3.18 The source of the authority to do those things will usually be the express terms of the party's rules or some direction from the national officers or committees of the party. In practice it is usual that the elected or appointed officers of the central or local parties carry out these sorts of activities, though sometimes ordinary members are appointed on an ad hoc basis in local parties to do them.

ii. Members who Canvass the Public

3.19 The source of members' authority to talk to the public in the party's name is not usually the express terms of the party rules but, rather, an invitation or request from the party that the member should join particular canvassing sessions. A member does not usually possess any general authority to canvass on behalf of her party. See paragraphs 3.22–3.26 below for further discussion of the rules about canvassing; and

[36] See *Bowstead and Raynolds on Agency*, 23rd edn (Sweet & Maxwell, 2024) Ch 3, Art 23, para 3-011 and Art 27, para 3-022.

consider paragraphs 11.47–11.48 below for the position in respect of members who make discriminatory posts on social media in their own time without the authority of the party.

iii. Party Representatives

3.20 An agency relationship may arise when the party's members are given responsibility to represent the party publicly, for example on television or at fundraising events or at public meetings. Elected politicians are likely to be in an agency relationship with the party when they are representing the party's interests in accordance with their functions under the party's rules. Some very senior politicians (for example, the leader or deputy leader of the party) will almost always be in an agency relationship with the party when they undertake public activity by virtue of their authorised role to represent the party generally on a daily basis to the public.

3.21 The acts of politicians done in the exercise of their public functions as elected public representatives are not attributable in law to political parties under the doctrine of legal agency.[37] The reason is because the authority to exercise those functions does not come from the party. By way of example, it is not the party's rule book or constitution that entitles an MP to sit in Parliament, to sit as a select committee member (which forms part of core parliamentary business[38]) or to deal with matters of state as a minister or legislator. The authority for an MP to do these things is the common law and the Bill of Rights 1689. Similarly, the authority for Police and Crime Commissioners to carry out their duties is section 1 of the Police Reform and Social Responsibility Act 2011. The authority of elected mayors to undertake their mayoral functions is section 4 of the Cities and Local Government Devolution Act 2016. No implied authority from the political party is needed to explain why these elected representatives have the public powers they hold.[39]

F. Canvassing

i. Persuading Electors to Vote or Abstain

3.22 In practice the term 'canvassing' refers to two distinct activities. The first activity is the practice of party activists talking to electors and seeking to persuade them to vote one way or another, or not to vote. Attempting to persuade an elector to remain neutral,[40] or to vote against another candidate,[41] fall within the definition of this type of canvassing. It is unlawful to pay people to do it.[42] Party members who are members of

[37] For example attending legislative votes, speaking in local authority committees, undertaking constituency surgeries, etc.

[38] See the judgment of Lord Phillips in *R v Chaytor (David)* [2010] UKSC 52, [2011] 1 AC 684 at paras 62 and 122.

[39] See *Ministry of Defence v Kemeh* [2014] EWCA Civ 91, [2014] ICR 625 at para 34.

[40] *Westbury's case* (1869) 1 O'M & H 47.

[41] An intention to prevent the election of one candidate will involve also an intention to improve the chances of success of the remaining candidates, and therefore to promote them: *DPP v Luft* [1977] AC 962 at 983 per Lord Diplock.

[42] Representation of the People Act 1983, s 111. If this prohibition is broken then both the person canvassing and the person who has paid him will be guilty of illegal employment.

the police force are forbidden from engaging in it.[43] Party activists who undertake this sort of canvassing with the authority of the candidate or his election agent will act as agents of the candidate. The consequence is that illegal or corrupt practices proscribed by electoral law[44] that are committed by activists in the course of canvassing will be attributable to the candidate and may void his election.[45]

3.23 The candidate may also be responsible for the actions of local constituency party members who take steps to persuade electors to vote a particular way (or not to vote), even if those activists are not authorised to carry out the steps in question, and even if senior party members disapprove of those steps. The case of *R v Rowe* was an example of this.[46] In that case it was accepted that a group of Liberal Democrat local party members were acting as agents of the candidate. The local members created mock Labour Party leaflets, misleading in nature, and had them distributed to known Labour Party supporters at night by Liberal Democrat supporters who were not known in the electoral wards concerned, to avoid any risk that the recipient electors would identify the source of the material.[47]

ii. Obtaining Data on How Electors Will Vote

3.24 The second type of activity falling under the general label of 'canvassing' is the process of obtaining electoral data about which residents in an electoral ward are likely to vote and, if so, for whom. A party cannot target its election campaign efficiently or check whether its supporters have voted if it does not know where they live and how they intend to vote. Most party members who go out canvassing will often be undertaking this information-gathering exercise rather than persuading electors to vote a particular way. The process usually involves one member, in charge of a list of names and addresses drawn from the electoral register, who allocates residences to other members along with instructions to find out how the voters who live there intend to vote. The voter's response to the canvasser is recorded against the copy of the electoral register. This data is eventually processed by the local and central parties, who are then in a position to ascertain how much of the electorate the party has contacted and what proportion of the electoral area has pledged to vote for it.

3.25 Party members undertaking this second sort of activity are unlikely to be engaged in canvassing within the meaning of the Representation of the People Act 1983.[48]

[43] ibid s 100.

[44] For example treating: offering voters material incentives to vote a certain way.

[45] Representation of the People Act 1983, s 159.

[46] *R v Rowe* [1992] 4 All ER 821, [1992] 1 WLR 1059.

[47] The Court of Appeal decided that the Lib Dem candidate was not guilty of a corrupt practice under the Representation of the People Act 1983, despite the local party members' actions, as the lower court's findings (which were not challenged on appeal) were that none of the voters who had given evidence before him had been influenced by the deceptive leaflets.

[48] The basis of the statutory regime is Victorian and probably requires updating to account for modern electoral practices.

Members who do so are, therefore, very unlikely to act as agents of a candidate for whose corrupt or illegal practices the candidate is responsible.[49] Nevertheless, legal agency may well arise between these members and the local or national party, so that the party is liable for tortious acts by them.[50]

3.26 In all cases, though, the party will want to set out clearly what volunteer members are expected to do and what they must not do when canvassing for the party. In practice, it is advisable that canvassing sessions are officially organised and that one or several senior or experienced members of the local or national party are able to attend each session to ensure that local activists do not go off on an unauthorised frolic of their own. It should also be made clear in the party's rules or written policies that a member who carries out unauthorised campaigning or canvassing may be subject to disciplinary action by the party.

G. Members' Liability in Contract for Acts of a Party Agent

3.27 A member is unlikely to be able to recover damages against an unincorporated association for a breach of contract done by an agent who was acting on behalf of the whole party, including himself. In those circumstances the agent is acting on behalf of the membership as a whole, and the apparently wronged member is just as responsible for his conduct as any other member. Nevertheless, that exclusion of liability will not arise in the case of a party agent who makes disciplinary decisions in respect of a member, and who, in the course of making such determinations, breaches the contractual term of fairness (or another contractual term). In those circumstances, the interests of the party and the member in question are sufficiently separate so that the member may sue the party for the agent's breach.[51]

H. Members' Liability in Negligence

3.28 A member of an unincorporated association does not owe another member a duty of care simply arising from their joint membership. As a general rule, therefore, a member of an unincorporated political party will not be liable in negligence for injury or loss to another member save if particular circumstances are present.[52] A member may owe a duty of care to another if the former has assumed a particular duty (for example, as a steward) and he performs that duty in a negligent way that gives rise to a civil wrong.[53] A duty of care may also arise from the presence of dangerous circumstances.

[49] For an extended discussion of the limits of agency for corrupt and illegal practices, see R Price and V Sedgley, *Parker's Law and Conduct of Elections* (LexisNexis, looseleaf) Chs 6 and 19D.

[50] ie a tortious act is a civil wrong, for example an act of negligence in breach of a common law duty of care, or breach of various statutory duties, including those set out in the Equality Act 2010.

[51] *Bonsor v Musicians Union* [1956] AC 104 at 148–49 per Lord MacDermott.

[52] *Robertson v Ridley* [1989] 1WLR 872 (CA); *Jones v Northampton Borough Council* (1990) Times, 21 May (CA).

[53] ie a tortious act or omission: see *Prole v Allen* [1950] 1 All ER 476 (Assizes).

For example, a party secretary would have a duty of care to another member if the secretary were to arrange a meeting in premises on which there existed a danger of injury and the secretary had actual knowledge of circumstances that he knew gave rise to a risk of injury to members if not told of the cause of the danger.[54] If the rules of the party provide that a member shall have a duty of care to another, then a duty of care will arise.[55]

III. Governing Committees

A. Powers and Duties

3.29 Governing committees manage the day-to-day administration of political parties. The Conservative Party's National Board manages its affairs. The Labour Party, the Co-operative Party and the Scottish National Party are managed by their respective National Executive Committees. The Liberal Democrats are managed by a Federal Board. People serving on these governing committees are either elected directly or indirectly by the membership, or appointed. The legal principles underpinning internal elections, including of committee members, are dealt with in Chapter 5, Section II.

3.30 These committees have powers to govern only so far as the rules permit, including any rules implied by custom and practice. Extensive express terms of the constitution usually set the boundaries of these committees' decision-making powers. The implied term of rationality and good faith limits their powers even if the express contractual position provides that their powers are unlimited or if the contract is silent on the matter.[56] At least some committee members will serve on sub-committees. It is usual for committee members (sitting on main or sub-committees) to have authority, express or implied, to make decisions and to deal with situations as they arise.[57] In practice, committee members wield powers of discretion and approval over a broad range of decisions and functions, including:

i. the procedures used to select candidates; and the party's endorsement of candidates selected by local members; (see Chapter 6 on selecting candidates);
ii. disciplinary procedures; (see Chapter 12, Section III);
iii. party policy and manifestos;
iv. the management of local parties and affiliated organisations;
v. making or proposing changes to the party's constitution (see paragraph 2.18 above);
vi. endorsing or approving political strategies (for example, giving permission to enter into electoral or political alliances with other parties);
vii. approving the party's financial arrangements; and approving its statements of accounts for the purposes of PPERA 2000.

[54] *Jones v Northampton Borough Council* (1990) Times, 21 May (CA).

[55] *Robertson v Ridley* [1989] 1WLR 872 (CA).

[56] *Evangelou v McNicol* [2016] EWCA Civ 817; *Williamson v Formby* [2019] EWHC 2639 (QB).

[57] *Heatons Transport (St Helens) Ltd v TGWU* [1973] AC 15, [1972] 3 WLR 431; *Unite the Union v Nailard* [2017] ICR 121 at paras 49 and 52.

3.31 When committees act as final arbiters of internal disputes among members or subordinate party units the courts will defer to them on matters of political judgement. Yet, the committees cannot oust the jurisdiction of the courts. Party rules that attempt to do so by giving the committee sole jurisdiction over intra-party disputes have no legal effect.[58]

3.32 A committee member is liable for decisions taken by the committee when he knows of the matter decided. The committee has the power to enter into contractual relationships with third parties, for example, for the employment of staff, to hire premises, to rent offices or to obtain services. Where committee members enter into a contract with a third party on behalf of the committee, they will be bound personally under the contract as principals (ie parties to the contract) and not just agents of the party, unless the contract's terms expressly limit their personal liability.[59] Parties usually rely on members sitting on the governing committee on a voluntary basis without remuneration. It is therefore desirable that any contract into which the committee enters on behalf of the party limits the personal liability of committee members, otherwise the party may struggle to persuade ordinary members to take up a governing role. Governing committees usually have a power under the party constitution to establish subsidiary limited liability companies, through which significant commercial or property transactions can be undertaken, thereby limiting the legal exposure of committee members.

B. Duty to Act in the Party's Best Interests

3.33 Governing committee members, and local party executive officers, have a general implied authority to act in the interests of the party's members.[60] It has been held that governing committee members of an association have a fiduciary duty[61] to the membership such that they are trustees, having the management and the administration of the funds of the association.[62] It is axiomatic that governing committee members who are statutory directors of a party set up as a company have fiduciary duties to the company.[63] Governing committee members must, therefore, act in the best interests of the party as a whole and not in their personal interests or the interests of one faction of the committee. This does not mean that governing committee members cannot give effect to the priorities of a particular political faction or internal political group, so long as the member does so not because he or another will benefit personally, but rather because he believes that the party's electoral or general position is best served by the programme or propositions put forward by the political faction in question.

[58] eg *Evangelou v McNicol* [2016] EWCA Civ 817; *Barnett v British National Party* [2020] EWHC 1538 (QB).

[59] N Stewart KC et al, *The Law of Unincorporated Associations* (Oxford University Press, 2011) paras 7-18–7-20.

[60] *Heatons Transport (St Helens) Ltd v TGWU* [1973] AC 15 at 112.

[61] ie a duty of loyalty to act in the best interests of the membership.

[62] *Todd v Emly* (1841) 7 Meeson and Welsby 427, 151 ER 832 per Lord Abinger.

[63] Companies Act 2006, ss 170–77; eg *Bairstow v Queens Moat Houses plc* [2001] 2 BCLC 531.

3.34 It is not firmly settled whether a local party's executive committee members or branch officers have a fiduciary relationship with members by dint of their office; the existence of such a fiduciary duty has been tentatively approved in principle by the Court of Appeal.[64] A general secretary, president or chairman employed by the committee to manage the party from day to day is also likely to have a fiduciary duty to the committee as his employer, given his very senior status in the organisation and his authority to contract with others on behalf of the party, to manage its funds and to dispose of its property with delegated authority.[65]

C. Consultation on Matters of Policy

3.35 Governing committees are charged with determining the political direction of the party with the leadership. This may involve the party's ministers in government consulting with the committee on policy.[66] The committee's views on policy are advisory in those circumstances and public office holders must not unlawfully fetter their discretion by following them. The same is true for local councillors and other members holding executive office in local government.[67]

D. Delegation

3.36 It has already been observed that most parties will be governed by committees of volunteers. Those people will often have other commitments elsewhere, not least paid employment, which preclude them from meeting and taking party decisions at short notice. Nonetheless, political parties are often required to respond quickly to events and to changes in public opinion. For reasons of practicality, governing committees will usually wish to delegate ad hoc decision-making to sub-committees, officers and party employees. Governing committees are allowed to delegate the exercise of their powers to subcommittees and staff to avoid party management duties placing impractical expectations on volunteer members. This power to delegate, and its extent, should be set out unambiguously in the rules. Powers of delegation may nevertheless arise by way of an implied term even if the rules are silent on the matter. An implied power is likely to be necessary if the alternative would require the party to

[64] See *Unite the Union v Nailard* [2017] ICR 121 (EAT) at para 55 concerning the analogous organisational structure of a trade union.

[65] The duty arises because, by signing the contract of employment, he has contracted to undertake duties that impose more rigorous duties in the law of equity. See *University of Nottingham v Fishel* [2000] ICR 1462 at 1491 per Elias J.

[66] The Conservative Party's rules give its Board oversight of a policy forum the purpose of which is to discuss policy ideas with the Leader of the Party and, when in government, the forum should normally be chaired by a government minister: Conservative Party Constitution, Part VIII, paras 66 and 67. The Labour Party's rules provide that its National Executive Committee should confer with its elected representatives prior to the formulation of legislative proposals for the proceeding parliamentary session: *Labour Party Rule Book* Ch 1, cl VIII.3.F.

[67] eg *R v London Borough of Waltham Forest* [1988] QB 419 per Stoker LJ; *Bromley London Borough Council v Greater London Council* [1983] 1 AC 768.

interpret its rules impractically, for example, by necessitating a small group of people on the committee to execute every administrative act of the party.[68]

3.37 It is ultimately for the governing committee to decide how to exercise the power to delegate. The courts will be slow to decide that decisions made by a subcommittee with the governing committee's knowledge are outside the latter's powers.[69] No issue of wrongful delegation will arise where the governing committee subsequently ratifies a subcommittee's decision.[70] The rules may expressly require the governing committee to approve the decisions of a subcommittee. If so, the subcommittee's decisions must not be presented as final in the absence of the parent committee's approval.[71] It is sensible for many of the day-to-day responsibilities of the governing committee to be delegated to an elected or employed Chairman, General Secretary or President with oversight of the central party's apparatus and the ability to employ staff.

IV. Statutory Officers

3.38 Each registered political party must have a leader, a treasurer and a nominating officer.[72] These officers are referred to here as 'statutory officers' because PPERA 2000 requires them. Parties may also appoint a campaigns officer. Among these officers the leader and the treasurer are the most significant for regulatory purposes. A party may have numerous political officers that are not statutory officers, such as chairs of committees or executive officers for various groups (eg a chair of a national executive committee, a local party secretary or a women's officer). This latter group of non-statutory officers is a product of the party's constitution and rules. The powers and duties of those officers will be prescribed by the parties in their respective constitutions or in other contractual documents, and so it is unnecessary to deal with all the various permutations here. Further detail about the scope of the party's constitution is set out in Chapter 2; and paragraphs 3.29–3.37 above explain the powers of governing committee members, many of which will apply with equal force to the officers of other kinds of party committee.

A. The Leader

3.39 The PPERA 2000 requires a person to be registered as the party's leader.[73] The leader must be the overall leader of the party.[74] For most parties this will be self-explanatory: it will be the leader of the national party elected or appointed in accordance with the party's rules.[75] Some parties, notably the Green Party, have co-leaders.

[68] eg *Choudry v Treisman* [2003] EWHC 1203 (Comm) paras 71–72.
[69] ibid para 72.
[70] ibid para 73.
[71] *Williamson v Formby* [2019] EWHC 2639 (QB) para 49.
[72] Unless they are a minor party, in which case, they are not required to have a person registered as treasurer.
[73] PPERA 2000, s 24(1)(a).
[74] ibid s 24(2)(a).
[75] See Chapter 5, Section III for further detail about leadership elections.

The PPERA 2000 permits a person to be registered as the leader of a party for a particular purpose where there is no single overall leader.[76] For example, one of the co-leaders may be the final decision-maker on internal party matters and, therefore, registered as the statutory leader.[77] The registered party leader, unlike the other statutory officers, may also hold all the other mandatory statutory offices so that he is the registered leader, treasurer and nominating officer.[78] The leader will also become the statutory treasurer of the party if the treasurer dies in office or if his tenure is terminated for any other reason, save that if the leader was registered as the treasurer too, the nominating officer will become the treasurer instead (and if the leader was registered as both the treasurer *and* the nominating officer, then another registered officer of the party will become the treasurer).[79]

3.40 For minor parties, the obligation to notify the Commission that the party's registered details are accurate each year falls on the registered leader. The leader must notify the Commission of this in the period of one month before the anniversary of the party's registration and six months after the anniversary, at the latest. The notification must state that the party's details in the register remain accurate or,[80] if they are not, the notification must include an application to correct them or to notify the Commission that the leader has changed.[81]

B. Treasurer

3.41 Every party that is not a minor party must have a person registered as its treasurer.[82] The treasurer may not also be the nominating officer (unless both posts are held by the leader).[83] He may not be the treasurer if he has been convicted of an electoral offence in five years preceding his registration (ie an offence under PPERA 2000 or any other offence committed in connection with an election or referendum or a recall petition of an MP under the Recall of MPs Act 2015). The treasurer's appointment will automatically terminate upon his conviction for an electoral offence (and the termination will be effective on the date of the conviction).[84] The person registered as the treasurer has responsibility on behalf of the party for its compliance with financial obligations under PPERA 2000. Among other things, he must:

i. ensure that the party keeps accounting records that are sufficient to show and explain the party's transactions;[85] and he must ensure that those accounting

[76] PPERA 2000, s 24(2)(b).
[77] 'How to Register your Political Party', Electoral Commission, www.electoralcommission.org.uk/full-guidance/how-register-your-political-party.
[78] PPERA 2000, s 24(1).
[79] ibid s 24(6) and (7).
[80] ibid s 34(3), (4).
[81] ie an application under PPERA 2000, s 30 or notification under s 31.
[82] PPERA 2000, s 24(1)(c).
[83] *Erlam and Others v Rahman* [2015] EWHC 1215 (QB) at para 273.
[84] PPERA 2000, s 24(8).
[85] ibid s 41(1).

records are preserved for at least six years from the end of the financial year of the party in which they are made;[86]

ii. prepare a statement of accounts for each financial year,[87] to be approved by the party's management committee if there is one, or its leader if not;[88] and the treasurer must ensure that the statement of accounts is preserved for at least six years from the end of the financial year to which the statement relates;[89]

iii. deliver the annual statement of accounts (or revised accounts[90]) to the Electoral Commission (and, if the accounts have been audited, a copy of the auditor's report);[91]

iv. notify the Electoral Commission that the party's particulars are accurate in the register of political parties within six months of the deadline to deliver the annual statement of accounts to the Electoral Commission;[92] if the party's particulars are not correct then the treasurer must include an application to amend the particulars (eg the party's name or emblem etc), notification of a change in the names of registered officers, or any other information required to correct the register;[93] and any amendments the party has made to its constitution since registration or the last notification of particulars;[94]

v. prepare quarterly donation reports (for periods January–March, April–June, July–September and October–December);[95] and deliver the reports to the Electoral Commission within 30 days of the end of the quarter period;[96]

vi. prepare weekly donation reports in a general election period (ie every seven days starting with the day Parliament is dissolved up to and including polling day and, if so provided for by the relevant secretary of state, for elections to the Scottish Parliament, the Welsh Senedd and elections of police and crime commissioners)[97] recording each donation of more than £11,180 received in each week by the central party (or by the whole party if it has no separate accounting units);[98] and deliver the reports to the Electoral Commission within seven days of the end of each weekly period;[99]

[86] ibid s 41(4).
[87] ibid s 42(1).
[88] ibid s 42(2)(b).
[89] ibid s 42(6).
[90] ibid s 48.
[91] ibid s 45.
[92] ibid s 32(1).
[93] ibid s 32(2).
[94] ibid s 32(3).
[95] ibid s 62. Sometimes, especially for smaller or minor parties, recordable donations might dry up between general elections. Where no recordable donations have been received or dealt with in four consecutive quarters the treasurer is not required to prepare any donation report until a recordable donation is next received or dealt with by the registered party: ibid s 62A.
[96] ibid s 65(1).
[97] ibid s 67.
[98] ibid s 63. Note that the threshold amount was increased from £7,500 in 2023 by secondary legislation and may be varied again. The requirement to submit weekly donation reports is dispensed with if the party has declared its intention to field no candidates in the general election and it does not, in fact, field any candidates: ibid s 64.
[99] ibid s 65(2).

vii. take all reasonable steps to ascertain if a donor is a permissible donor and,[100] if not, to return his prohibited donation to him within 30 days of its receipt;[101]

viii. authorise expenditure to be incurred (or give somebody else, in writing, authority to do so) in respect of a petition recalling an MP under the Recall of MPs Act 2015;[102] and authorise payments to be made in respect of campaigning related to such a petition;[103]

ix. return donations from impermissible or unidentifiable donors in MP recall campaigns;[104]

x. make a recall petition return[105] with the appropriate declaration[106] and secure the report's delivery alongside accompanying documents to the Petitions Officer;[107] the return should give details of all payments incurred in the campaign, any unpaid expenditure claims that a person has sought or is about to seek in an application to the court of which the treasurer is aware and details of any disputed claims.[108]

3.42 The treasurer must fulfil his responsibilities and risks committing a criminal offence (being a corrupt or illegal practice penalised by electoral law) if he does not. By way of example, the treasurer will be guilty of a criminal offence if he fails without reasonable excuse to submit a proper statement of accounts or fails without reasonable excuse to deliver a donation report that complies with PPERA 2000. Similar penalties apply in respect of the making and delivery of recall petition returns.

3.43 The duties of the treasurer are, therefore, extensive and important; and he may appoint up to 12 deputy treasurers on such terms as he sees fit.[109] The purpose of that power is to allow the treasurer to delegate his functions to authorise campaign expenditure – otherwise, it would be impractical for one person to deal with campaign spending where a party is contesting a large number of seats. PPERA 2000 envisages that 12 deputy treasurers would enable 'a Great Britain-wide party to appoint a deputy to cover each of Scotland, Wales, and the nine English regions', though of course it is up to the registered treasurer to confine a deputy to a particular geographical area or not.[110]

3.44 A person is ineligible to be appointed as a deputy treasurer if he has been convicted of an electoral offence under PPERA 2000 or in connection with any relevant election or a recall petition within the preceding five-year period.[111] He will commit a

[100] A permissible donor is one which is listed in ibid s 54(2).
[101] ibid s 56.
[102] Recall of MPs Act 2015, Sch 3, para 8.
[103] ibid Sch 3, para 9.
[104] ibid Sch 4, paras 14(3) and 15(4).
[105] ibid Sch 5, para 1.
[106] ibid Sch 5, para 5(1).
[107] ibid Sch 5, para 6.
[108] ibid Sch 5, para 2.
[109] PPERA 2000, s 74(1).
[110] PPERA 2000, Explanatory Notes, para 146.
[111] ibid s 74(3).

criminal offence if he accepts the office of deputy treasurer when he is ineligible by reason of such conviction(s).[112] As with the treasurer, the deputy treasurer's appointment will terminate automatically upon any conviction of any electoral offence.[113]

3.45 To appoint a deputy treasurer the treasurer must notify the Electoral Commission of the name of the deputy, the address of the deputy's office (which will usually be the party's registered address) and a declaration of acceptance signed by the proposed deputy.[114] The registered treasurer must notify the Electoral Commission within 14 days if the appointment of the deputy is terminated for any reason (including on death in office) or within 28 days if there is any change to the address of his office.[115] To do all this, parties should use Electoral Commission form RP5.

C. Campaigns Officer

3.46 A party may register a person as its campaigns officer.[116] The campaigns officer is responsible for the party's compliance with various campaign and referendum expenditure rules which would otherwise be the treasurer's responsibility. As with the treasurer, PPERA 2000 allows the campaigns officer to appoint up to 12 deputy campaigns officers to assist with the control of campaign expenditure.[117] The campaigns officer may also be the registered party leader or nominating officer.[118] The eligibility for, appointment to and termination of, the role of campaigns officer or deputy campaigns officer mirrors that of the treasurer, so the same information must be registered with the Electoral Commission and the same offences will be committed if a person with relevant electoral offence convictions is appointed to and accepts the role.[119]

3.47 The campaigns officer (or a deputy campaigns officer as the case may be) has the following responsibilities (which, in the absence of a campaigns officer, the treasurer or deputy treasurer must carry out):

i. authorising notional campaign expenditure[120] and authorising campaign expenditure to be incurred by the party;[121]
ii. making payments of authorised campaign expenditure[122] and, in the case of a deputy campaigns officer, notifying the campaigns officer that the payment has been made and providing a supporting invoice or receipt;[123]

[112] ibid s 74(4).
[113] ibid s 74(5).
[114] ibid s 74(2).
[115] ibid s 74(6) and (7).
[116] ibid s 25(1).
[117] ibid s 25(4).
[118] ibid s 25(1)(b).
[119] ibid s 25(3) and (5)(a).
[120] ibid s 73.
[121] ibid s 75(1).
[122] ibid s 76(1).
[123] ibid s 76(3).

iii. ensuring that the party adheres to the limits on campaign spending set out in PPERA 2000;[124]
iv. preparing campaign expenditure reports and campaign payment statements;[125]
v. organising and securing the preparation of an auditor's report of campaign expenditure reports where relevant incurred campaign expenditure exceeds £250,000;[126]
vi. delivering or securing the delivery of campaign expenditure reports and any related auditor reports to the Electoral Commission;[127] and signing the required declaration.[128]

3.48 The campaign officer also has the following responsibilities in respect of referenda (which, in the absence of a campaigns officer, the treasurer or deputy treasurer will carry out):

i. authorising referendum expenses to be incurred, or authorising in writing another person to authorise referendum expenses;[129]
ii. making payment of referendum expenses or authorising in writing another person to make such payment (in which case that person must notify the campaign officer that he has made payment and provide supporting receipts or invoices as soon as possible after the payment is made);[130]
iii. ensuring that the party does not incur referendum expenses above the limits set out in PPERA 2000;[131]
iv. submitting returns to the Electoral Commission setting out information about referendum expenditure;[132] and organising and securing the preparation of an auditor's report of referendum expenditure returns where relevant incurred campaign expenditure exceeds £250,000;[133]
v. delivering, or securing the delivery of, referendum returns and auditors reports of referendum returns to the Electoral Commission within six months of the end of the referendum poll;[134] and signing the relevant declarations in the return.[135]

3.49 In the rare circumstances that a political party is registered but campaigning in support of another political party rather than standing its own candidates, the campaigns officer will also have the responsibilities in respect of third-party national election campaigns set out in Part VI of PPERA 2000,[136] and which are addressed in Chapter 10.[137]

[124] ibid s 79.
[125] ibid s 80.
[126] ibid s 81.
[127] ibid s 82.
[128] ibid s 83.
[129] ibid s 113.
[130] ibid s 114(1) and (3).
[131] ibid s 118(2).
[132] ibid s 120.
[133] ibid s 121.
[134] ibid s 122.
[135] ibid.
[136] ibid Explanatory Notes, para 30.
[137] Two circumstances can be readily imagined: the Co-operative Party does not stand joint candidates with the Labour Party in every constituency and may wish to support a Labour Party candidate in a constituency in

D. Nominating Officer

3.50 The nominating officer has responsibility for three things. First, for the party's representatives' submission of the party's lists of candidates for elections.[138] Second, for issuing certificates authorising the candidates' descriptions on nomination papers.[139] The description that may be authorised is either the name of the political party registered with the Electoral Commission or the description of the party registered with the Commission.[140] Nominating officers will naturally want to avoid the error made in one Lincolnshire parish election nomination paper in the 2023 local elections whereby approval was given for nomination papers in which candidates put as their respective descriptions 'white, female, average build, long hair', 'overweight, beard' and 'database administrator'.[141] The third thing for which the nominating officer is responsible is the approval of descriptions and emblems used on ballot papers at elections.[142]

E. Additional Officer

3.51 The role of the additional officer only arises if a single person is registered as holding the roles of leader, nominating officer and treasurer. In that case, the party must also register another officer with the Electoral Commission so that the party has two registered officers and one person is not responsible for everything. This is important because, if the person dies who is at once the leader, treasurer and nominating officer, the party must have a person who can take up the role of treasurer until a replacement treasurer is registered.[143] The additional officer must have some specified office in the party.[144] The Electoral Commission's guidance simply says that the additional officer must 'have an official role of some kind in the party'. This may be, therefore, a person who is chair of the national board or governing committee, a party chairman, or a senior director of the party, or a deputy leader, etc.

F. Minor Parties

3.52 Minor parties are not required to register a treasurer and the provisions in PPERA 2000 about treasurers, campaign officers and their deputies do not apply to minor parties.[145] (See the definition of minor parties at paragraphs 2.24 and 2.46 above.)

which the Co-operative Party is not standing. Similarly, smaller right-wing parties may not stand candidates in seats held by the Conservative Party, but may wish to support that party's candidates instead.

138 PPERA 2000, s 24(3)(a).

139 ibid ss 24(3)(b) and 22(6).

140 Representation of the People Act 1983, Sch 1, r 6A; The Local Elections (Parishes and Communities) (England and Wales) Rules 2006, Sch 2, r 5.

141 Statement of Persons Nominated East Lindsey (Binbrook), published by the Returning Officer, East Lindsey District Council, April 2023.

142 PPERA 2000, s 24(3)(c).

143 ibid s 24(7)(b).

144 ibid Sch 4, para 4.

145 ibid s 34(2)(a).

But minor parties must nevertheless register a leader and a nominating officer. The leader of a minor party has a responsibility additional to those set out above. He must also notify the Electoral Commission that the party's registered particulars are still accurate. The notification must be given annually and the time to do so is within the period starting one month before the anniversary of registration and ending with the deadline of six months after the anniversary of registration.[146] The notification should be done using Electoral Commission form RP8M, which must be signed, returned either by post or by fax and accompanied by a fee, currently £25 (in 2024).[147]

3.53 If the party's registered details are not accurate, the leader should provide up-to-date information in the following ways:

i. by giving notice under section 31 of the PPERA 2000 that includes details of any change to the name of the registered leader or nominating officer or any other registered officer; or of the home address of the officer(s); or the address of the party's headquarters or the address to which communications may be sent.[148] This should be done using Electoral Commission forms RP2 (to alter an entry in the register), RP3 (to notify a change in registered details) or RP4 (to register a replacement party officer).
ii. by making an application under section 30 of the PPERA 2000 to change the party's registered name; to change the part or parts of Great Britain in respect of which it is registered (if it is on the Great Britain register); to add, alter, substitute or remove a registered description of the party; or to add, substitute or remove a registered party emblem.[149] This can be done within Electoral Commission form RP8M.[150]

3.54 A minor party may decide to register itself as a party that can stand candidates more widely than merely in community and parish elections. In that case the party must make an appropriate application to the Electoral Commission and it will be required to register a treasurer in the same way the major parties must do (because it ceases to be a minor party).[151]

V. Party Conferences

A. Annual Party Conference

3.55 Party conferences are influential events on the political calendar that can generate significant media coverage. They provide an opportunity for disparate parts of the

[146] ibid s 34(3) and (4).
[147] www.electoralcommission.org.uk/sites/default/files/2022-05/form-rp8m_updated.pdf.
[148] PPERA 2000, s 31.
[149] ibid s 30(1).
[150] All relevant forms may be found online on the Electoral Commission's website at www.electoralcommission.org.uk/i-am-a/political-party/political-parties-pef-online-and-forms.
[151] PPERA 2000, s 34(7) and (8).

party, from local constituency parties to MPs and peers, to coalesce, plot the party's course and, depending on the powers afforded to members by the party concerned, to confirm or reject central party proposals. Conferences also provide parties with an opportunity to raise funds.

3.56 The membership convening in conference is for many parties the supreme governing body, holding the power to change the party's rules. Thus, the work of the Labour Party is subject to 'the direction and control of Party conference',[152] the Liberal Democrat conference is the party's 'sovereign representative body',[153] the Scottish National Party's conference is 'the supreme governing body of the Party',[154] and Plaid Cymru is subject to its conference which is 'the highest authority of the party'.[155] But the Conservative Party's 'supreme decision making body' is its board and not conference[156] and the Co-operative Party is managed by its National Executive Committee, on which the resolutions of party conference are merely advisory.[157]

3.57 Hundreds of members and guests attend conferences of the major political parties. Many parties have detailed rules addressing rights of attendance, voting procedures and meeting arrangements. Rules governing admission to party conferences must comply with the Equality Act 2010.[158] Many legal principles that apply to meetings more generally apply to conference meetings, though the prevalence of extensive contractual arrangements governing these mass meetings' procedures may have the effect of excluding some terms implied by common law (for example, the right to a ballot, which is dealt with in paragraphs 4.28–4.29 below).

3.58 Often, parties establish committees the sole purpose of which is to regulate the rules and arrangements for the annual conference.[159] These conference committees, although prominent but once a year, have significant influence over the procedures and structures of the conference and, by extension, over the party as a whole.

3.59 It is usual for parties' constitutions to require party office holders (the Chief Executive or General Secretary, for example) to be re-elected at party conference by the membership, or delegates thereof. If the annual election does not happen, the office-holder will hold his authority in breach of the rules and his subsequent decisions will be void. Committee members should resign and stand for re-election (if permitted) once their terms have elapsed.[160] The rules of the party should therefore provide a mechanism for the extension of tenures in the event that the annual conference cannot be held.

[152] *Labour Party Rule Book*, Ch 1, VI.
[153] Federal Constitution of the Liberal Democrats, Art 6.
[154] Constitution of the Scottish National Party, cl 9.
[155] Constitution: Plaid Cymru – the Party of Wales, cl 15.
[156] Conservative Party Constitution, Part IV.
[157] Co-operative Party Rule Book, cl 6.8.
[158] See Chapter 11, Section III.C.
[159] See the Labour Party's 'Conference Arrangements Committee', the Liberal Democrats' 'Federal Conference Committee' and the Conservative Party's 'Committee of the Board on Party Conferences' as examples.
[160] See *Faruk and Others v Rahman and Others* (30 May 2000, unreported) (ChD) para 7 per Neuberger J (as he then was).

VI. Uniforms, Insignia and Militarism

A. Uniforms

3.60 The wearing of uniforms and other apparel by, and associated with, political organisations is forbidden in particular circumstances prescribed by the Public Order Act 1936 and the Terrorism Act 2000.

3.61 The Public Order Act 1936 prohibits members of political parties from wearing party-political uniforms or insignia at public meetings or in public places. (Note that this prohibition does not prevent political party members wearing party badges, rosettes or stickers.) These provisions were brought into force principally to stop fascist political organisations from marching in the streets of London's East End, causing riots and breaches of the peace.[161] A recent example of the provisions' use was the arrest of uniformed members of Britain First.[162]

3.62 A person commits an offence if he wears any uniform or insignia signifying his association with any political organisation or with the promotion of political objects in a public place or at a public meeting.[163] The component requirements of this offence, most of which were clarified in the leading case of *O'Moran v DPP*, are addressed below.[164]

i. 'Wearing'

3.63 The 1936 Act requires a person to be wearing an item of apparel, so the simple donning of a badge on the lapel would not meet the definition of wearing a uniform. Nor would the wearing of something very trivial (for example, a stud earring). Dark glasses, black berets, dark clothing and shirts have been held to fall within the Act's scope.[165]

ii. 'Uniform'

3.64 Whether or not a particular article of dress is to be described as a uniform depends on all the circumstances of the case.[166] Generally, for the purposes of the 1936 Act a uniform is:

i. clothing that is recognised as uniform worn by a single person, for example, the uniform of a soldier or police organisation;

[161] *Wilson v Skeock* (1949) 113 JP 294, 65 TLR 418.

[162] N Zatat, 'Britain First's "Christian Patrol" has ended very badly for them' (*The Independent*, 3 August 2016). In 2016 Britain First operated a uniformed group called the 'Britain First Defence Force'. The group's leaders were arrested following a political march in Luton.

[163] Public Order Act 1936, s 1.

[164] *O'Moran v DPP; Whelan v DPP* [1975] QB 864.

[165] ibid at 873. The position in respect of sashes is not easily apparent from the Act or associated jurisprudence. The practice since 1936 appears to be to permit the wearing of sashes, which presumably do not fall within the definition of apparel.

[166] ibid.

ii. a distinct article of clothing that is recognised and known to be the uniform of a relevant political organisation (for example, a swastika armband or a Ku Klux Klan hood);
iii. a distinct article of clothing that is not already recognised to be the uniform of a political organisation but which, nevertheless, is an identical article which a number of people deliberately adopt for the purposes of showing an association between them. For example, in the 1970s members of the Irish Republican movement adopted black berets which were not previously known to be the uniform of a relevant organisation but which were worn to indicate their association to promote the cause of Irish republicanism.[167]

iii. 'Association with a Political Organisation or Promotion of Political Objects'

3.65 There are two relevant categories of association with an organisation:

i. circumstances where a particular article of clothing is adopted by a recognised political organisation and is proven to be associated with it. It is not necessary for the particular organisation to be specified or named (as the organisation may change its name) so long as it can be proven that the article in question has been associated with a political organisation capable of identification in some manner.
ii. circumstances where there is no previous association between the item of clothing and a recognised political organisation but the circumstances in which it is worn make clear an association between several people and activity of a political character. For example, the wearing of a beret or armband by people at a funeral associated with a member of the Irish republican movement at which a speech is delivered of a political character.[168]

iv. Public Place or Public Meeting

3.66 This is self-explanatory, but the definition of a public meeting for the purposes of the 1936 Act is broad enough to include a meeting of a private organisation that is visible to the public. For example, it was determined in one case that a private meeting of the British Ku Klux Klan near Rugby (Warwickshire) was a public meeting for the purposes of the Act because the press had been invited to it and at the meeting the Ku Klux Klan had burned a cross, visible for miles around.[169]

B. The Terrorism Act 2000

3.67 The prohibitions of the Terrorism Act 2000 are wider in scope than those of the 1936 Act. Section 13(1) of the Terrorism Act 2000 prohibits not only the wearing

[167] ibid at 873–74.
[168] ibid at 874.
[169] *R v Robert Edward Relf and Others* (1965) Times, 8 October.

of clothing but the wearing, carrying or displaying of 'an article' in such a way or in such circumstances as to arouse reasonable suspicion that a person is a member or supporter of an organisation proscribed under the 2000 Act. The term 'article' is wide enough to include the carrying of flags or even the wearing of an item of jewellery.[170] To be guilty of the offence a person must know that he or she is wearing or carrying the item in question, but aside from that the offence is a strict-liability one and the person does not need an intention to support the proscribed organisation to be guilty of it.[171] The Supreme Court had to decide whether section 13 of the Terrorism Act 2000 was a disproportionate interference with the right to freedom of expression under Article 10 ECHR in *Pwr and Others v Director of Public Prosecutions*. The Court ruled unanimously that it was not. The provision is highly focused and aimed at ensuring that proscribed organisations do not obtain a foothold in the UK through the agency of people in this jurisdiction. Section 13 of the 2000 Act is about a restriction, or deterrence, designed to avoid violence, not the prevention of a situation in which there is an immediate threat of violence or disorder. That was a sufficient justification for the restriction on freedom of expression involved in section 13 to be lawful.[172]

C. Paramilitary Wings

3.68 The Public Order Act 1936 also bans political organisations from maintaining quasi-military (or paramilitary) organisations, including any body organised, trained or equipped for the purpose of using or displaying physical force in promoting any political objectives.[173] The 1936 Act also prohibits the organising, training or equipment of an association's members in such manner as to arouse reasonable apprehension that they are organised and either trained or equipped for the purpose of using or displaying physical force to promote political objectives.[174] The fact that there is no evidence of actual attacks or plans for attacks on opponents does not necessarily remove grounds for 'reasonable apprehension'.[175]

VII. Overview of Election Campaign Finance Controls

A. Summary

3.69 The rules about political campaign finances relating to political parties are detailed and lengthy. The following paragraphs set out a brief overview of the relevant statutory regimes controlling political campaign expenditure.[176] Two different statutory

170 *Rankin v Murray* 2004 SLT 1164, 2004 SCCR 422.
171 *Pwr and Others v DPP* [2022] UKSC 2, [2022] 1 WLR 789 at paras 25 and 58.
172 ibid at para 77.
173 Public Order Act 1936, s 2(1).
174 ibid s 2(1)(b).
175 *R v Jordan v Tyndall* [1963] Crim LR 124 (NICA).
176 Further guidance about the detailed provisions governing this area can be found in B Posner et al, *Schofield's Election Law* (Sweet & Maxwell, looseleaf); and R Price and V Sedgley, *Parker's Law and Conduct of Elections* (LexisNexis, looseleaf).

regimes regulate the election finances of candidates and of political parties. The first is set out in the Representation of the People Act 1983, which regulates candidates' election campaign spending. The second regime, which is found in the Political Parties, Elections and Referendums Act 2000, controls donations to, and election expenditure by, political parties themselves. The two regimes' controls on election campaign expenditure are mutually exclusive, irrespective of whether in practice they may overlap.[177] This is because PPERA 2000, section 72(7) provides that regulated political party election campaign expenditure does not include any expenses that a candidate must account for under the Representation of the People Act 1983.

B. Controls on Candidates' Election Spending

3.70 The regulation of candidates' election expenses is longstanding. It evolved from Victorian statutes which had as their purpose the reduction of electoral corruption. The basic structure of the current regime was set out in the Representation of the People Act 1949 and amended through the enactment of various consolidation acts, of which the Representation of the People Act 1983 is the latest. The 1983 Act has several important effects. It defines election expenses, which are closely regulated. Election expenses are any expenses, incurred at any time, which are used for the purposes of the candidate's election after the date when he becomes a candidate at the election, and which relate to:[178]

i. advertising of any nature;
ii. unsolicited material addressed to electors;
iii. transport by any means of persons to any place;
iv. public meetings of any kind;
v. the services of an election agent or any other person whose services are engaged in connection with the candidate's election;
vi. accommodation and administrative costs.

3.71 These categories are defined in detail in Part 1 of Schedule 4A to the RPA 1983. Various exemptions are set out in Part 2 of that schedule (notably the candidate's deposit, the publication of any matter in a newspaper or periodical other than an advert, and the provision of voluntary services by an individual, in his own time, free of charge).

3.72 The controls on election expenditure apply to the 'short campaign' during a general election, once Parliament has been dissolved and a person formally becomes a candidate.[179] The controls apply to election expenses incurred by prospective Westminster Parliamentary candidates during the 'long campaign' of a general election, even before an election is declared, but only when a Westminster Parliament

[177] *R v Mackinley* [2018] UKSC 42, [2019] AC 387 at [7].
[178] RPA 1983, s 90ZA(1).
[179] For the purposes of election expenses, the earliest date that a person can formally become a candidate in a Westminster general election is on the date of the dissolution of Parliament: see RPA 1983, s 118A.

runs for the maximum five-year term, or close to it.[180] The controls also have effect in respect of Parliamentary by-election campaigns (once a person becomes a candidate after the vacancy leading to the by-election arises);[181] as well as local government campaigns.[182]

3.73 The requirements imposed by the RPA 1983 on candidates and their agents are intricate. The basic architecture of the legislation is as follows. The RPA 1983 imposes spending limits on the election expenses incurred by or on behalf of a candidate for the purposes of the candidate's election.[183] Expenses include what is known as 'notional' expenditure, in other words, property, goods or services that have been provided free or at a discount of more than 10 per cent of their market value. The 1983 Act treats candidates as having incurred notional expenses equal to the market value of whatever may have been supplied free of charge and, if supplied at a discount, equal to the difference between the market value and what the candidate actually paid.[184] As set out below in Chapter 10, the 1983 Act bans anybody other than the candidate, his agent or somebody authorised in writing by the agent, from incurring election expenses of over £700.[185]

3.74 Candidates' agents must account for the election expenses that have been incurred by or on behalf of the candidate, as well as donations received by him, through a return to the returning officer within 35 days after polling day.[186]

3.75 It is a criminal offence to incur expenses in excess of the spending caps, or to fail to provide the various returns required by the Act (though there are various defences). Various offences also amount to a corrupt or illegal practice under the 1983 Act and may, depending on the offence concerned, restrict the candidate's ability to stand in future elections.

C. Controls on Political Parties' Campaign Finances

3.76 The second statutory expenditure regime limits the expenditure of political parties rather than candidates. The political party regime was introduced in its current form by PPERA 2000. The architecture of PPERA 2000 is similar to that set out in the RPA 1983 affecting candidates; PPERA 2000 was designed to extend a similar regime to political parties. The 2000 Act provides a definition of election expenditure (which is dealt with in detail in Chapter 10). Political parties are subject to spending caps on election expenses the purpose of which is to advance the position of the party's candidates

[180] RPA 1983, s 76ZA(1).
[181] ibid s 118A(2)(a).
[182] ibid s 118A(3).
[183] ibid ss 76, 76ZA and 90ZA.
[184] ibid s 90C.
[185] ibid s 75.
[186] ibid s 81.

at an election. (These are summarised in Table 1 near the beginning of Chapter 10). Political parties are prohibited from accepting donations from anonymous or non-permissible donors. Parties (other than minor parties) must account for the donations they have received and the expenditure they have incurred by sending returns on a quarterly basis to the Electoral Commission. During a general election campaign after the dissolution of Parliament, parties must submit returns on a weekly basis (see 3.41 above). As with the RPA 1983, it is a criminal offence to flout PPERA 2000's controls on electoral finance (and there are defences in various circumstances). The 2000 Act also imposes obligations on membership associations and individual members of political parties, including MPs (which are addressed in Chapters 4 and 5).

4

Local Political Parties

I. Introduction

4.1 Most people engaged in party-political activity organise on a local level within constituencies, primarily the constituencies of the Parliament at Westminster but also those of the Scottish Parliament and the Welsh Senedd. There are 650 constituencies in the UK, each of which returns an MP to Parliament.[1] This chapter begins by setting out the principal types of political entity which operate on the constituency level: the local constituency parties of national or regional political parties, residents' associations and other groups with an exclusively local focus, registered trade union branches and minor political parties which operate at the parish level. The following sections of this chapter address the legal relationship between central or 'national'

[1] Sinn Fein candidates who are elected to the House of Commons do not take their seats in Westminster.

parties and their subordinate constituency and branch parties, and the regulation of constituency parties' financial affairs. Thereafter, we turn to the rules regulating order and participation at local party meetings and the legal provisions relevant to political clubs, which are particularly important in the structure of the Conservative Party (ie Conservative Clubs).

II. Local Political Bodies

A. Constituency Parties

4.2 Four broad categories of party-political entities carry out political activity on a local level. This chapter is concerned mainly with the first category: the local constituency parties of national or regional parties (eg the Labour Party, the Conservative Party, the Liberal Democrats, the Scottish National Party, Plaid Cymru, the Green Party and the parties in Northern Ireland). These constituency parties are separate legal entities from their central or national counterparts. They often have a degree of financial autonomy. A political party must state when it applies to register whether, for financial purposes, it has both a central organisation *and* one or more constituent or affiliated organisations, each of which is to be responsible for its own financial affairs and transactions for accounting purposes.[2] Where they are registered as financial units separate from the central party (called 'accounting units') these constituency parties must register officers with the Electoral Commission, submit their accounts to the Commission in specific circumstances and they must comply with financial and accounting rules in the Political Parties, Elections and Referendums Act 2000 (PPERA 2000) separately from the central party. Notwithstanding that they may be separate legal entities, these constituency parties are not independent from their respective central parties; and they are not registered as parties in their own right with the Electoral Commission.

B. Residents' Associations and Single-Issue Groups

4.3 In the second category are residents' associations, groups of independent candidates and groups campaigning about local issues having a single, unitary structure. They are dedicated to standing candidates only in one particular constituency or a particular local area comprising a handful of constituencies (or, where the group only stands candidates in local elections, in the electoral wards comprising a specific local authority area). These groups are registered as political parties with the Electoral Commission. They usually have no wider policy or activity than participating in the politics of a specific geographic location.

[2] PPERA 2000, s 26(2)(b).

C. Trade Unions

4.4 Registered trade unions are a third category of political entity that organise within local constituencies. Trade unions do so by affiliating branches of their members who are registered to vote in particular constituencies with local Constituency Labour Parties (see paragraph 8.31 for further detail). These trade union branches are legal entities separate from the Labour Party; they are not registered as political parties.

D. Minor Parties Standing in Parish or Community Elections

4.5 In the fourth category are minor political parties. These are parties that contest parish or community elections only.[3] These minor parties have a unitary structure and usually restrict their operations to a few specific electoral wards.

III. Legal Status of Constituency Parties

4.6 The major parties all operate local parties on a constituency level. These constituency parties are not mere branches of their respective central parties. Rather, they are separate unincorporated associations with their own rules, their own executive officers and members. The constituency parties may be sued, and may hold property and membership dues, in their own right.[4] Note, however, that where a central party is established as a company, its local parties are not also separate corporate entities that are capable of being sued as one single entity. A member wishing to sue a constituency party in such circumstances must either sue the central party as responsible for one of its legal agents, or sue the local party in a representative capacity (ie sue the chair or secretary or other nominated head of the local party as a representative of all members except the claimant).[5]

4.7 Constituency parties have a degree of autonomy but they are not independent organisations. The relationship between the constituency parties and their national parent organisations was aptly summarised by the Court of Appeal in the case of *Lewis v Heffer*.[6] That case was about the Labour Party, but the key principles set out in the judgment apply with equal force to all other main political parties in Britain, given their broadly similar structures:

> a constituency Labour Party cannot be regarded as independent of the national party. Nor can its members. It is like a regiment of an army or a ship of a fleet. Each individual is a member of

[3] ibid ss 160(1), s 28(2)(d).

[4] See *John v Rees* [1970] Ch 345 and *Lewis v Heffer* [1978] 1 WLR 1061. Both cases concern the Labour Party but the relevant principles therein are relevant to all parties. Unincorporated associations must be sued in a representative capacity.

[5] See *UKIP v Hardy* [2011] EWCA Civ 1204 at para 35.

[6] *Lewis v Heffer* [1978] 1 WLR 1061.

> his unit but he is also a member of the whole. His unit is subject to the directions of the High Command: and so is he.[7]

4.8 The legal relationship between local constituency and central parties varies depending on the political party concerned. For example, Conservative Associations traditionally have a higher degree of autonomy than Constituency Labour Parties. Nevertheless, the legal relationship between local and central political units is broadly similar across the party-political spectrum. The following are points common to all the major parties:

i. **Members**: party members who join a political party enter into two separate legal contracts: one with the national party and another with the constituency party.
ii. **Rules**: constituency parties have their own rules, a breach of which may give rise to a legal claim by constituency party members. But the rules of the constituency parties must conform with specifications dictated by the central party. Constituency parties, primarily through their executive officers, must comply with the rules of the national or central party. If they do not, the rules of the party usually permit the central party to control it directly.
iii. **Property**: constituency parties may hold property and money for the benefit of their members. The powers of the constituency parties to hold property is, however, tightly controlled by the national party, which determines, and may change, the powers and functions of local parties.
iv. **Staff**: constituency parties may enter into employment contracts and employ staff. If the employer is the constituency party then it will be liable for unfair dismissal and other breaches of the Employment Rights Act 1996. See, for example, the case of *Bourne v Davyhulme Constituency Conservative Association*.[8]
v. **Multi-area parties**: local parties are permitted to combine into multi-constituency parties with the consent of the central party (and the Liberal Democrats permit local parties to be made up of several local council areas too).
vi. **Hierarchy**: constituency parties are subject to direction from the national or central party and the central party may suspend local parties in various circumstances. In the case of the main parties that stand candidates across Britain, the affairs of constituency parties are co-ordinated by a hierarchically superior regional body (called the Regional Party in the Labour Party, the Liberal Democrats and the Green Party and the Area Management Council in the Conservative Party). Constituency or local parties may themselves have subordinate local branches that operate in particular electoral wards. If so, those subordinate ward branches may also be legal associations in their own right; however, they are not accounting units for the purposes of financial regulation.
vii. **Party democracy**: the selection of party candidates primarily takes place within local parties (although central parties usually retain powers to interfere and regulate the selection competition: see paragraph 6.7 below). Representatives on central

[7] ibid at 1071.
[8] *Bourne v Davyhulme Constituency Conservative Association* (unreported, 18 November 1985) IT/20219/85 at para 6.

or governing party committees may be appointed by local party executives or elected by local party members as the case may be.

4.9 Different political parties have local party structures which can vary considerably, as the following examples show:

i. **The Conservative Party**: the Conservative Party operates local constituency associations. The associations are technically separate operational units that are themselves 'members' of the central party. Their own membership is restricted to natural persons[9] who are members of the party.[10] The associations may receive membership subscriptions.[11] Individual members may hold membership of more than one association but, if so, they will not be entitled to more than one vote in internal party elections.[12] Each association has at its head a chairman, who is entitled to a place in the National Conservative Convention (a body that serves as a link between the Board, members, the national party leadership and the associations) and in the relevant Area Council (which co-ordinates the activities of the party and its associations on a regional level). The associations each have an executive body as well as members and each association is charged with adopting candidates for Westminster elections and promoting the activities and objects of the Conservative Party in their respective constituencies.
ii. **The Labour Party:** the Labour Party has Constituency Labour Parties (CLPs). CLPs are established in constituencies as the Labour Party National Executive Committee so determines. They have their own individual members who must be members of the Labour Party. CLPs may also have affiliated organisations, being local branches of the trade unions and socialist societies that are affiliated to the national party, local co-operative society branches and branches of the Co-operative Party (with whom the Labour Party has had an electoral alliance for almost 100 years). Local trade union branches are only eligible to affiliate to CLPs if they have members who are registered as electors in the constituency.
iii. **The Green Party:** the Green Party's structure affords a relatively high degree of autonomy to local party entities. It has Local Parties, which are formed by local members. The Central Party encourages autonomy of the Local Parties.[13] The Local Parties may decide to merge with each other or to split.[14] Local Parties may federate at any level within or across the boundaries of Regional Party boundaries. Regional Parties are established by the Central Party constitution to cover particular geographical regions. The Regional Parties are represented on the Green Party Regional Council.[15] The Green Party differs from the Conservative and Labour Parties in that the function of its Board and National Executive Committee respectively are, in the Green Party, split between two different bodies. The Green Party's

[9] ie living people rather than companies.
[10] Conservative Party Constitution (2021), Pt I, cl 4.2.
[11] ibid cl 6.
[12] ibid cl 8.
[13] Constitution of the Green Party, cl 5.i.
[14] ibid cl 5.x.
[15] ibid cl 5.ii.

Regional Council operates as an internal legislative body that advises the Green Party Executive. The Regional Council has overall responsibility for interim policy statements between party conferences and for the party's internal democratic procedures. The Regional Council also has the power to recall the Green Party's co-leaders and to impose a fresh ballot to determine the leadership.[16] The Green Party Executive manages the day-to-day running of the party.[17]

IV. Financial Affairs of Constituency Parties

4.10 A national party's constituency parties do not need to be financially autonomous. But if the local parties are responsible for their own finances, then they will be accounting units for the purposes of PPERA 2000. Note that affiliated trade unions and co-operative societies are not accounting units for the purposes of electoral legislation.[18]

A. Local Party Treasurers

4.11 Constituency parties that are accounting units must have a person registered as the treasurer of the local party. The treasurer is responsible for the constituency party's compliance with the regulation of financial affairs, so far as relevant, as set out in PPERA 2000.[19] Constituency parties must also register an additional person who is an officer of the local party able to assume the responsibilities of the treasurer if the role of treasurer falls vacant.[20]

4.12 The constituency party's treasurer has exclusive duties in respect of the local party's financial record-keeping and accounting, in the sense that the registered treasurer of the central party has no responsibility for those things.[21] It is important that local party members undertake the role of treasurer seriously and carefully. The constituency party treasurer will be guilty of an offence if he fails to comply with the statutory requirements in PPERA 2000.[22] The Electoral Commission's guidance recognises that the people responsible for conducting the local party's financial affairs are, in the main, volunteers. The Commission suggests that it will take the facts of each case into account and will only take formal action when necessary or proportionate to do so.[23] A treasurer who deliberately or recklessly breaches his obligations to the Electoral Commission is also likely to be liable to be disciplined by the central party.

[16] ibid cl 6.
[17] ibid cl 7.
[18] PPERA 2000, s 26(8).
[19] ibid s 27(2).
[20] ibid s 27(2)(b) and (3). See Ch 3 for further details about what should happen when the post of registered treasurer becomes vacant.
[21] ibid Sch 5, paras 2(1)(a), 3(1)(a) and s 49.
[22] ibid s 47.
[23] Electoral Commission guidance, 'Overview of accounts for accounting unit treasurers' at 7.

4.13 The constituency treasurer must ensure that accounting records are kept that are sufficient to show and explain the constituency party's transactions and financial position and its assets and liabilities.[24] Essentially the records should give a reasonably accurate picture of the party's finances at any time. The accounting records must contain entries showing from day to day all money received and spent by the constituency party, what money is spent on and received for and a record of the assets and liabilities of the constituency party.[25] Maintaining proper records will help party treasurers to prepare the party's annual statement of accounts.[26] The treasurer must ensure that the records are kept for a minimum of six years from the end of the financial year in which they are made.[27] The constituency party's financial year is the same as that of the central party.[28]

B. Statement of Accounts

4.14 The treasurer must also prepare an annual statement of accounts,[29] approved by the constituency party's management committee or its secondary registered officer.[30] The treasurer is obliged to submit the constituency party's statement of accounts to the Electoral Commission only if the local party's total expenditure or gross income exceeds £25,000 in any financial year,[31] and if so, the treasurer must ensure that the statement of accounts is submitted within four months after the financial year's end.[32] Note, however, that the Commission has a general power to inspect the constituency party's financial records, including a power to demand that statements of accounts are sent to the Commission. If a demand is made then the treasurer must comply with it within specified deadlines.[33] Note also that, where submitted to the Electoral Commission, the local party's statement of accounts is available for inspection by the public.[34] The treasurer may make subsequent revisions to correct deficient statements of accounts that have already been sent to the Commission.[35] The Electoral Commission has created a standard Microsoft Excel template spreadsheet statement of accounts that local parties can use if they wish.[36] Local parties are encouraged to use the Commission's online service, PEF, to submit the statement of accounts.[37]

[24] PPERA 2000, s 41(1) and Sch 5, para 1(2)(a) and (b).
[25] ibid s 41(3).
[26] Electoral Commission guidance, 'Overview of accounts for accounting unit treasurers' section 4.
[27] PPERA 2000, s 41(4).
[28] ibid Sch 5, para 1(3).
[29] ibid s 42(1).
[30] ibid Sch 5, para 3(2).
[31] ibid Sch 5, para 6(1).
[32] ibid s 45(1). If the accounts are required to be audited because the party's gross income or expenditure exceeds £250,000 in any financial year, the statement of accounts and associated documents must be submitted to the Commission no later than 6 months and 7 days after the end of the financial year. See ibid ss 45(2) and 43(3).
[33] ibid Sch 5, para 6(3).
[34] ibid s 46 and Sch 5, para 7.
[35] ibid s 48 and Sch 5, para 9.
[36] Available at www.electoralcommission.org.uk/i-am-a/political-party/guidance-submitting-your-statements-accounts.
[37] See the Electoral Commission's guidance on PEF for how to use it and how to submit a return using it: 'PEF Online user guide'.

4.15 The statement of accounts may be prepared using either the cash or the accrual method of accounting. Under the cash accounting method one records financial transactions only when sums of money change hands. Accruals accounting is different: one accounts for transactions when the party has received, or given, a benefit, even if money has not been parted with. For example, if a local party were to have some leaflets printed, under the cash accounting method it would record the transaction when it *paid* for the leaflets; whereas under the accrual method the party would record the transaction when it *received* the printed leaflets (even if it had not yet settled the bill for them). It is usual for the central party to direct which accounting method local parties should use, so local treasurers should confirm the position with the central party.

4.16 Local party treasurers should keep in mind, among other things, that membership income includes not only membership subscriptions received by and kept within the local party, but also any membership subscriptions that have been transferred from the local party to the central party and vice versa. If money transferred to the local party by the central party can be identified as directly relating to membership fees then the local party should record that money under 'membership'. If the money cannot be identified as relating directly to membership fees then it should be recorded under the category 'transfers in' and the party should record the payment's purpose in the accounting note as 'membership income'.[38] The expenditure and income of a constituency party's ward branches should be included in the constituency party's statement of accounts and the accounts should state to which branch the sums refer.[39] Local party treasurers who need further information or support about completing account statements should ask their central parties for help in the first instance and then, if necessary, consult with the Electoral Commission online or by telephone.

4.17 If the constituency party's gross income *or* total expenditure in any financial year exceeds £250,000, which will be unlikely for smaller local parties and those not in target seats, the treasurer must arrange for the accounts to be audited.[40] (NB: the financial thresholds set out above and in PPERA 2000 are subject to change from time to time by primary and secondary legislation.)

V. Local Party Meetings: Order and Participation

A. Powers of the Chair

4.18 The chair of a party meeting, or of a party committee, is usually elected by the membership. The chair of party sub-committees will usually fall to be elected by the members of the relevant committee. The powers of a chair elected by the membership, for example the chair of a local branch party, should be set out in the rules.

[38] Electoral Commission guidance 'Cash accounting for accounting units' at 10–11.
[39] ibid 12.
[40] PPERA 2000, s 43(1) and Sch 5, para 4.

4.19 The common law affords powers and duties to chairs in addition to those set out in the party's constitution. The first duty of the person chairing is to preserve order.[41] He must ensure that the proceedings are conducted in a proper manner and that the sense of the meeting is properly ascertained with regard to any question which is properly before it.[42] He must ensure that the business of the committee does not exceed the jurisdiction permitted under the party's constitution.[43] The chair should regulate the proceedings so as to give all persons entitled a reasonable opportunity of voting.[44] He must also ascertain whether a quorum is present and oversee the validity and the result of any votes.[45] He may order a recount of any vote if there is doubt as to the result.[46] He must act not as a dictator but as a servant of the members.[47]

4.20 The chair should act neutrally and allow different opinions to be fully and fairly debated in accordance with any standing orders.[48] He must ensure that members do not tyrannise the meeting and may bring speeches to a close with the support of a majority of members present.[49]

4.21 Where the chair has a power to exercise a casting vote under the rules, he may exercise it as he thinks fit, but he must do so honestly and in accordance with what he believes to be the best interests of those who may be affected by the vote.[50]

4.22 The Chair has an inherent power to adjourn a meeting in the case of disorder; that power must be exercised in good faith for the purposes of facilitating the meeting and not for the sake of procrastination or interruption. Any adjournment must be no longer than necessary.[51]

4.23 Disorder must be addressed by the chair where it arises. The Court set out guidance for doing so in *John v Rees*, which concerned a 'robust political meeting' of a Welsh Labour Party that had descended into chaos. If there is disorder, the chair ought first to make earnest and sustained efforts to restore order, summoning to his aid if necessary any officers or others whose assistance is available. If the disorder persists, the chair should attempt to apply any provisions for adjournment provided for in the rules, for example by obtaining a motion to adjourn. If this proves impossible, the chair should exercise his inherent power to adjourn the meeting for a short while, such as 15 minutes, taking due steps to ensure so far as possible that all members present know of the adjournment. If serious violence breaks out, the chair should exercise his inherent power to adjourn as soon as possible.[52]

[41] *John v Rees* [1970] Ch 345 at 382.
[42] *National Dwellings Society v Sykes* [1894] 3 Ch 159 at 162.
[43] *Abbot v Sulivan and Others* [1952] 1 KB 189 (CA).
[44] *R v D'Oyly* (1840) 12 Ad & El 139 at 159.
[45] *Labouchere v Earl of Wharncliffe* (1879) 13 ChD 346 para 354.
[46] *Hickman v Kent or Romney Marsh Sheepbreeders Association* [1920] 37 TLR 163 (CA).
[47] *R v Bradford City Metropolitan Council, ex p Wilson* [1990] 2 QB 375 at 380, [1990] 2 WLR 255.
[48] ibid at 380.
[49] *Wall v London and Northern Assets Corpn* [1890] 2 Ch 469 at 438.
[50] *R v Bradford City Metropolitan Council, ex p Corris* [1990] 2 QB 363 at 371, [1990] 2 WLR 247.
[51] *John v Rees* [1970] Ch. 345 at 382.
[52] ibid.

B. Rights of Participation During Meetings

4.24 A member's right to attend a party-political meeting is founded in contract. His primary remedy for interference with that right will be an injunction or a declaration. Members are only entitled to attend meetings to the extent that the party's rules allow.[53] Thus, members may be permitted to attend general meetings but not meetings of a committee.[54] Barring a member from a meeting when he is eligible to attend it will constitute a breach of the membership contract. Members who are eligible to attend have a common law right to be heard at the meeting unless the rules expressly provide otherwise.

4.25 Members have a right to neutral treatment from the chair and a right to present their opinions, subject to the party's rules and standing orders.[55] Members have no right to monopolise the meeting and the majority is only bound to listen to reasonable arguments from the minority for a reasonable length of time.[56]

C. Rights to Vote at Meetings

4.26 A member's right to vote at meetings is determined by contract and it should be delineated by the express terms of the rules. Members may have a right to attend meetings but not to vote at them; that will often be the case where the rules for meetings draw a distinction between elected party delegates and ordinary, non-voting members, ie at party conferences or general meetings of constituency parties.

4.27 Some subordinate party organisations are incorporated; for example companies under which property is held, incorporated associated clubs or affiliated organisations.[57] Members of these bodies have rights of participation in meetings delineated by statute, for example, rules relating to the elections of directors, quorums, voting and proposing resolutions under the Companies Act 2006.

D. Right to Demand a Poll

4.28 Most voting takes place by a show of hands at meetings of political parties, particularly those of local branch parties and governing committees, save that contentious votes or votes of confidence are usually done by secret ballot. After a vote is taken by a show of hands, any member present at the meeting has the right to demand that the

[53] See eg *Evangelou v McNicol* [2016] EWCA Civ 817: members only have rights that the rules permit.

[54] Ordinary members are rarely permitted to attend the meetings of parties' governing committees. Members are often permitted to attend meetings of constituency parties other than their own, with the permission of the relevant party's executive committee, but not to vote in them.

[55] *R v Bradford City Metropolitan Council, ex p Wilson* [1990] 2 QB 375 at 380, [1990] 2 WLR 255.

[56] *Wall v London and Northern Assets Corpn* [1890] 2 Ch 469 at 483.

[57] eg Friendly Societies or working men's clubs. See Ch 2 for types of legal structures prevalent in political parties.

chair takes a poll (ie a recorded vote) of the members present.[58] But there is no obligation to hold a poll until one of the contending voters or parties expresses dissatisfaction with the decision of the chair upon a show of hands and demands one: it is effectively an appeal against a vote by a show of hands.[59] The right can be excluded by express contractual terms in the party's rules.[60]

4.29 The common law right does not extend to a *secret* ballot (a poll is not necessarily secret). Unless the rules expressly provide otherwise, the organisers of the poll are entitled to know how members voted, not least for the purposes of scrutiny.[61] A poll may be used to verify whether those voting are in fact eligible to vote.[62] In practice, when many local parties vote in a poll on a matter, the poll is treated as a secret ballot and members are simply required to cast their vote by handing in a slip of paper without any identifying mark.

E. Public Meetings

4.30 Attempts to break up or obstruct a public political meeting amount to a breach of the peace.[63] Political meetings are also protected during election periods by the Representation of the People Act 1983. A political meeting for those purposes is defined as a public meeting during the election campaign for the purpose of furthering the candidature of a parliamentary or local government candidate for election.[64] It is an illegal practice under election law (and therefore a criminal offence) for any person (including therefore a member of a rival political party) to break up or disrupt a lawful public political meeting during an election period.[65] Where a person is suspected of causing such disruption at a relevant meeting in Great Britain, the chair of the meeting may request the police to require the disruptor to declare immediately his name and address. It is an offence to refuse to do so or to give a false name and address.[66] Misuse by the police of their powers to silence hecklers at a public political meeting will amount to an unlawful infringement of the hecklers' rights to free expression and free assembly under Articles 10 and 11 ECHR.[67]

VI. Political Clubs

4.31 For completeness it is necessary briefly to mention political clubs that operate in local areas. They have a particularly important role in promoting the political ideology

[58] *Campbell v Maund* (1836) 5 Adolphus & Ellis 865.
[59] ibid at 881.
[60] ibid.
[61] *Haarhaus & Co GmbH v Law Debenture Trust Corpn* [1988] BCLC 640 at 651.
[62] *R v Wimbledon v Local Board* (1882) 8 QBD 459 at 465.
[63] *Sleigh and Russell v Moxey* (1850) J Shaw 369.
[64] Representation of the People Act 1983, s 95(1).
[65] ibid s 97(1).
[66] ibid s 97(3).
[67] *R (Gillan and Another) v Commissioner of Police of the Metropolis and Another* [2006] UKHL 12, [2006] 2 AC 307, para 30.

and programmes of the Conservative Party (and, historically, of the Labour Party, though Labour Clubs are not such an important part of the Labour movement today). Because of their enduring importance to the wider organisation of the Conservative Party, the focus of the following paragraphs is on examples relating to Conservative Clubs; materially similar legal principles are likely to apply to clubs affiliated to the other political parties.

A. Structure and Purpose

4.32 These clubs are usually established as companies or unincorporated associations and the laws that apply to those types of organisations apply with equal force to political clubs. The purpose or objects of Conservative Clubs are generally to widen the public's political involvement and engagement with the Conservative Party. They publish magazines that have articles about political matters; and hold social and other events, including about political issues. The clubs are focal points for local political campaigning and electioneering and often their premises are used to promote the Conservative Party's candidates, for example, by holding Conservative Party events and hosting the party's candidates. But there are often non-political elements to these sorts of clubs, for example, a subsidised bar and social events.[68] It is usually not a requirement for membership that prospective members are also members of a Conservative Association. But party members are often recruited from club members.

4.33 Conservative Clubs play an active part in the Conservative Party by affiliating to the Association of Conservative Clubs. An affiliated club may pay a subscription or donation to the constituency association in which it is located. If so, the club's members will be deemed club members of the party. Only a party member may represent the club or the Association of Conservative Clubs on the party's various internal committees.[69] Conservative Associations may choose to arrange themselves so that each club in their area that is affiliated to the Association of Conservative Clubs shall send a representative to sit on the executive council of the local Conservative Association[70] (or, where associations merge into a Federation covering more than one constituency, on the Federation's executive committee).[71]

B. Donations and VAT

4.34 The clubs donate money to the Conservative Party. Note that, although the motivation for these clubs' establishment is political, where the most significant of its

[68] *Shanklin Conservative and Unionist Club v HMRC* [2016] UKFTT 0135 (TC).
[69] Conservative Party Constitution (as amended), Art 25.
[70] ibid Sch 7, para 6.
[71] ibid.

activities is the provision of social amenities to its members the club will not be able to benefit from a VAT exemption on its membership subscriptions.[72]

4.35 The PPERA 2000 regulates donations to members' associations that consist wholly or mainly of members of a political party, where the donation is for the association's use or benefit in connection with political activities.[73] Political activities include promoting or procuring the selection of a person to be a political party's candidate in a public election, or their election to an internal office within the party (eg as the party's leader). Political activity for these purposes also includes a membership association's promotion and development of policies to be adopted by the political party in question.[74]

4.36 If the association falls within the scope of those provisions, then it should record any donations of more than £500 and must record any donations of more than £11,180, made either as a single sum or by aggregate sums of more than £500[75] – PPERA 2000 is not concerned with donations of minor value of £500 or less.[76] The membership association must then report those donations to the Electoral Commission within the time limits specified in PPERA 2000, Schedule 7 and provide the mandatory details set out in Schedule 7 paragraph 11 (the donor's name, address, the amount and the date received, etc). An association must not accept a donation if the donor is not a permissible donor,[77] or if the donor is anonymous (or the association is unable to determine whether the donor is a permissible one for some other reason).[78]

4.37 Unincorporated associations that donate more than £37,270 to political parties in any calendar year must register with the Electoral Commission.[79] A single donation of more than £37,270 will trigger the duty to register with the Commission; so too will a series of donations which together amount to more than £37,270.[80] As above, only donations of more than £500 count towards the threshold total.[81] A loan of money counts as a donation for the purposes of PPERA 2000.[82] The club must notify the Electoral

[72] *Shanklin Conservative and Unionist Club v HMRC* [2016] UKFTT 0135 (TC).

[73] PPERA 2000, Sch 7, para 1(3)(b).

[74] ibid Sch 7, para 1(4).

[75] ibid Sch 7, para 10.

[76] ibid Sch 7, para 4(3)(b). But associations must be alert to donors who attempt to evade the regulatory regime by making several or many payments of less than £500 – if that happens, the association should contact the Electoral Commission for advice.

[77] ie an individual on the register of parliamentary or local government electors maintained under the Representation of the People Act 1983, a company incorporated and carrying on business in the UK, a trade union on the register of trade unions, a building society or a friendly society, a limited liability company carrying on business in the UK, or an unincorporated association of more than two people which carries on business or other activities in the UK: PPERA 2000, s 54(2).

[78] PPERA 2000, Sch 7, para 6.

[79] But note that this obligation does not apply to unincorporated associations that are accounting units of a political party, eg local parties.

[80] PPERA 2000, Sch 19A para 1(1).

[81] ibid Sch 19A, para 1(3).

[82] ibid Sch 19A, para 1(2)(b) and (d).

Commission within 30 days of the donation that takes it over the £37,270 threshold. The club should keep records of all and any gifts of more than £500 it receives if the club intends to donate more than £37,270 to a political party. Clubs that fall under the obligation to register with and notify the Commission of political donations must also submit a report to the Electoral Commission detailing every gift of more than £11,180 received; detailed rules in PPERA 2000, Schedule 19A prescribe the detail and timing of such reports.[83] These financial thresholds are set out in primary and secondary legislation and are susceptible to amendment.

[83] ibid Sch 19A, para 2.

5

Internal and Leadership Elections

I. Introduction

5.1 This chapter sets out rules about the conduct of internal elections in parties, whether for the position of leader, the election of committee members or the election of candidates for public elections. (Chapter 6 explains the rules that relate to the selection of party candidates in further detail). Political parties are private organisations governed by contractual constitutions (see Chapter 2). That means that the conduct of internal party-political elections is a private matter for the party. A party's constitution should set out detailed rules for members' eligibility to vote and their participation, as well as rules about systems of voting, the declaration of results and other matters. The rules that apply to elections in private bodies (companies, associations and so on) apply with equal force to political bodies and parties, but particular legal considerations are relevant to political parties due to their unique status as private bodies with an important place in public democracy. The mechanisms to appoint or remove a party leader are especially important: the leader of a national party has enormous scope to alter its political fortunes and policy. Legislation requires all registered political parties to have a registered leader of the party overall. Section II of this chapter explains the principal rules relevant to internal elections generally. Section III considers the operation of leadership elections, how party leaders may be deposed and, last, the powers leaders hold over the rest of the party upon their election.

II. Internal Elections

A. Eligibility to Vote

5.2 A member has no entitlement to vote in a party's internal election simply by being a member of the party.[1] She will have the right to vote only as provided in the party's rules and if she satisfies any eligibility criteria therein. Eligibility to vote may vary from one election to another.

5.3 A political committee charged with a broad power under the rules to delineate rights of participation in elections is entitled to define eligibility criteria both to stand and to vote. This power is not limited to mere 'gap filling' of uncertainties in the rules. It may include a power of discretion over matters of substance to do with participation as well as with matters of procedure.[2] Any decision about eligibility must comply with the implied contractual terms of rationality and good faith.

5.4 The 'freeze date' for an internal election is the date by which a particular state of affairs (usually party membership status) must exist in order for a member to be eligible to vote. The imposition of a freeze date will usually mean that some members have voting rights while others do not.[3] A freeze date may be prospective (requiring people to have become members by a future date) or retrospective (members must have been

[1] *Evangelou v McNicol* [2016] EWCA Civ 817 para 38.
[2] ibid para 40.
[3] ibid para 52.

admitted to membership from a date in the past).[4] The decision to set the freeze date must accord with the provisions in the rules and must be made on a proper factual and legal basis, otherwise it will be void and susceptible to judicial interference.[5]

B. The Election

i. No General Right to Re-election

5.5 Neither a sitting member of a committee nor an elected officer has a right to be re-elected unless the constitution of the party says so.[6] Generally, and unless otherwise provided for in the constitution, the election to a committee or an office thereof (for example, chair of an executive committee) is in no sense connected to the election of different people to those positions previously. It is an entirely independent and unconnected creation.[7] Thus, there is generally no entitlement to rotation by seniority ('Buggins' turn'). The rules may provide for different nomination requirements depending on whether a candidate is an incumbent.

ii. Notice and Rules of the Election

5.6 Notice of an internal election must be given or the result will not bind those eligible members who did not receive notice and who did not vote.[8] However there is usually no obligation to circulate papers specifying the key dates for an election, or nomination papers relating to the election, to members who have not paid their subscriptions up to date.[9] The election of committee members must follow the terms of the procedural rules set out in the party's constitution otherwise the committee will be invalidly constituted and its subsequent decisions will be void.[10]

5.7 Minor errors of procedure will not necessarily render the election a nullity: the crucial question is whether the conduct of the election has been substantially in accordance with the procedure laid down in the rules. Thus, an election will not be void merely because ballots have been sent out to members but not received in time or at all. Any postal ballot is, by nature, subject to the vagaries of the postal service. Mere administrative errors disrupting an election will not vitiate it if the error is not directly to do with the conduct of the ballot.[11]

[4] *Evangelou v McNicol* [2016] EWCA Civ 817; *Jeffers v The Labour Party* [2011] EWHC 529 (QB).

[5] *Khan v Scottish Executive Committee of the Scottish Labour Party* [2018] CSOH 68 para 19.

[6] *Weinberger v Inglis (No 2)* [1918] 1 Ch 517 (CA).

[7] *Weinberger v Inglis* [1919] AC 606 (HL).

[8] *Baird v Wells* (1890) 44 Ch D 661 at 671.

[9] *Jeffers v The Labour Party* [2011] EWHC 529 (QB).

[10] *Hussain v Wycombe Islamic Mission and Mosque Trust Ltd and Iqbal* [2011] EWHC 971 (Ch). The executive committee of a mosque was appointed with the agreement of political factions within its membership, rather than a vote of its members. The committee was not validly elected and its decisions to enter into contractual arrangements and trust agreements were void.

[11] *Brown v Amalgamated Union of Engineering Workers and Another* [1976] ICR 147 at 157.

iii. Voting in Internal Elections

5.8 Rules for internal elections may specify a particular system of voting, for example by first past the post or by single transferable vote. Contractual provisions may also be made for the election to take place by a vote of different membership colleges or by the membership as one constituency. A power under the constitution to set procedural rules for elections is likely to include the power to determine not only matters of procedure but also matters of substance about participation in the ballot (eg who may participate in it),[12] and the system of voting. Where the governing committee has broad contractual powers to manage the party, and the rules are silent as to the procedure and method for election, the committee may choose any means and procedure for the election so long as their choice is not tainted by irrationality, capriciousness or bad faith.[13]

5.9 A member's right to vote is exercised when he completes the ballot paper. The right is recognised and effected when his ballot paper is counted.[14]

iv. Independent Scrutineers and Independent Returning Officers

5.10 A party may appoint an independent body or independent returning officers to conduct the election on its behalf if the rules permit such delegation. If so, the party will normally be under a duty to abide by the independent returning officer's decision. No claim for breach of contract will lie against the party for procedural irregularities in the conduct of the election on the part of the independent returning officer. Where the conduct of the election is properly delegated by the party, it will have fulfilled its obligations under the rules and will be bound by the result of the ballot.[15]

5.11 Where a party appoints an independent scrutineer to conduct the election yet the party's rules are silent on important elements of the electoral system, it may be appropriate to imply as terms into the party's rules the methods of election usually adopted by the scrutineer.[16]

5.12 Political parties may for various reasons establish associated legal entities other than unincorporated associations, for example to hold real property. Clubs affiliated to the political party may also be incorporated legal entities. In those cases, particular statutory and contractual provisions will regulate elections to those

[12] *Evangelou v McNicol* [2016] EWCA Civ 817 para 55.
[13] *Cassel v Inglis* [1916] 2 Ch 211 at 231.
[14] *RMT v CD* [2001] IRLR 808, [2002] CLY 1424 para 20.
[15] *Veness and Another v National Union of Public Employees and Others* [1992] ICR 193 at 196.
[16] See *RMT v CD* [2001] IRLR 808, [2002] CLY 1424. The RMT's elections to its executive committee were conducted to a single transferrable vote system that resulted in a tie. The RMT's rules were silent on what to do in the event of a tied result and it was appropriate for the rules of the Electoral Reform Service, who was the scrutineer, to be implied into the RMT's procedure for the election.

incorporated entities' governing bodies,[17] potentially to the exclusion of the party's accepted procedural rules.

v. Results

5.13 The election will conclude when the result is declared or published.[18] At that moment the person with the highest number of votes has been elected. There is no implied power to remove him from the position by purporting to cancel the election, unless it can be shown that the whole process was a nullity. The party is subject to a duty at that stage to give effect to the wishes of the membership as expressed in the ballot and as declared.[19] The declaration bars any fresh ballot being undertaken for the election in question, unless some factor emerges which renders the election null and void. Factors rendering the election void include the candidates being ineligible to be elected in the first place, or voting that was marred by fraud.[20]

5.14 Generally, and commonly in trade union elections, the effect of the declaration of the result is to waive irregular practices by the candidates. Fairness requires that any objections to the validity of an election are presented within narrow time limits.[21] It is questionable whether this principle applies with equal force to political parties, given the public interest that their affairs be free from corruption. Significant corruption on the part of candidates for a major office of a main political party is likely to present legitimate grounds for the party to invalidate their election. Given the public interest that political parties be free from corruption, less serious infractions of the rules by candidates for minor office may justify disciplinary action by the party (for further detail on principles of good governance for political parties see Chapter 12, Section II).

5.15 A member of a party who stands for election to a committee and is elected in a ballot conducted in accordance with the rules will be entitled to serve on the committee.[22]

5.16 Members have a right to know the result of a ballot at their local branch or at the regional or sub-regional office where they cast their vote. However, there is no general right to inspect the results save as permitted by the party's rules or by express direction of its governing committee.[23]

[17] eg Co-operative and Community Benefit Societies Act 2014, s 14; Companies Act 2006, ss 160 and 284; Friendly Societies Act 1974, s 7(2); Friendly Societies Act 1992, s 27.

[18] *Veness and Another v National Union of Public Employees and Others* [1992] ICR 193 at 196.

[19] *Douglas v Graphical Paper and Media Union* [1995] IRLR 426 paras 22 and 23.

[20] *Brown v Amalgamated Union of Engineering Workers and Another* [1976] ICR 147 at 160.

[21] ibid.

[22] See *Sinclair v UKIP* [2003] EWHC 2675 (Ch) para 35.

[23] *Hughes v Transport and General Workers Union* [1985] IRLR 382 at 385.

vi. Revoking, Cancelling, or Postponing Elections

5.17 Those charged with the conduct of the election must act fairly in deciding to adjourn, rerun or cancel the ballot.[24] Where members are required to submit notice of nominations not by a specified date but simply by the day of the election, and the election is adjourned, the deadline for nominations will be the day to which the election is adjourned.[25]

5.18 If irregularities in the election are so significant as to require a fresh ballot in the opinion of the governing committee, the committee must canvass the observations of any person who has been announced as the winner of the election, especially where the office in question is a remunerated one.[26] If a fresh election is held it will be a new event for which new nominations and candidates will be required.[27] An election may only be cancelled or set aside if there is good evidence that irregularities are likely to have had a significant effect upon the result.[28]

5.19 Candidates have nothing more than an expectation of acceding to the office in question until the result is declared.[29] Once a candidate's victory has been declared, however, the successful candidate has rights to the elected position that can only be removed by a fair exercise of the powers of the general meeting or by the executive committee.[30]

5.20 An elected member or officer of an executive committee (eg of a constituency party) may be removed by the general meeting of the membership that was eligible to elect him, for reasonable cause in a reasonable opinion of the members.[31] However, the rules of natural justice must be followed before passing resolutions stripping officers of their powers or role.[32]

vii. Standing to Challenge an Election in Court

5.21 Sufficient legal standing is required to challenge an internal election of a political party. Only party members, being contractual parties to the party constitution, will have a legal basis to bring a challenge. Even among these members, the class of people who have standing will often be drawn narrowly. Generally, only those members who can demonstrate some interference with a right or power under the constitution which affects them as a member of the party will have standing to sue.[33] In an election open to

[24] *Brown v Amalgamated Union of Engineering Workers and Another* [1976] ICR 147 at 169.
[25] *Catesby v Burnett* [1916] 2 Ch 325.
[26] ibid.
[27] *Douglas v Graphical Paper and Media Union* [1995] IRLR 426 para 42.
[28] ibid.
[29] *Brown v Amalgamated Union of Engineering Workers and Another* [1976] ICR 147 at 169.
[30] ibid at 160.
[31] *Inderwick v Snell* (1850) 2 Macnaghten & Gordon 216, 42 ER 83.
[32] *John v Rees* [1970] Ch 345 at 382. For the requirements of natural justice, see Ch 12, Section III.B.
[33] *Howell v Evans & McNicol* [2020] EWHC 2303 (QB).

all members of a political party – for example a leadership election – all members are likely to be affected by the result and, therefore, are likely to have sufficient standing. So, in *Evangelou v McNicol* an individual, ordinary member of the Labour Party had standing to challenge the Labour Party's decision to set eligibility criteria to vote in the 2016 Labour Party leadership election which had disenfranchised her.[34]

5.22 The vast majority of political elections will concern, at most, those members of the local parties or organisational units in which a person has been elected, such that there is no standing for members outside that group to challenge the result. A party member is unlikely to have sufficient standing to challenge the election of a person by a parliamentary party to a position in that parliamentary group, unless the wider party's rules provide for some contractual association between the parliamentary group and the rest of the membership. The case of *Conservative and Unionist Central Office v Burrell* serves as an example of this point. At the time the case was decided the leader of the Conservative Party was elected solely by the party's MPs. (The case was actually about what sort of legal body the Conservative Party was for tax purposes.) In its examination of the party's structure the Court of Appeal decided that no member of a local constituency association, simply by reason of being an association member, could claim he had a contractual right under the Conservative Party's constitution to challenge the parliamentary party's election of its leader.[35] There was an insufficient contractual relationship between the parliamentary party and an individual member for any such challenge to have a proper basis.

III. Leadership Elections

A. Electing Political Leaders

5.23 The election of the main parties' leaders is an event of high drama which the public is left to witness as mere spectator. Examples are the 1990 Conservative Party leadership election deposing Mrs Thatcher, the unsuccessful attempt by Labour MPs to depose Mr Corbyn in 2016 and the election of Ms Truss as Conservative Party leader in 2022. The election of a political party's leader is a matter for that party alone, through its agreed contractual arrangements involving its party members and machinery.[36] Because these leadership elections are governed by the rules set out in the parties' respective constitutions they are subject to the law of contract; they may, therefore, be challenged by party members in the courts.[37] Judges have cautiously ventured into

[34] *Evangelou v McNicol* [2016] EWCA Civ 817 at para 3.

[35] *Conservative and Unionist Central Office v Burrell* [1982] 1 WLR 522 at 557 per Lawton LJ.

[36] eg *R (on the application of Tortoise Media Ltd) v Conservative and Unionist Party* [2023] EWHC 3088 (Admin) per Fordham J. The principle of autonomy set out in that High Court case is concordant with the jurisprudence of the ECtHR on the autonomy of political parties under Art 11 ECHR, although that body of case law was apparently not before the Court in *Tortoise Media Ltd.*

[37] See *Foster v McNicol* [2016] EWHC 1966 (QB); *Conservative and Unionist Central Office v Burrell* [1982] 1 WLR 522.

leadership disputes when called on to do so, though they have adopted a narrow focus on specific contractual terms and principles and declared themselves entirely uninterested in the political result of their application.[38]

i. The Campaign

5.24 Political actors have a great deal of latitude in organising and fighting battles for political leadership so long as they do not infringe the party's rules and the campaign is free from corruption. Campaigns that offend statutory duties may be tainted by unlawfulness, but such unlawfulness is unlikely to vitiate the election so long as the contractual and common law rules governing the leadership election itself have been followed. For example, a mishandling of membership data may amount to a breach of the Data Protection Acts; however, the remedy for the breach lies in a private law action for damages by a member for breach of their personal data rights, rather than in an injunction striking down the results of the election.

5.25 There may be campaigning acts done in bad faith in the course of a leadership battle, but the presence of bad faith alone is unlikely to nullify a leader's victory. This is because bad faith actions will usually be done in contexts where no relevant legal relationship can be established between rival interested parties, not because the court is uninterested in the presence of bad faith. The law implies a duty into all political party constitutions, in common with all contracts, that the powers under the rules will be exercised in good faith (see Chapter 2, Section II.B). The duty of good faith exists between those acting on behalf of the political party on one hand and its members on the other, who are all signatories to the rules. The duty is not owed by one individual member to another, still less from a candidate standing for leadership to another candidate. But a candidate may sue the party for breach of contract where those acting on behalf of the party (for example its governing committee, or the incumbent leader) take decisions in bad faith in respect of the candidate (eg a decision to bar him from standing taken in bad faith).

5.26 Party members who campaign for the leadership themselves or on another person's behalf may become regulated donees subject to the controls on donations under the Political Parties, Elections and Referendums Act 2000 (PPERA 2000). The rules are materially similar to those that apply to membership associations set out above at paragraphs 4.35 and 4.36. A member of a political party will be a regulated donee where he receives one or more donations over £500 for the purpose of promoting or securing a person's election to the leadership of the party. In that case the duties to keep records and to report donations within the time limits set out in PPERA 2000, Schedule 7 will apply. Any donation by one person or organisation of more than £2,230 (whether made in a single sum or in aggregate) should be reported to the Electoral Commission. Regulated donations include not only sums of cash but also the provision of non-cash benefits, for example free office space (in which case the value of the donation is the

[38] *Evangelou v McNicol* [2016] EWCA Civ 817.

market value of the benefit).[39] No donation may be accepted from an impermissible donor,[40] an anonymous donor, or where it is not possible to ascertain whether the donor is a permissible one. A report must be sent to the Electoral Commission of all donations received (and returned) of more than £500 from impermissible or unidentifiable donors. The report should set out the amount, nature and value of the donation, the name and the address of the donor (if known), the date the donation was received, the date it was returned and who it was returned to.[41] (The financial thresholds above are those that apply in 2024 and may be subject to subsequent amendment by legislation.) It is an offence to retain donations from impermissible donors. Note that some political parties also place their own limits on the amount of money that candidates may lawfully expend campaigning for their election. Those internal limits are purely a matter for the party; their breach may give rise to grounds for barring a candidate from the leadership contest or for disciplinary action under the party's rules, depending on the position adopted by the party in question.

ii. The Election

5.27 The main political parties have seen a transformation in the processes to elect their leaders over the last 40 years; from exclusive affairs in smoke-filled rooms and tiny franchises to open, transparent mass-membership voting. Until 1965 the Conservative Party did not elect its leader through a transparent ballot: a leader 'emerged' following deliberations among Conservative MPs. That system has been described as 'an opaque process of negotiation and "soundings" involving senior party figures'.[42] Thereafter, until 1997, only Conservative MPs were entitled to vote for the party's leader. Until 1983, only Labour Party MPs were entitled to vote for the Labour Party leader. In the 1980 leadership election of Michael Foot, therefore, only 269 Labour Party members were entitled to vote. Notwithstanding that the Party had several hundred thousand individual members in addition to affiliated trade unions with millions of members in their ranks, victory was carried with merely 139 votes. None of the major parties operate these sorts of restricted electoral systems today. The electoral processes for the main Westminster parties, as they stood in 2024, are summarised below.

5.28 The Conservative Party operates a two-stage voting system. The 1922 Committee (comprising all back-bench MPs, who elect its executive committee) has a duty to present to the membership a choice of candidates for election. The 1922 Committee has the power to determine by what procedure candidates will be shortlisted for presentation.[43] In the 2019 and 2022 leadership elections candidates were shortlisted by eliminating ballots of the party's MPs.[44] A candidate achieving more than 50 per cent

[39] PPERA 2000, Sch 7, para 10.
[40] See Ch 4, fn 77 for the list of permissible donors.
[41] PPERA 2000, Sch 7, para 11(3).
[42] N Johnston, *Leadership Elections: Conservative Party* (House of Commons Library, 2019); P Webb, *The Modern British Party System* (Sage, 2000) 197–98.
[43] UK Conservative Party Constitution, Sch 2(3).
[44] N Johnston, *Leadership Elections: Conservative Party* (House of Commons Library, 2019) 3.

of the vote among the party membership will be declared elected leader of the party.[45] Where there is only one valid nomination at the close of nominations prior to the first ballot being held by the parliamentary party, the election of the nominee may be ratified by a ballot of the membership.[46] The Chairman of the 1922 Committee is the returning officer.[47]

5.29 The Labour Party also operates a two-stage system. Where a vacancy for leader arises, candidates must secure nominations from five per cent of Constituency Labour Parties, or nominations from at least three affiliate bodies (at least two of which must be trade unions) comprising five per cent of affiliated membership. Where the incumbent leader is challenged, candidates must be supported by 20 per cent of Labour Party MPs. Both the incumbent leader and deputy leader are entitled to be on the shortlist of candidates automatically in their respective elections.[48] In the past, voting took place in electoral colleges of ordinary members, affiliated trade unions and affiliated socialist societies. Now, the current rules require a candidate to obtain the support of a majority of members and affiliated members who vote in a single college.[49] The General Secretary is the returning officer. Reflecting the practice required by statute elsewhere in the Labour movement,[50] an independent scrutineer must be appointed to oversee and verify the ballot.[51] The election takes place by single transferrable vote.

5.30 Contenders for the leadership of the Liberal Democrats must obtain nominations from at least 10 per cent of other Liberal Democrat MPs (ie not including the candidate) and from at least 200 members in aggregate in not less than 20 local parties and official youth organisations.[52] Candidates passing that threshold will be put to a ballot of all eligible members using the alternative vote system.[53] The Returning Officer is the Chair of the Federal Appeals Panel and the Acting Returning Officer is the Chief Executive of the party.[54] The Scottish Liberal Democrats' rules differ from those of the federal party in that their leader is elected for a fixed term of no longer than five years, after which she must stand for re-election.[55]

5.31 The Scottish National Party requires its leader to be elected annually by all eligible members of the party. Candidates for leader must obtain the nominations of at least 100 members, who must be drawn from at least 20 branch parties. However, the incumbent leader will automatically stand nominated for the election and, where only one candidate is nominated for leader, it is unnecessary to hold an election.[56]

[45] UK Conservative Party Constitution, Sch 2(6).
[46] ibid Sch 2(7).
[47] ibid Sch 2(9).
[48] *Labour Party Rule Book*, Ch 2, II, 2, B.
[49] ibid Ch 2, II, 2, C.
[50] eg for the election of a trade union's President. See Trade Union and Labour Relations (Consolidation) Act 1992, s 49.
[51] *Labour Party Rule Book*, Ch 2, II, 2, C.
[52] Federal Constitution of the Liberal Democrats, cl 18.5.
[53] ibid cl 9.6.
[54] Federal Constitution of the Liberal Democrats, 'Leadership Election Regulations', cl 1.
[55] The Constitution of the Scottish Liberal Democrats, cl F3.
[56] Scottish National Party Constitution, cl 15.7.

iii. Registration

5.32 Once an overall leader of a registered party has been elected, he or she must be registered as the party leader with the Electoral Commission.[57] (For further detail about registration see Chapter 3 Secton IV.A.)

iv. Elevation to Government

5.33 A person who is elected to lead a party when the party holds a legislative majority does not automatically assume public executive power. Rather, in each case, a consequential constitutional process is required, as set out below.

i. The Prime Minister is appointed by the sovereign on advice. The advice is the identification of the person who will have the support and confidence of the House of Commons. The advice will usually identify as that person the leader of the largest party in the Commons, who has the support of a majority of MPs.[58] When a party deposes a leader who is Prime Minister between general elections, the party will need to select a new leader. The new leader will normally become Prime Minister, providing that the party concerned still holds a majority in the House of Commons. In this way, the change in party leader results in a change in Prime Minister without a general election. It is important to remember, however, that the appointment of Prime Minister has not been outsourced to the political party in these circumstances. The party's choice of leader and the appointment of Prime Minister are distinct processes. As set out above, a party's choice of leader must be a matter for the party to decide autonomously according to its internally agreed process. Separately, the Prime Minister is appointed by the King on advice. Usually, based on the outcome of the political party's selection process, the advice will be that the emergent party leader has the support and confidence of the Commons.[59]
ii. First Ministers of Scotland and Wales are appointed by the sovereign. Their respective Parliaments must nominate them to be First Minister and the Presiding Officer of the Parliament will recommend to the King that the nominated person should become First Minister.[60] The First Minister must enjoy the confidence of the Scottish Parliament and the Welsh Senedd respectively; the First Minister must resign if the respective assembly resolves that it no longer has confidence in him or her (in the Senedd the condition is that the Senedd resolves that the Welsh Ministers no longer have confidence in the First Minister – the effect is materially the same).[61]

[57] Political Parties, Elections and Referendums Act 2000, s 24(1).

[58] *R (on the application of Tortoise Media Ltd) v Conservative and Unionist Party* [2023] EWHC 3088 (Admin) per Fordham J.

[59] ibid. In that case a claim for judicial review failed which challenged the Conservative Party's election of Liz Truss as leader: 'The political party has no legal power to select or appoint the Prime Minister. That is an act of the Sovereign, on advice to the Sovereign. That is the true reality' (at paras 35–38).

[60] Scotland Act 1998, ss 45(1) and 46; Government of Wales Act 2006, s 46.

[61] Scotland Act 1998, s 45(2); Government of Wales Act 2006, s 47(2).

iii. As for Leaders of local authorities: many local authorities operate a 'leader and cabinet model'. Under that system, the full council elects the Leader of the Council. This will usually be the leader of the political group[62] having a majority of seats. The members of that political group will choose their leader by election amongst themselves. In practice, where a particular political party holds a majority of seats on a local council, the leader of that party's group in the council will usually be Leader of the Council (but not always – especially if there are deep political divisions within political parties and a coalition is required).

v. *The Leader of the Opposition*

5.34 The Leader of the Opposition in Parliament is the leader of the largest party after the governing party. The Speaker is the final arbiter of who is the Leader of the Opposition if there is any doubt (ie for the purpose of who shall receive the salary associated with that position[63]).

B. Removing Political Leaders

5.35 The lack of any directly-elected element to the executive branch places MPs (and local councillors in local authorities that operate a leader and cabinet system) in primary position to curtail the tenure of political party leaders, even those who enjoy a democratic mandate. Popular political movements and currents are, in this sense, subservient to parliamentary forces, because MPs can break their leadership and block them from leading the country. Most Prime Ministers since 1990 have been undone by their own party organisations while the party's majorities in the House of Commons were left unscathed. The premierships of Thatcher, Blair, May, Johnson and Truss were all extinguished by their parties and, chiefly, by members of the parliamentary party; only Major and Brown resigned following a general election defeat. (Cameron resigned a year after a general election, and when he had a parliamentary majority, following the defeat of his policy in a referendum.) This is a peculiarity of the representative Westminster system. In jurisdictions with a directly-elected president, political leaders have a direct mandate to lead the country which cannot be extinguished merely at the whim of legislators in their own party (short of constitutionally recognised mechanisms for removal, eg impeachment).

5.36 The removal of a party leader relies on a loss of confidence in him on the part of a parliamentary party. The loss of confidence may be formalised with a vote by simple

[62] A local authority political group is a group of two or more local councillors recognised under the Local Government (Committees and Political Groups) Regulations 1990, SI 1990/1553, regs 7 and 8. Local authority councillors are only divided into political groups where there is more than one political group on the council. The group is validly constituted once councillors provide written notice to the relevant council officer appointed to receive it, stating that the council members who have signed it wish to be treated as a political group, alongside the name of the group and the name of one of the signatories who is to act as the group's leader.

[63] Ministerial Salaries Act 1975, s 2(2).

majority that triggers a contested leadership election depending on the party. It is very unlikely that a vote of no confidence in the leadership of a political party, even if done in Parliament, would fall within the scope of parliamentary privilege such that the court's jurisdiction is entirely ousted. The vote, even if it were to take place within the parliamentary precinct, would not be part of Parliament's core business but, rather, the act of a private association on parliamentary premises.

5.37 A no confidence motion is not needed to remove a Labour Party leader. A motion of no confidence in Jeremy Corbyn was passed by a large majority of the Commons members of the Parliamentary Labour Party in 2016. Mr Corbyn declared that the vote had no constitutional standing in the party's rules and refused to resign. The Labour Party's rules provide that a leadership challenge should move to a membership ballot only if 20 per cent of Labour Party MPs nominate a challenger. Once the threshold is reached, the leadership election must take place, as it would in the case of a vacancy. The Conservative Party, however, does require a formal vote of no-confidence to trigger a leadership contest. This is not a condition of the Conservative Party constitution, but of the rules of the 1922 Committee. A vote of no confidence may be triggered by 15 per cent of Conservative MPs submitting letters of no confidence to the Chair of the 1922 Committee. If the incumbent leader wins the vote of no confidence by a simple majority, he may continue as party leader and no further challenge may be brought within a year.

5.38 As a matter of law, an incumbent leader subject to a challenge has no inherent right to be on the ballot or to be re-elected (see paragraph 5.5 above). The right to participate once more is defined by the party's constitution. Thus, a challenged incumbent Labour Party leader has the right automatically to be on the leadership election ballot, but a challenged Conservative Party leader is barred from participation once a no-confidence vote has been lost. In the Labour Party it is therefore possible to have a conflict between the Parliamentary Labour Party and the wider party. This is precisely what occurred in 2016. Mr Corbyn was re-elected as Party leader with 313,209 votes, or 61 per cent of members and affiliates voting. No such conflict is possible in the Conservative Party: the parliamentary party has the final word.

C. Leaders' Powers on Election

i. Generally

5.39 The starting point is that a party leader only has power over his party to the extent that its constitution permits. Most political parties draw the boundaries of their leader's powers broadly. Many leaders will also have powers that are not specified by the constitution but which fall to them by long-standing custom and practical, operational necessity. The terms of the constitution are contractual terms, as Chapter 2 explains more fully. Contract law provides some limitations on the exercise of the leader's powers through the implied terms of good faith and rationality. Chapter 7, Section II sets out in further detail the application of those terms to decisions of a purely, or mainly, political character.

5.40 We are concerned here with an elected leader's power to make decisions within his own party. Nonetheless, it is useful to deal briefly with two principles of public administrative law that are relevant to the exercise of a leader's public executive powers. First, a party leader holding public executive office must only use his public powers for the purpose for which they have been conferred and not for electoral advantage. It is lawful if, by exercising public powers for a proper public purpose,[64] a leader hopes that his party will earn the gratitude and support of the electorate and thus strengthen his electoral position. But it is entirely unlawful for a leader to exercise executive powers to promote the electoral advantage of his party or himself.[65] An archetypal example of the unlawful merging of political and public power was when the leader of Westminster City Council, Dame Shirley Porter, executed a policy to sell council homes in marginal electoral wards with the express purpose of increasing her party's prospects in the 1990 local elections. That conduct was declared to be 'disgraceful' in the judgment of the House of Lords.[66]

5.41 Second, when a party leader is the Prime Minister, he will advise the sovereign on the exercise of prerogative powers and, by constitutional convention, the King is obliged to follow that advice. The Prime Minister is the only person with the power to advise the sovereign in this way. He has, therefore, a constitutional responsibility to have regard to all relevant interests, including the interests of Parliament; he is not simply the leader of the government of the day seeking to promote its own policies. So, it was unlawful for Mr Johnson to advise Queen Elizabeth II in 2019 to prorogue (ie to suspend) Parliament for five weeks during the period in which the UK was negotiating its exit from the European Union. There was no evidence that Mr Johnson had any reason to advise a five-week prorogation, nor any hint of his special constitutional responsibility as more than simply the leader of the governing party.[67]

ii. Power to Set the Party's Policy

5.42 A leader's power to set the party's policy is a significant one due to its effect on the political movement and its reception among voters. The extent of the power varies from party to party. For example, the Conservative Party leader has the power to determine the political direction of the party but must have regard to the views of members and the Conservative Policy Forum.[68] The Labour Party's leader does not have the formal power to set policy unilaterally in Opposition. That power is afforded to the party's national conference and to its governing committee, of which the leader is a member, and to the representatives of the party's principal constituent parts which, among other things, have a role in drawing up election manifestos.[69] The power to set the policy

[64] ie the purpose for which the powers were conferred.
[65] *Porter v Magill* [2001] UKHL 67, [2002] 2 AC 357 para 21 per Lord Bingham.
[66] ibid para 48.
[67] See *R (on the application of Miller) v Prime Minister* [2019] UKSC 41, [2020] AC 373 at paras 30 and 60 per Baroness Hale of Richmond.
[68] Conservative Party Constitution, Part III, cl 11.
[69] *Labour Party Rule Book*, Ch 1, cll V.2–4.

direction of the Liberal Democrats is held by its Federal Policy Committee and its conference, which must generally approve policy.[70] The Scottish National Party's conference also has the power to determine the party's policy.[71] In practice, though, the leader of each party may articulate policy positions on his or her own initiative.

5.43 Where a leader holds public executive office in local government and the devolved nations, his party may not act as the 'puppet master' dictating policy to him, nor may it curtail his right to exercise his executive discretion freely. In so doing, the leader would be impermissibly following decisions of a third party that purported to rob him of his discretion.[72] Some prerogative powers exercised by the Prime Minister are not amenable to judicial scrutiny, and so the rule against fettering of discretion has no practical application to them.[73] The Prime Minister is precluded from undertaking parliamentary activities under the dictation or instruction of an extra-parliamentary body (as are all MPs).[74] In practice, therefore, the policy role of a political party and its committees can at most be consultative when its leader holds public executive office, whether at national or local level.

iii. Power to Enter into Political Agreements with Other Parties

5.44 When no party has a majority it will fall to party leaders to decide whether to enter into political agreements with one or more rival political groups. That is a political decision to which it is problematic to apply the legal concept of rationality. The ability of the courts to interfere with the decision is probably limited to ensuring that the party adheres to any relevant procedural requirements in its constitution. The decision's legitimacy is based on the democratic mandate of those involved and the need to form a functioning majority government, not on an objective process of rational, fact-based decision-making.[75]

5.45 Confidence and supply or coalition agreements made between MPs concerning their allegiance in Parliament are political acts that cannot be challenged or struck down by a court. A court is unable to question those agreements without contravening the doctrines of parliamentary privilege and exclusive cognisance (which are explained in further detail in Chapter 7, Section II). The decision, nominally by Conservative Prime Minister Theresa May, to enter into a confidence and supply agreement with the Democratic Unionist Party following the loss of her House of Commons majority

[70] Constitution of the Federal Liberal Democrats, Art 18.

[71] Constitution of the Scottish National Party, cl 9.1(a).

[72] The principle that discretion should not be fettered is a central principle of administrative law enumerated in many cases, eg *R (on the application of West Berkshire District Council) v Secretary of State for Communities and Local Government)* [2016] EWCA Civ 441. See further Lord Woolf et al, *De Smith's Judicial Review*, 8th edn (Sweet & Maxwell, 2018) at paras 9-001–9-029.

[73] *R (Sandiford) v Secretary of State for Foreign and Commonwealth Affairs* [2014] UKSC 44. For example, the defence of the realm.

[74] See further Ch 13.

[75] See further Ch 7, Section II.

in the 2017 general election, serves as an example. The agreement was followed by government spending commitments in accordance with it, primarily for the benefit of Northern Ireland. Ciaran McClean, a Green Party member, sought to challenge the agreement by judicial review in England. The Divisional Court refused permission for judicial review because, among other things, all political parties seek to promote particular interests and particular interested points of view. That is the nature of the political process, and the disciplines to which they are subject are the usual political ones of needing to be able to command majorities in the House of Commons on important votes and of seeking re-election at the appropriate time. In the Court's view, 'the law does not super-impose additional standards which would make the political process unworkable'.[76] There is no reason why the same logic should not apply in the case of political agreements in local government.

iv. Power to Appoint Portfolios and Party Spokespersons

5.46 It is usual for political leaders to have a unilateral power to appoint associates to cabinet or similar positions, including shadow executive posts in legislatures (including local councils). Nevertheless, it is open to parties to limit that power by providing for the election of those posts by the party's elected representatives. Such was the case over many decades for the Labour Party's appointment of its Shadow Cabinet in the House of Commons. From the mid-twentieth century to 2011 the Parliamentary Labour Party elected the members of the Shadow Cabinet, although the leader retained the power to allocate particular portfolios.

5.47 Once the leader of a local authority political group has been elected, she usually has an unfettered power under the party's rules to appoint other members of the group to cabinet positions (if she is Leader of the Council) or to shadow cabinet or spokesperson positions (if the party is in opposition). The situation is different for the appointment of the group's councillors to local authority committees. Frequently, local authority officers determine the allocation of committee seats to different political groups on the council. In so doing the authority must give effect to the wishes of the various political groups about whom among their members should be appointed to each committee seat.[77] The wishes of a political group for this purpose are those expressed either by the leader of the group or by a majority of the members of the group in a written statement. Leaders of political groups may be overruled by their fellow party councillors in decisions about who should sit on local authority committees: where the leader's wishes conflict with those expressed by the majority in their written statement, the latter prevails.[78]

[76] *R (on the application of McClean) v First Secretary of State* [2017] EWHC 3174 (Admin) at para 21 per Sales LJ.

[77] Local Government and Housing Act 1989, s 16(1).

[78] Local Government (Committees and Political Groups) Regulations 1990, SI 1990/1553, reg 13. Under reg 15 the local authority may make the decision itself where a political group fails to express its wishes within three weeks of being notified.

v. Remuneration

5.48 The Leader of the Opposition in Parliament is entitled to receive a substantial supplement to his salary as an MP.[79] Leaders of local authority political groups in England may receive a special responsibility allowance in addition to their basic councillor allowance. The entitlement to the additional allowance is to be pro rata where the leader does not hold that position throughout the whole of a year.[80] Similar provision is made for leaders of local council political groupings in Wales. In Scotland the Leader of the Council of a local authority is entitled to be paid an amount additional to his allowance as a councillor.[81] It is uncommon for political parties (local or national) to pay their leaders a salary for assuming that role; the position of leader is not an employed post but a voluntary one appointed by election.[82]

[79] Ministerial Salaries Act 1975, s 1(1)(b).

[80] Local Authorities (Members' Allowances) (England) Regulations 2003, SI 2003/1021, reg 5.

[81] Local Governance (Scotland) Act 2004 (Remuneration) Regulations 2007, SSI 2007/183, reg 6.

[82] Note that maintenance payments by a political party to its leaders would not breach the parliamentary standards regime: see Ch 13.

6

Selecting Candidates for Public Elections

I. Introduction

6.1 Thousands of people stand for election every year to represent communities as local councillors, mayors, police and crime commissioners, members of the devolved legislatures and MPs. In the case of independent candidates, no selection contest is necessary. But in political parties there is significant competition among members for selection as the party's prospective candidate. The main political parties have developed extensive rules to govern those competitions, a breach of which may be challenged in the courts. English jurisprudence has recognised that the honesty and integrity of parties' processes for the selection of the candidates who stand in their name is of the greatest importance in a democracy.[1] (The principle no doubt equally

[1] eg *Choudhury v Triesman* [2003] EWHC 1203 (Comm) at para 86 per Stanley Burnton, J. That general principle is also expounded in the case law of the ECtHR, especially with respect to the importance of the democratic integrity of parties' internal processes, as to which see Ch 1 and Ch 12, Section II.

holds good in Scotland, Wales and Northern Ireland.) The courts are content to defer to parties' judgements about the political benefits or disadvantages of particular potential candidates, which the courts are not in a position to judge. However, the courts are willing to scrutinise parties' decisions to ensure that they are untainted by corruption or dishonesty.

6.2 Political parties exert immense influence over who will populate the legislatures, and therefore, over the diversity of legislators' views and backgrounds. That influence is a product of the representative democratic system, which relies on registered political parties to supply the electorate with a choice of candidates. Political parties act as 'gatekeepers' to the legislature; and their approach to selecting candidates has the potential to undermine or to promote pluralism and democratic principles on which the electoral system depends. For that reason, the Equality Act 2010 prohibits unlawful discrimination in the selection of political parties' candidates on protected grounds (race, religion, sexual orientation etc). The law also recognises that some groups in society, particularly women and ethnic minorities, face historic and enduring barriers to fair political representation in the country. The Equality Act 2010 permits positive action in favour of selecting candidates from underrepresented groups in the circumstances outlined in Section III of this chapter.

6.3 Some countries with electoral systems similar to the UK's, for example, New Zealand, require political parties to select their candidates democratically.[2] There is no comparable statutory requirement in the UK. Nevertheless, the constitutions of the main political parties all provide for the selection of candidates using democratic methods and the involvement of the membership. The parties' rules usually permit internal democracy to be abridged and limited in various circumstances and 'parachuting' candidates preferred by the leadership into parliamentary contests has been relatively common.

II. Selecting Candidates

A. Methods of Selection

i. Generally

6.4 The method of selection is a matter for the party and no one else to decide. The rules and constitution of the party will usually set out detailed contractual procedures that the national party and local party units must follow. Adopting a selection process outside the scope of the rules risks exposing the party to legal liability for breach of contract. Officers and members who operate a selection process contrary to the rules

[2] Electoral Act 1993 (New Zealand), s 73. See Ch 3 for further detail about the legal and contractual relationship between different internal elements of political parties.

may themselves be subject to disciplinary action by the appropriate organs of the party. However, save if the party's constitution expressly provides otherwise, there is no sufficient direct contractual relationship between members permitting one to sue another personally for operating a selection process in breach of contract.[3]

6.5 Contractual selection procedures vary from party to party and in complexity. There are various points in common. Many parties operate approved longlists of eligible members from which local party units may shortlist or select prospective candidates. Shortlists of candidates are often compiled through interviews with committees established for that purpose. The shortlist is usually thereafter presented to the eligible membership to vote for a candidate. Sometimes the rules will be vague or partial. In that case, the party or its designated local constituency organisations should adopt a selection process that is consistent with the general scheme of the constitution. The usual principles of contractual construction will apply to the rules governing candidate selections, so the meaning of any rules that do exist must be assessed in the light of the natural and ordinary meaning of the words used and the overall purpose of the relevant clause in the party's constitution.[4] The party may have practices for selection that are not set out expressly in the rules, but which nevertheless form part of them by dint of longstanding and accepted usage; see paragraph 2.16 ff for rules implied by custom and practice.

6.6 Party members who aspire to be candidates for election sometimes campaign inside their parties to persuade fellow members to select them. Donations may be sought to support that activity. PPERA 2000 regulates donations to party members, and membership associations comprised mainly of party members, in these circumstances. A person or association in receipt of donations over a specified value must record donations and report them to the Electoral Commission. It is illegal to accept donations from impermissible or anonymous donors. The relevant rules are outlined in more detail in Chapter 4, Section VI.B and paragraph 5.24 ff. Some parties impose rules limiting how much candidates for election can spend on their selection campaigns. A breach of those rules may give rise to grounds for disqualification from the selection process or for disciplinary action, depending on the constitution and rules of the party in question.

ii. Intervention by Central Parties

6.7 The highest administrative body of a political party commonly has broad powers of party management under the rules which allow the central party to intervene in, or to modify, the selection processes operated by local parties. For example, the Conservative Party's Board has 'power to do anything which in its opinion relates to the management and administration of the Party'[5] and the Liberal Democrat's Federal Board has a power

[3] *Howell v Evans* [2020] EWHC 2303 (QB).
[4] *Evangelou and Others v McNicol* [2016] EWCA Civ 817 paras 19–23.
[5] Conservative Party Constitution, Part IV, cl 17.

to make and vary rules about party elections.[6] The Labour Party has similar rules. Two cases – one Labour and the other Conservative – demonstrate the significant extent to which central parties may intervene in local selection procedures.

i. In 2021 the High Court held that the Labour Party's National Executive Committee had a broad power to manage selection procedures and to intervene in them. The party had undertaken a selection exercise for the Mayor of Liverpool election. It had shortlisted three candidates to go before a ballot of members for selection. Those potential candidates issued promotional material and engaged in hustings events. However, just before the party was to issue ballots to its members in Liverpool to select one of the potential candidates, the National Executive Committee's shortlisting panel lost confidence in the candidates on the shortlist. The National Executive Committee decided to remove those candidates from the shortlist and to rerun the shortlisting exercise, shortlisting two new potential candidates instead. The High Court determined that the National Executive Committee's broad powers allowed it not only to impose candidates on local units but also to decide who could be put on a shortlist and to reinitiate a selection process that was already underway.[7]
ii. Mr Story was a candidate for the Conservative Party in the 2014 European Parliament elections. If the party had won enough votes for two MEPs from its list to be returned, he would have been the second. In the event, it did not and he was not elected. In October 2016 the sitting Conservative MEP accepted a peerage and resigned as an MEP. Mr Story alleged that he should have become the party's replacement MEP as he was on an approved list of candidates already. The party contended, among other things, that it was entitled to refuse to put him on its approved list of potential candidates from which the candidate to fill the 2016 vacancy would be selected, even though Mr Story had been admitted to, and remained on, an approved candidate list which had been submitted for the purposes of the 2014 European Parliament election. The High Court determined that there was no rule in the party's constitution that governed the situation which confronted the Conservative Party's national Board. The Board therefore had power under the constitution to decide what to do and it was not constrained by the rules to decide in any particular way. The Board was entitled to decide what weight, if any, to give to the fact that Mr Story was already on the 2014 list of approved potential candidates.[8]

B. Factors Relevant to the Selection Decision

i. *Trust of the Electorate*

6.8 An overriding consideration for any party is whether a prospective candidate will win the trust and confidence of the electorate. A party's electoral position might be

[6] Federal Constitution of the Liberal Democrats, cl 9.6.
[7] *Rothery v Evans* [2021] EWHC 577 (QB) paras 138, 141 and 171.
[8] *Story v Mcloughlin* [2017] EWHC 3350 (QB) at paras 8 and 36.

so traditionally weak in a particular electoral area that even the best candidate has no hope of winning. But a weak candidate will make matters worse. If a candidate is *really* unsuitable then she might distinguish herself by serving as an embarrassing distraction from a party's electoral campaign more widely. The selection of candidates is also an opportunity for various internal political factions and pressure groups to promote like-minded people into legislative assemblies where they will vote according to shared values.

ii. Political Factors

6.9 The decision to shortlist one candidate over another in a selection process is an exercise of political judgement.[9] It is legitimate to exercise political judgement with regard to the potential perceptions of the electorate and the risk of political smears that may be levelled at a candidate and the party.[10] Thus, the shortlisting decision may be taken on the basis of factors that are significantly subjective and which may be harsh, or not entirely fair in the normal or colloquial sense of the word.[11]

6.10 Legitimate subjective political factors include: views formed about how a candidate's actions and words in the past may be seen by the electorate when she is in the public eye;[12] genuinely held concerns about the honesty or integrity of the selection process and how any procedural deficiencies may taint the selection of an otherwise entirely proper candidate; and rational fears that the party or the public will infer that those responsible for corruption of a selection process want a particular candidate to be selected.[13] A conclusion that other candidates appear on rational grounds to be better or electorally stronger is another legitimate political factor to take into account;[14] so too is a perception that a candidate is vulnerable to political attack, or that he would, by his selection, expose the party to a political risk that it was going to be open to attack and so vulnerable to defeat;[15] and doubts about the candidate's ability to win the election, or doubt that the candidate is the best placed to win the election.[16]

6.11 The aims and values of the party enumerated in its constitution are legitimate aids to the identification of political factors that may be taken into account in the selection process. The primary objective of a political party in a selection context is to select candidates who will reflect well on the party and have the greatest chance of being elected, thereby advancing the party's aims.[17] Parties have generally expressed that primary objective in two ways. The Labour Party and the Federal Liberal Democrats have

[9] *Rothery v Evans* [2021] EWHC 577 (QB), para 185.
[10] But note that it is not permissible to discriminate in contravention of the Equality Act 2010 on the basis of political expediency: see Ch 11, para 11.21.
[11] *Rothery v Evans* [2021] EWHC 577 (QB) para 171.
[12] *Nattrass v UKIP* [2013] EWHC 3017 (Ch) para 12.
[13] *Choudry v Treisman* [2003] EWHC 1203 (Comm) para 86.
[14] *Nattrass v UKIP* para 12.
[15] *Rothery v Evans* [2021] EWHC 577 (QB) paras 187–88.
[16] ibid paras 171 and 186.
[17] ibid para 171.

an express purpose to win elections for their parties' benefit. The Conservative Party, the Scottish National Party, the Co-operative Party and Plaid Cymru have as their declared objects the promotion or maintenance of their interests, being political activity, mutual ownership and democratic control, and independence, respectively.[18]

6.12 The public interest requires that the proceedings of political parties are free from corruption.[19] That is an important reason to ensure that selection procedures are transparent. There is no reason for political parties to shy away from making shortlisting or selection decisions on legitimate political factors. A decision-maker's open consideration and clear exposition of the political risks associated with a candidate is likely to result in a decision that is less susceptible to challenge. On the other hand, to give one reason for the decision and to act on another may demonstrate bad faith, thus vitiating the selection decision if bad faith is established.[20]

iii. Duty to Put Aspiring Candidates on Notice of Perceived Deficiencies

6.13 The law is unsettled about whether parties must give aspiring political candidates a fair opportunity to respond to perceived deficiencies in their candidature before a longlisting or shortlisting decision is taken. It seems that parties should give an aspiring candidate an opportunity to set out her position on any allegations of dishonesty made against her, or on any allegations of misconduct relevant to an extant party disciplinary procedure, before the party decides to bar her from the selection process on that basis. But where a selection decision is simply an appraisal of a candidate's relative qualities and her ability to attract the support of voters, the party is unlikely to be required to give the candidate notice of any concerns about her general aptitudes or failures.

6.14 It seems that parties must comply with principles of natural justice[21] where a selection decision involves some investigation into alleged wrongdoing by the candidate. In a case about the selection of a shop steward by a trade union's district committee,[22] the Court of Appeal distinguished cases where: (i) a committee was minded to take into account adversely any allegation of dishonesty against a candidate on one hand; and (ii) other considerations not based on dishonesty. In cases where dishonesty is alleged and taken into account as a relevant factor against a person, he should be entitled to know about it and to make representations to the decision-maker before the decision is taken.[23] A majority of the Court concluded that it was unnecessary to put other considerations relevant to a candidate's fitness for the post to him before approving his position. In general, and in the absence of a special reason, a committee would not act unfairly if it failed to give the candidate in question the opportunity to speak on

[18] See the parties' respective constitutional documents.

[19] *Choudry v Treisman* [2003] EWHC 1203 (Comm) para 82.

[20] See *D'Arcy v Adamson* (1913) 29 TLR 367; *Khan v Scottish Executive Committee of the Scottish Labour Party* [2018] CSOH 68.

[21] ie basic fairness. See Ch 12, Section III for further detail.

[22] *Breen v Amalgamated Engineering Union and Others* [1971] 2 QB 175.

[23] ibid at 195 and 200.

his own behalf before deciding whether to approve him. A duty to comply with 'elementary fairness' was recognised by the High Court in *Jones v McNicol*. That case concerned a Labour Party member who was unable to take part in a selection process because he had been subject to an administrative suspension following allegations of wrongdoing some two years earlier.[24] In *Choudry v Treisman*, the Labour Party decided to carry out an investigation into the selection processes of a constituency branch. The court expressly accepted that the principles of natural justice applied such that the Labour Party ought to have put the claimant on notice of any concerns raised in order to allow him to address those concerns.[25]

6.15 The duty to follow natural justice is unlikely to apply in the same way in circumstances where the selection decision is simply an appraisal of competing candidates' strengths and weaknesses in the absence of disciplinary allegations. Thus, in *Nattrass v UKIP* the party was under no duty to observe the rules of natural justice in declining to re-select a member on the basis of perceived disloyalty. To apply a duty of natural justice in those circumstances would mean that 'every candidate should presumably have a free rein to comment upon other candidate's comparative weaknesses', which is not the case.[26] *Ramsay v Hackett Pain* concerned a Conservative Party member who sought to challenge a decision to discuss his deselection from the Senedd Cymru. The High Court reached the conclusion that it was unnecessary to import natural justice principles in addition to those imposed by the need for honesty and rationality.[27] In *Rothery v Evans*, a Labour Party case, the High Court considered the decisions in both *Ramsay* and *Nattrass*. The Court concluded that it would take something exceptional to render a candidate selection decision unfair or irrational, even if the decision was harsh in the colloquial sense.[28] Because the decision is an exercise of political judgement, the standard of fairness required is that which is fair in a political selection decision and not in a disciplinary or investigative process.

C. Nominating the Selected Candidate

6.16 Once the party has selected its candidates it will fall to its registered nominating officer to nominate them for public election and to authorise the relevant nominating certificate. Each candidate must be nominated by a separate nomination paper. The rules governing the nomination of parliamentary candidates are set out in Schedule 1 to the Representation of the People Act 1983 and, for local authority candidates, in the Local Elections (Principal Areas) (England and Wales) Rules 2006[29] and the Scottish Local Government Elections Order 2011, as amended. Of particular interest for present purposes are the rules about who is disqualified from standing as a candidate in a public

[24] *Jones v McNicol* [2016] EWHC 866 (QB).
[25] *Choudry v Treisman* [2003] EWHC 1203 (Comm) para 77.
[26] *Nattrass v UKIP*, paras 11 and 12.
[27] *Ramsay v Hackett Pain* [2020] EWHC 3655 (Ch) para 15.
[28] *Rothery v Evans* [2021] EWHC 577 (QB) para 177.
[29] See R Price and V Sedgley, *Parker's Law and Conduct of Elections* (LexisNexis, looseleaf) for further detail in respect of the rules relating to England and Wales.

election; parties will plainly wish to avoid selecting and nominating a person who is not, in fact, entitled to be elected. The following paragraphs set out the principal categories of disqualification in relation to local government and to the House of Commons:

A person is disqualified from being a candidate in a local government election in cases of:

i. **Bankruptcy**: a person who is subject to a bankruptcy restrictions order.[30]
ii. **Imprisonment**: a person who has been convicted in the UK, the Channel Islands or the Isle of Man and who is given a custodial sentence (whether suspended or not) for a period of not less than three months (without the option of a fine) within five years before the day of election.[31]
iii. **Electoral offences**: a person who has been convicted of a corrupt or illegal practice, or who has been reported by an election court as personally guilty of a corrupt or illegal practice at a parliamentary or local government election pursuant to the Representation of the People Act 1983 (the disqualification is five years in respect of a corrupt practice and three in respect of an illegal practice).
iv. **Sexual offences**: a person subject to various sexual-offences orders where the opportunity to appeal has been exhausted.[32]
v. **Disqualifying occupation**: paid local authority staff (whether an office-holder or employee of the local authority);[33] people holding a politically restricted office of a local authority.[34]

A person is disqualified from being a candidate in an election for the House of Commons in cases of:

i. **Bankruptcy**: a person who is subject to a bankruptcy restrictions order.[35]
ii. **Imprisonment**: a person who has been convicted and sentenced to imprisonment indefinitely or for more than one year in the British Islands or the Republic of Ireland.[36] Note that this disqualifies a person from being nominated for election at all, not just from being elected.[37]
iii. **Electoral offences**: a person who has been convicted of a corrupt or illegal practice, or who has been reported by an election court as personally guilty of a corrupt or illegal practice at a parliamentary or local government election pursuant to the Representation of the People Act 1983 (the disqualification is five years in respect of a corrupt practice and three in respect of an illegal practice).
iv. **Treason**: a person convicted and detained for treason (this disqualification applies to elections in England, Wales and Northern Ireland).[38]

[30] Local Government Act 1972, s 80(1)(b).
[31] ibid s 80(1)(d).
[32] ibid s 81A. It has been suggested that the commission of sexual offences should be a ground of disqualification from parliamentary elections. At the time of publication, no such ground applies in respect of parliamentary elections.
[33] ibid s 80(1)(a) and 80(2)(a).
[34] Local Government and Housing Act 1989, s 1(1) and (1A).
[35] Insolvency Act 1986, s 426A.
[36] Representation of the People Act 1981, s 1.
[37] Representation of the People Act 1983, Sch 3, para 12(2)(c).
[38] Forfeiture Act 1870, s 2.

v. **Disqualifying occupation**: peers entitled to sit in the House of Lords;[39] Crown officers, government officers, and county dignitaries;[40] employed civil servants and members of the armed forces;[41] most judges (but not deputy district judges in magistrates' courts;[42] members of the Police Force (but not special constables);[43] foreign law-makers, namely members of the legislature of any country or territory outside the Commonwealth (save for the Republic of Ireland).[44]

III. Positive Action

A. Selection Arrangements

6.17 Registered political parties are permitted to adopt selection arrangements that promote protected groups who are underrepresented among a party's elected representatives. This 'positive action' in selection arrangements is lawful only if it complies with the criteria set out in section 104(3) of the Equality Act 2010, addressed in paragraphs 6.18–6.20 below.

i. Purpose

6.18 The selection arrangements must be made for the purpose of regulating the selection of candidates in one of the following elections: parliamentary elections, elections to the Scottish Parliament or the Welsh Senedd; City of London municipal elections (to the offices of mayor, alderman, common councilman or sheriff, any officer elected by the mayor, alderman and liverymen in common hall, corporate offices and the town clerk of the city[45]); elections for members of the Greater London Assembly, London borough councils, English and Welsh county, district, parish and community councils; and Scottish local government elections.[46] Elections for the Mayor of London are expressly excluded and therefore fall under the general provisions forbidding discrimination in the selection of candidates.[47]

6.19 The selection arrangements must have as their purpose the reduction of inequality in the party's representation in the relevant legislative body concerned.[48] Inequality here refers to a numerical inequality, between the number of the party's elected members who share a particular protected characteristic and those who do not share it. The

[39] House of Lords Act 1999, ss 1 and 3.
[40] House of Commons Disqualification Act 1975, Sch 1, Pts II, III and IV.
[41] ibid s 1(1)(b).
[42] ibid s 1(1)(a) and Sch 1, Pt I.
[43] ibid s 1(1)(d).
[44] ibid s 1(1)(e).
[45] Representation of the People Act 1983, s 191(1)(e).
[46] Equality Act 2010, s 104(3)(a) and (8).
[47] ibid s 104(8)(e).
[48] ibid s 104(3)(b).

pool for this comparison is not the party's elected politicians in general but those in a particular legislative body,[49] for example, in the Scottish Parliament. The candidates in the comparison are the current, incumbent members of the legislative body; not prospective candidates.[50] For the purposes of section 104(3) of the Equality Act 2010, people share the protected characteristic of disability if they have any disability and not merely if they share the same disability.[51]

ii. Proportionality

6.20 If the criteria set out above are met, then a party may put in place any selection arrangements it deems appropriate, so long as the arrangements are a proportionate means of reducing underrepresentation.[52] 'Selection arrangements' are not defined under the 2010 Act and they therefore encompass myriad arrangements. The Explanatory Notes to the Equality Act 2010 suggest reserving places on a shortlist for particular groups as one example. That is how many political parties have approached the provisions of the Act in practice. Other arrangements may be adopted instead. For example, appointing people who share a particular characteristic to a selection interview panel, weighting selection interview criteria to prioritise people from underrepresented groups where it is proportionate to do so, or stipulating that a percentage of approved selection lists are set aside for members of the party sharing a particular protected characteristic. Other measures may include encouraging applications from those in protected groups, or mentoring them, or giving particular training opportunities or other opportunities for participation in the party or its activities.[53]

6.21 Selection arrangements that focus exclusively on improving the representation of a particular group sharing a single protected characteristic are unlikely to be proportionate if the arrangements would further reduce the selection prospects for people in other under-represented groups. Where a party identifies that it has disproportionately low numbers of both female councillors and those from British Asian heritage in a particular council, it would be disproportionate to prioritise female candidates at the expense of British Asian candidates. However, it would be proportionate to adopt selection arrangements that prioritised the representation of both.[54]

6.22 The only selection arrangement that the High Court has scrutinised so far under these legislative provisions concerns the Liberal Democrats' organisation of a priority list of candidates for elections to the European Parliament (Yorkshire and the Humber region). Those elections were decided by proportional representation: seats were allotted to each party proportionally to its share of the vote. Each party had a list of candidates;

[49] ibid s 104(4).
[50] *Dhamija v The Liberal Democrats in England* [2019] EWHC 1398 (QB) para 25.
[51] Equality Act 2010, s 104(5).
[52] ibid s 104(3)(c).
[53] *Dhamija v The Liberal Democrats in England* [2019] EWHC 1398 (QB) para 10.
[54] Services, Public Functions and Associations: Statutory Code of Practice (EHRC, 2011) para 12.59.

the first seat won by the party would be allotted to the first person on the party list, the second seat won to the second person on the list and so on. In reality, it was unlikely that the Liberal Democrats would win more than one seat for the Yorkshire and the Humber region, so the candidate at the top of the Liberal Democrat list was most likely to be elected to the European Parliament. The issue in *Dhamija v The Liberal Democrats in England*[55] was that the Liberal Democrats operated a selection arrangement that sought to rearrange the order of their list of candidates to promote BAME candidates. Normally, the person that secured the most votes from Liberal Democrat members in that party's selection competition would have first place on the list. The Liberal Democrats sought to adjust the final selection result reflected in the order of the list to ensure that one of the two first-placed candidates was from a BAME background. The protocol also sought to ensure that one of the two first-placed candidates was female. That meant that if the first two places on the list were won by men, one of the men would be moved down the list and a woman moved up to take his place. The Liberal Democrats referred to this reordering of the priority list as 'zipping'.

6.23 The Court concluded that the practice of zipping was one of the more intrusive measures designed to ensure proper representation of protected groups. The Court decided that both aspects of the selection arrangement (the promotion of BAME and female candidates) had been unlawful, falling outside the exemption in section 104 of the Equality Act 2010. Given that the Liberal Democrats in the region were represented by a single member of the European Parliament who was female (the incumbent), it could not be said that women were underrepresented in that region. Selection arrangements prioritising women, therefore, could not be justified. Neither could the policy of 'zipping' a member of one protected group be justified to remedy inequality: it would have the effect of disadvantaging a member of another, similarly underrepresented group, which could not be regarded as a proportionate response.

B. Single Characteristic Shortlists

6.24 It is not permissible for parties to insist on shortlists of people of only one particular protected characteristic (save for the characteristic of sex, as set out below). This means that a political party could not insist on shortlisting (by way of example) only Black candidates for a local government by-election. However, if Black members are under-represented amongst a party's elected councillors on a particular council, the party could choose to reserve a specific number of seats for Black candidates on their selection shortlists.[56] (Note that it is not unlawful for all the candidates on a shortlist to share the same protected characteristic, so long as the party has not operated selection arrangements to impose a single characteristic shortlist.)

[55] *Dhamija v The Liberal Democrats in England* [2019] EWHC 1398 (QB).
[56] Equality Act 2010, Explanatory Notes, para 338.

C. Single Sex Shortlisting

6.25 Single sex, and therefore all-women, shortlists are a selection arrangement that is permitted under the Equality Act 2010.[57] All-women shortlists will be allowed only where women are underrepresented among a party's incumbent, elected members of a particular legislative body, for example among its MPs or councillors in a particular county council. There is no requirement for all-women shortlists to be a proportionate means of reducing imbalance between the sexes in order to use them.[58] The provision in the Equality Act 2010 for all women shortlists is time-limited until 2030.

6.26 For the purposes of the Equality Act 2010, sex is defined as 'a reference to a man or to a woman'[59] and a woman is defined as 'a female'.[60] Consequently, as the law presently stands, a transgender woman who has not changed her legal sex to female by obtaining a full gender recognition certificate will be ineligible to be included in an all-woman shortlist[61] (ie it is not possible for a legally male person who simply self-declares their gender to be that of a woman or non-binary to be included on an all-woman shortlist). But a transgender woman who has been issued with a full gender recognition certificate under section 9 of the Gender Recognition Act 2004 is considered to be a person of the female sex pursuant to section 9(1) and (2) of that Act and should therefore be treated as eligible to stand on a single sex female shortlist. A failure to permit her to do so is likely to amount to discrimination because of, or harassment related to, the protected characteristic of gender reassignment.[62]

6.27 The Equality Act 2010 also has a provision, yet to be brought into force, obliging a political party to publish information about diversity in its selection of candidates. In 2015 the Women and Equalities Select Committee noted that 'the Coalition Government decided instead to pursue a voluntary approach in the first instance, and has worked with political parties to encourage greater transparency and report on the diversity of their political candidates'.[63] The number of women elected to the House of Commons reached an historic high in 2019. Yet the level of underrepresentation is striking. There have only ever been, across all Parliaments, less than 600 female Members of Parliament. Over half of those have been Labour Party MPs. In 2016 there were more male MPs sitting in the Chamber of the House of Commons than there had ever been female MPs throughout history.[64] Nevertheless, for the first time, following the 2019 election, half of the Labour Party's MPs were female. Where equal representation of

[57] Equality Act 2010, s 104(7).
[58] ibid.
[59] ibid s 11(a).
[60] ibid s 112(1).
[61] Gender Recognition Act 2004, s 9.
[62] Equality Act 2010, ss 7, 13, 26 and 101.
[63] *Memorandum to the Women and Equalities Select Committee on the Post- Legislative Assessment of the Equality Act 2010* (House of Commons, 2015) CM 9101, para 3.51.
[64] Richard Kelly, 'Female Members of Parliament' Research Briefing (House of Commons Library, 7 March 2022).

women is secured in a party's legislative cohort, the party is thereafter precluded from operating any further all-women shortlists in candidate selections for that legislative body until a disparity emerges again.

D. Members of the House of Lords

6.28 Neither the prohibitions against unlawful discrimination nor the prescription of justified positive action in the Equality Act 2010 apply to the nomination of Members of the House of Lords, where 28 per cent of members are women. The application of the Equality Act 2010 to political office holders is addressed in further detail in Chapter 11, Section III.D.

7

Political Discipline: The Whip and Political Factions

I. Introduction

7.1 A political party's members do not always agree about what is to be done. Nor do they necessarily share the same political ideas. But the political factions that compete within parties must be controlled if the party is to be an effective political force. In December 2001 the BBC reported that a Labour MP, opposed to military action in

Afghanistan, said colleagues verbally and physically attacked him because he opposed government legislation:

> He claimed that MP Jim Dowd prodded him in the back, another MP resorted to swearing and name-calling and Labour Whip Gerry Sutcliffe warned him he would be attacked again if he failed to stop criticising the government. All the accused MPs have denied Mr Marsden's allegations, which follow previous claims by him that Chief Whip Hilary Armstrong compared him to appeasers of the Nazis. On Wednesday Mr Marsden released a statement 'Labour thugs attack MP' in which he outlined his allegations … Senior Conservative MP Gerald Howarth … said: 'I have a document headed: "Labour Thugs Attack MP" and in this document, Mr Marsden makes a number of deeply serious allegations against other Labour Members including whips. He alleges both verbal and physical attacks on himself. What action can you take to protect Members of this House from attack by other Members – particularly to protect dissident members of the government from physical attack and intimidation from their own whips?[1]

7.2 In 2022 *ITV News* opened with the following report:

> It has been a night of astonishing scenes at Westminster with reports of jostling, manhandling, bullying and shouting outside the parliamentary lobbies in a supposed vote of confidence in the government. The deputy Chief Whip was reported to have left the scene saying 'I'm absolutely effing furious I just don't effing care anymore' before he resigned along with the Chief Whip. But we have just been told they have now officially unresigned. The Home Secretary has, however, definitely gone. In short, it is total, absolute, abject chaos.[2]

7.3 Few would identify the preceding events, if reported accurately, as an acceptable or successful assertion of political management by leaders over their colleagues. But how does the law delineate acceptable political management and unacceptable political pressure? This chapter sets out the legal principles that regulate the political management of party representatives by the political leadership. Chiefly, we are interested in how party leaders may enforce political discipline among party members who are public representatives in the legislatures.

7.4 This chapter starts by outlining how the courts treat political decisions. Judges are extremely reticent to interfere in political questions because it is difficult, and at times impossible, to analyse them objectively and judiciously. Nonetheless the law will intervene to protect individual legal rights, to ensure the lawful administration of public authorities and for reasons of public policy. Section III of the chapter sets out legal principles governing the exercise of the party whip. The whip is the most important direct device through which parties may assert legislative political discipline. The oppressive exercise of the whip in local authorities can lead to ultra vires public decision-making in which the courts do interfere. There is far less scope for any judicial scrutiny of the parliamentary whip, though some legal principles limit its use in theory and one can distil

[1] 'Colleagues "attacked" me, says MP' (*BBC News*, 5 December 2001), http://news.bbc.co.uk/1/hi/uk_politics/1694282.stm.

[2] 'There's chaos in Westminster as Liz Truss hangs on as PM' (*ITV News*, 20 October 2022).

common principles of good practice. Section IV of this chapter turns to how internal political differences are treated within the general party body, including the arrangement of political factions.

II. Political Decisions

7.5 Decisions about political matters will often fall outside the purview of the courts. Legal authorities have repeatedly cautioned the courts against trespassing into the political arena; they must recognise 'the vital dividing line between the world of politics and the world of the law'.[3] In a case concerning the 2016 Labour Party leadership election, the Court of Appeal endorsed the proposition that 'the courts must be careful not to interfere in political matters'.[4] Courts in other cases have declined to interfere in the selection of political parties' candidates on a similar basis.[5] It has been said that political acts cannot be challenged, declared unlawful or struck down in a court of law.[6] In *R (on the application of Miller) v Prime Minister*[7] the Supreme Court determined the illegality of the then-Prime Minister Boris Johnson's prorogation of Parliament. Lady Hale, delivering the Court's unanimous judgment, reiterated that the courts cannot decide political questions. Nevertheless, although the courts cannot decide political questions, the fact that a legal dispute concerns the conduct of politicians, or arises from a matter of political controversy, does not preclude the courts from considering it.[8]

7.6 Whether a political decision is capable of judicial scrutiny (ie whether it is justiciable) depends in large part on the source of the decision's legitimacy and the subject matter. Some political issues are beyond the constitutional competence assigned to the courts under the principle of the separation of powers. Once a court has identified an area forbidden to it, no adjudication may take place on the matters within that area, even if it is necessary to do so to decide some other justiciable issue. An archetypal example is proceedings in Parliament, which the courts may not question.[9]

7.7 A much broader category of non-justiciability comprises political matters that the courts are simply not in a position to judge, and which are not justiciable for that reason. For example, the legitimacy of decisions about the maintenance and security of legislative majorities is derived from the democratic credentials of the people taking them, who must attempt to resolve political differences through agreement, compromise and

[3] *Foster v McNichol* [2016] EWHC 1966 (QB) para 59.

[4] *Evangelou v McNicol* [2016] EWHC 2058 (QB) para 74 and [2016] EWCA Civ 817 at para 28. Note that the judgment of the High Court was overturned by the Court of Appeal on other grounds.

[5] See, for example, *Nattrass v United Kingdom Independence Party* [2013] EWHC 3017 (Ch) para 15; *Choudhry v Treisman* [2003] EWHC 1203 (Ch).

[6] *R (on the application of McClean) v First Secretary of State* [2017] EWHC 3174 (Admin), [2018] 1 Costs LO 37.

[7] *R (on the application of Miller) v Prime Minister; R (on the application of Cherry and Others) v Lord Advocate* [2019] UKSC 41, [2019] 3 WLR 589.

[8] *R (Miller) v Prime Minister and Others* [2019] UKSC 41, [2019] 3 WLR 589 at para 31. See also para 5.40 above.

[9] See *Shergill v Khaira* [2014] UKSC 33, [2015] AC 359 at paras 41–43.

the exercise of their democratic mandate. This sort of decision-making includes the strategic political dealing and trading involved in passing legislation. It is incapable of rationalisation according to the transparent and reasoned analysis deployed by judicial decision-makers;[10] not least because it is difficult to apply a relevant standard of impartiality or objectivity (and sometimes it will be impossible to do so).[11] Decisions about such matters are, therefore, incapable of judicial determination or regulation. Another example is the appointment or dismissal of a minister, or the decision of the Prime Minister to retain a minister in office; those are purely political decisions and there are no judicial standards which can be used to judge them. For the same reason, it has been held that most of the provisions of the Ministerial Code involve political matters that the courts are not in a position to interpret.[12]

7.8 At the other end of the scale to political horse-trading lie the quasi-judicial disciplinary decisions of political committees which require findings of fact to be made after investigation (for example, disciplinary investigations into members' alleged misconduct). The legitimacy of those decisions is derived from a transparent process of independently-minded logical reasoning.[13] That decision-making must comply with judicial principles of rationality and good-faith.[14] Although the context of these sorts of decisions may be political, the courts will readily scrutinise them and intervene if necessary to protect individual contractual rights.

7.9 Where a party officer's exercise of contractual discretion calls for, or principally depends on, the exercise of political judgement (eg the selection of a candidate under a party's rules) the requirement of rationality and fairness may persist so that the court can apply an objective standard and intervene to remedy unlawfulness. That said, any unfairness must be seen in the context of a political process, not a disciplinary, investigative, or punitive process and so there would have to be something exceptional to make these sorts of political judgements irrational or unfair.[15]

7.10 Of course, a political act or decision may be unlawful because of the manner in which it is carried out or by its nature; and to that extent political decisions may be impugned in broadly the same way as any other. For example, a decision might entail an infraction of the criminal law (eg bribery) or the commission of a tort (eg harassment or negligence); or it might be taken for an impermissible reason (eg discrimination

[10] *R (SC and Others) v Secretary of State for Work and Pensions and Others* [2021] UKSC 26, [2022] AC 223 at paras 168–69; *Attorney General for Bermuda v Ferguson and Others (Bermuda)* [2022] UKPC 5 at para 57.

[11] *R (on the application of McClean) v First Secretary of State* [2017] EWHC 3174 (Admin), [2018] 1 Costs LO 37 para 21.

[12] See eg *R (FDA) v Prime Minister and Minister for the Civil Service* [2021] EWHC 3279 (Admin), [2022] 4 WLR 5. Nevertheless, the court found that there are some elements of the Ministerial Code that are not so associated with political decisions that the courts cannot interpret them; for example the meaning of provisions therein which define bullying and harassment, which provide a standard of conduct in the workplace.

[13] *R (SC and Others) v Secretary of State for Work and Pensions and Others* [2021] UKSC 26, [2022] AC 223 at para 169.

[14] ie those set out in *Braganza v BP Shipping Ltd* [2015] UKSC 17, [2015] 1 WLR 1661 at para 30. See further para 2.15 above.

[15] *Rothery v Evans* [2021] EWHC 577 (QB) at para 176.

contrary to the Equality Act 2010 or subjecting a person to a detriment for whistleblowing contrary to the Employment Rights Act 1996).

III. The Whip

7.11 The party whip may refer to three distinct things. First, the person (or people) responsible for organising a party's legislators to vote a particular way in Parliament or councils are called whips. The whips also facilitate the nomination and appointment of a party's representatives to legislative committees. The whips have a disciplinary role in respect of their colleagues' conduct. It is common for the whips to address alleged infractions of agreed rules or standards by public representatives. Second, the request or instruction to vote a particular way is also referred to as 'the whip', and it may be a one-, two- or three-line whip, the final of these being the most insistent. Third, a person who is a member of the party's group in a legislature is said to have the party whip. A person can lose the whip, which may be withdrawn, thus ending his or her formal allegiance with the political group. All three elements of the whip enforce political discipline by working to ensure that representatives vote in accordance with the leadership's position on legislation and legislative motions.

7.12 Whips do not have free rein to act however they wish in the pursuit of political discipline. The provisions of the general law bind their actions as much as anyone else's. Thus, physical pressure brought to bear by the whips may amount to assault or battery in contravention of the criminal or the civil law; repeated campaigns of intimidation may amount to harassment contrary to the Protection from Harassment Act 1997; and discriminatory acts by a whip towards other party members may contravene the Equality Act 2010, and so on. It appears that criminal acts (but not criminal speech) done in Parliament do not fall outside the ordinary course of criminal justice.[16] The fact that a crime is committed within the parliamentary precincts is not a bar to the jurisdiction of the criminal courts (in 1812 John Bellingham was tried and convicted of the murder of the then Prime Minister Spencer Percival in the Palace of Westminster). Parliament and the courts have overlapping, but different, jurisdictions in respect of crimes committed on parliamentary precincts such that a crime committed within the House of Commons may also constitute a contempt of Parliament.[17]

7.13 The following general principles (which are set out in more detail in the rest of this chapter) may be distilled from a variety of sources.

i. Malicious, vindictive or coercive measures taken against legislators are impermissible.
ii. It is permissible for a parliamentary party to make public spending commitments to encourage a legislator to vote a particular way.

[16] *Bradlaugh v Gosset* (1884) 12 QBD 271.

[17] See *Chaytor* [2010] UKSC 52, [2011] 1 AC 684 at paras 80 and 81. Nor is it the case that an act attracts parliamentary privilege merely because it is done in the precincts of Parliament. For a more detailed exposition of the operation of the criminal law in Parliament see *Erskine May: Parliamentary Practice*, 25th edn (LexisNexis, 2019) 'Proceedings, precincts and criminal acts', Chapter 11 at para 11.18.

iii. A robust statement of the whip is acceptable so long as it does not preclude a legislator from coming to his own conclusion about how to vote.
iv. The whip must be withdrawn concordantly with any rules the party has for that purpose. Withdrawal of the whip may not be done with malice, capriciousness or for discriminatory reasons.
v. Loyalty to the whip must not be blind. Legislators must exercise independence of mind and vote according to their own judgement.
vi. MPs must not follow the whip if by doing so they would contravene their duty to the Crown, the country, or the interests of their constituents. A conflict between personal and public interests must be resolved immediately in favour of the public interest.
vii. Legislators may exercise their votes by following the whip on the basis of party-political advantage.
viii. The duty to attend a legislative vote as instructed by the whip is subordinate to extra-political duties of regulated professions (eg barristers).
ix. Contractual agreements purporting to oblige legislators to vote with a particular group in return for a benefit are void for reasons of public policy.

A. Who are the Whips?

7.14 Party legislators carry out the functions of the whip on behalf of their party leader, who appoints them. Those people are referred to as whips in Parliament, the devolved legislatures and local authorities.[18] The whips manage legislative business. Especially, they facilitate the passage of draft legislation through the legislature. That task usually involves cooperation between rival party whips on administrative matters, as well as organising the mechanics of voting in the chamber (for example, by agreeing pairing).[19] The head of a party's team of whips is known as the Chief Whip.

7.15 Party leaders have a very broad discretion to appoint colleagues to the office of whip.[20] The government whips in Parliament hold long-standing, formal Ministerial roles in the executive. The Chief Whips in the Commons and the Lords are members of the government, alongside various junior assistant whips. By convention the Deputy Chief Whip in the Commons is also Treasurer of the Household (ie His Majesty's Household),[21] an assistant Commons Whip is Vice-Chamberlain of the Household,[22] and another is Comptroller of the Household.[23] (These are ceremonial titles that serve

[18] For a history of the practice of whipping, see V Larminie, '"The Parliament driver": Walter Long, party politics and the whip', *The History of Parliament online* (19 April 2019); and R Kelly et al, 'The Whip's Office', House of Commons Library Research Briefing (10 October 2008).

[19] The practice by which legislators from rival parties are 'paired' together so that the absence of one from a vote will entail an arranged absence of their counterpart. This effectively cancels out the numerical disadvantage caused by a legislator's inability to attend to vote.

[20] Note that the whip is a political office and, therefore, the prohibition of discrimination in the appointment of office-holders under the Equality Act 2010 does not apply to it: Equality Act 2010, Sch 6, para 2.

[21] See www.gov.uk/government/ministers/deputy-chief-whip-comptroller-of-hm-household.

[22] See www.gov.uk/government/ministers/government-whip--2.

[23] See www.gov.uk/government/ministers/comptroller-of-hm-household-government-whip.

to denote a position in the executive arm of government.) The 'Chief Opposition Whip' and the 'Assistant Opposition Whip', whether in the Commons or the Lords, are defined by statute as the people nominated as such by the Leader of the Opposition in the Houses of Parliament.[24] Whips in the devolved legislatures and local authorities have no equivalent statutory rank, though their work is no less significant. The Chief Whips in the Scottish and Welsh Parliaments are members of the devolved cabinets.

B. Exercising the Whip

7.16 The rules about how parties should exercise the whip are especially important to the work of local authorities, where abuse of the whip may provide grounds to challenge the authority's decisions in court. The law accepts the reality that political parties in legislative assemblies may need to exert some pressure on their members to enforce the party line on policy and legislation. The point at which that pressure becomes illegitimate is ill defined. There are no commonly agreed party rules about whipping. The courts have addressed some aspects of whipping in local authorities, but not comprehensively. The following general propositions can be discerned from legal authorities and other guidance; they provide a basic framework regulating whipping practices. Many of those principles have arisen in public law cases challenging local councils' decisions. It must be borne in mind that the question whether whipping arrangements contravene public law principles is wholly distinct to whether they breach a political party's contractual duties to its members. So, whipping that removes a legislator's ability to vote independently may render the act of a local authority unlawful but provide no actionable suit by the legislator against his party. On the other hand, the suspension of the whip from a local councillor in contravention of the party's rules may amount to a breach of contract but be irrelevant to the lawfulness of the local authority's decisions. Other whipping behaviour may not breach any recognised legal standard but nevertheless contravene accepted codes of conduct relevant to legislators, for example the House of Commons Code of Conduct or party codes of conduct.

i. Parliamentary Business

7.17 The government and opposition whips in Parliament make decisions about the organisation of parliamentary business between the opposition and the government.[25] Decisions made in these 'whipping' activities are not capable of judicial scrutiny in court. To the extent that those activities concern the core business of Parliament (for example, passing legislation), they will fall within the ambit of Article 9 of the Bill of Rights 1689: the courts must not question proceedings in Parliament. Even if those activities do not concern the core business of Parliament, they are very unlikely to be justiciable so far as they relate to political negotiation and debate outside the work of the

[24] The Ministerial and Other Salaries Act 1975, s 2(1).

[25] For example, stipulating which votes to attend, organising pairing, negotiating parliamentary time via 'the usual channels', organising the nomination of members to committees, and so on. For the meaning of 'usual channels' see www.parliament.uk/site-information/glossary/usual-channels.

chamber or committees for the purposes of resolving political opinion in Parliament. The courts must be careful 'not to undermine Parliament's performance of its functions by requiring it, or encouraging it, to conform to a judicial model of rationality'.[26]

ii. Enforcing Political Discipline

7.18 Case law has asserted a distinction between a sanction imposed to ensure party discipline and a punishment for defying the whip, though the difference between the two is not particularly clear. It would seem that the imposition of a sanction that is a recognised consequence of voting against the whip is permissible if its principal purpose is to attain political discipline in a legislature. On the other hand, meting out punishment is not acceptable if its purpose is simply to deter a legislator from voting in the future in a manner which the majority would find distasteful.[27] 'Punishment' here includes a penalty or any action that is vindictive or malicious or impermissibly coercive.[28] Such a penalty would amount to impermissible pressure that may void a legislative decision in local authorities (but not in Parliament, given the doctrines of parliamentary privilege and exclusive cognisance[29]).

7.19 Party discipline in this context means attempts to keep the party group together.[30] The fact that sanctions may flow as a consequence of failing to accept and vote with the party whip such that a legislator is deterred from doing so does not by itself invalidate his vote, so long as he has considered all the available options and considers that the maintenance of party unanimity is of greater value to his constituents than insistence on his own view.[31] So, an increasing scale of sanctions for failing to 'toe the party line' from a reprimand, to removal from committee chairmanships and to withdrawal of the whip was held lawful in one Court of Appeal case concerning a local authority party group.[32] In another case, where a councillor had been removed from a committee by her party for failing to follow the whip, it was held that there was nothing intrinsically wrong in a decision to change a party's representation on a committee or sub-committee so as to advance the policies which the party considers desirable.[33]

iii. Withdrawing the Whip

7.20 Withdrawing the whip from a legislator does not mean that he can no longer vote, but it does mean that he is no longer considered to be a member of the party's group of legislators. In *R v London Borough of Waltham Forest* various Labour councillors voted with the whip to raise rates (local taxes), notwithstanding that they personally

[26] *R (SC and Others) v Secretary of State for Work and Pensions and Others* [2021] UKSC 26, [2022] AC 223.
[27] *R (Lovelace) v Greenwich London Borough Council* [1991] 1 WLR 506 (CA) at 523.
[28] ibid at 520.
[29] ie the right of each House to regulate its own proceedings and internal affairs without interference from outside bodies.
[30] *R (Lovelace) v Greenwich London Borough Council* [1991] 1 WLR 506 (CA) at 520.
[31] *R v Waltham Forest London Borough Council, ex p Baxter* [1988] QB 419 (CA) at 428.
[32] ibid.
[33] *R (Lovelace) v Greenwich London Borough Council* [1991] 1 WLR 506 (CA) at 520.

disagreed with the rise. The Labour Group's standing orders stated that the whip would be withdrawn from councillors who voted against it. The rise was challenged in legal proceedings. The court held that expulsion from the party group (ie withdrawal of the whip) pursuant to a party's standing orders would not in itself invalidate the councillor's vote:

> so long as councillors are free to remain members despite the withdrawal of the whip and so long as they remember that whatever degree of importance they may attach to group unity and conformity with group policy, the ultimate decision is for them and them alone as individuals.[34]

7.21 Quite separate from the public law position is the lawfulness of withdrawing the whip under the private law of contract. If the party whip is withdrawn as a sanction, it should be done in accordance with any internal rules the party has for that purpose. Different considerations apply depending on whether the whip is withdrawn for failing to vote with the leadership or whether it is removed as the outcome of disciplinary proceedings for a breach of the party's constitution. The withdrawal of the whip as a political sanction is a political act. It is unlikely to amount to a breach of the implied terms of rationality or fairness save in exceptional circumstances. On the other hand, the removal of the whip as a disciplinary outcome is a quasi-judicial act to which the rules of natural justice and rationality will apply in the usual way. So, expulsion from a political caucus as punishment for a disciplinary infraction must be done in accordance with the party's rules; with the principles of natural justice; and avoiding capriciousness, arbitrariness, bad faith and bias. Nevertheless, removing the whip from a member capriciously or maliciously for no cause is likely to contravene the terms of fairness and rationality in the contract of membership. The court has intervened in circumstances where, by withdrawing the whip from an MP, the party had precluded him from standing for the party in the next round of public elections, putting his livelihood at risk.[35]

iv. Welsh Scrutiny Committees

7.22 Unlike in the rest of Britain, Welsh legislation prevents the votes of local authority scrutiny committees being whipped.[36] A 'prohibited party whip' for this purpose is defined as an instruction (however expressed) which is given on behalf of a political group on a local authority to a member of that political group sitting on an overview and scrutiny committee of the local authority. An instruction will be an exercise of the whip if it is an instruction as to how the member should vote on a question falling to be decided by the committee; and, if not complied with, it would be likely to make the member liable to disciplinary action by the political group which gives the instruction.[37] A member of an overview and scrutiny committee must not vote on a question at a

[34] *R v Waltham Forest London Borough Council, ex p Baxter* [1988] QB 419.

[35] See *Williamson v Formby* [2019] EWHC 2639 (QB).

[36] Local Government (Wales) Measure 2011, s 78.

[37] ibd s 78(10).

meeting of the committee if, before the meeting, the member has been given a prohibited party whip.[38] The vote must be disregarded if it falls foul of the prohibition.[39]

C. Following the Whip

i. Loyalty to the Whip

7.23 Loyalty to the whip must not be blind.[40] The law expects legislators in all chambers to cast their votes with independence of mind. One traditional constitutional position[41] was updated for modern times by Lord Justice Staughton:

> The law, when it impinges on the issue at all, expects that a person elected to a representative assembly will exercise his own judgment upon every question which the assembly has to decide. Inevitably there will be pressures upon him to vote one way or the other – pressure from his colleagues, from the party whip, from the newspapers and from his constituents. He must necessarily have regard to those opinions; but in the end he will exercise his vote in accordance with his own judgment. The law does not forbid pressure in general; to do so would be to ignore reality. Nor does it forbid all sanctions which may be imposed for voting contrary to the wishes of those who have power to impose them. The party whip may be withdrawn, newspapers may comment unfavourably, constituents may decline to re-elect, the local party may deselect. None of those measures is unlawful or an improper fetter on the representative's judgment.[42]

7.24 The fundamental function of MPs and peers in the constitutional principle of the Crown in Parliament is to advise the sovereign freely;[43] they are also intermediaries between the people and the government.[44] That requires MPs (and peers) to maintain the independence of their judgement when undertaking their constitutional functions voting, and advising, on legislation.[45] MPs must not place themselves under an obligation to organisations outside Parliament which influences them in the performance of their official duties, including voting in Parliament.[46] Therefore, whipping should only

[38] ibid s 78(1).

[39] ibid s 78(2).

[40] *R (on the application of McClean) v First Secretary of State* [2017] EWHC 3174 (Admin), [2018] 1 Costs LO 37 para 30.

[41] The traditional principle being set out by Edmund Burke in his speech to the electors of Bristol on 3 November 1774: 'Parliament is not a congress of ambassadors from different and hostile interests; which interests each must maintain, as an agent and advocate, against other agents and advocates; but Parliament is a deliberative assembly of one nation, with one interest, that of the whole; where, not local purposes, not local prejudices ought to guide, but the general good, resulting from the general reason of the whole. You choose a member indeed; but when you have chosen him, he is not a member of Bristol, but he is a member of Parliament.'

[42] In *R (Lovelace) v Greenwich London Borough Council* [1991] 1 WLR 506 (CA) at 523–24.

[43] See eg *Amalgamated Society of Railway Servants v Osborne* [1910] AC 87 (HL); *Attorney-General of Ceylon v de Livera* [1963] AC 10, [1962] 3 WLR 1413.

[44] See for eg *R v Rule* [1937] 2 KB 375 (CA); *De Buse and Others v McCarthy* [1942] 1 KB 156 (CA).

[45] *Amalgamated Society of Railway Servants v Osborne* [1910] AC 87 (HL); *Attorney-General of Ceylon v de Ceylon v de Livera* [1963] AC 10, [1962] 3 WLR 1413.

[46] See Ch 13 below and the House of Commons' 'Resolution of 15 July 1947, amended on 6 November 1995 and 14 May 2002: Conduct of Members': 'It is inconsistent with the dignity of the House, with the duty

be done by a party's MPs. To the extent that an extra-parliamentary party unit seeks to enforce a political instruction about how to vote, MPs should not consider themselves compelled to follow it.

7.25 Nor should MPs follow the party whip if, in doing so, they would contravene their duty to the Crown, the country more generally or what is right in the interests of their constituents.[47] MPs must not follow the whip if, by voting in compliance with it, they consider they are acting against the interests of constituents or the nation as a whole.[48] MPs have a duty to avoid any conflict between personal interests and the public interest. A conflict between the two must be resolved immediately in favour of the public interest.[49] Where following the whip would cause a conflict of interest to arise, or resolve a conflict of interest in favour of an MP's private interests, MPs should not do so.

7.26 Councillors must not toe the party line blindly either.[50] They must not follow the whip in a way that amounts to a fettering of their discretion.[51] To do so risks their votes being disregarded, and dependent council decisions invalidated. A councillor will follow the whip impermissibly where he has failed to apply his own mind to the question in issue and failed to weigh voting with the whip against other relevant considerations. So, a councillor must not treat himself as irrevocably bound to carry out pre-announced policies contained in election manifestos.[52] Nor should he exercise a pre-determined acceptance of a decision made by his political party, to the exclusion of all other considerations.[53] The fact that a party issues an instruction to follow the whip in robust or strong language is not something alone that indicates a councillor is prevented from freely exercising his vote, provided he is able to weigh the whip against other material considerations and reach a different conclusion if he judges that is merited.[54] The mere fact that all members of one party vote the same way is not evidence that they were not each exercising an independent judgement.[55]

of a Member to his constituents, and with the maintenance of the privilege of freedom of speech, for any Member of this House to enter into any contractual agreement with an outside body, controlling or limiting the Member's complete independence and freedom of action in Parliament or stipulating that he shall act in any way as the representative of such outside body in regard to any matters to be transacted in Parliament'.

[47] *R (on the application of McClean) v First Secretary of State* [2017] EWHC 3174 (Admin), [2018] 1 Costs LO 37 para 30. Thus, MPs must not follow the whip in circumstances where voting with the party line would cause them to be unfaithful to the monarch and his heirs and successors.

[48] The principle was enumerated in *The Code of Conduct together with the Guide to the Rules Relating to the Conduct of Members* (House of Commons, 10 October 2019, HC 1882) in 'Duties of Members', para III.6. The principle has not been replicated in the most recent Code published in 2023 (HC 1083), though a Resolution in which the principle is set out has been included in the 2023 publication's appendix (Resolution of 15 July 1947, amended on 6 November 1995 and 14 May 2002: Conduct of Members: 'the duty of a Member being to his constituents and to the country as a whole, rather than to any particular section thereof').

[49] *The House of Commons Code of Conduct* (10 February 2023 HC 1083), 'The Code of Conduct for Members of Parliament', 'General Principles of Conduct', Part D para 2.

[50] *Bromley London Borough Council Respondents v Greater London Council and Another Appellants* [1983] 1 AC 768.

[51] eg *R v London Borough of Waltham Forest* [1988] QB 419.

[52] *Bromley London Borough Council Respondents v Greater London Council and Another Appellants* [1983] 1 AC 768 para 829 per Lord Denning.

[53] *R v London Borough of Waltham Forest* [1988] QB 419 per Stoker LJ.

[54] *R (on the application of IM Properties Development Ltd) v Lichfield District Council* [2014] EWHC 2440 (Admin), [2014] PTSR 1484 at para 80.

[55] *Jones v Swansea City Council* [1990] 1 WLR 54 para 83.

7.27 It is permissible to follow the whip's instruction to vote a particular way despite vehement disagreement with the political position. It is also permissible for a councillor to vote with the whip against his own personal assessment of a policy if he considers he could serve his constituents better by maintaining the political unity of his political grouping while influencing his party internally;[56] or because he fought the election on the basis of policies for the future put forward in the election manifesto of a particular political party and received a majority of votes;[57] or because of the views of his party colleagues;[58] or because the proposal in question has the support of members of his party, some of whom will have carefully considered the merits of the proposal in the light of general shared party values.[59]

ii. Party Political Advantage

7.28 MPs and peers are entitled to exercise their votes in Parliament on the basis of both party-political advantage and the party line. Legislators will not have acted in bad faith, nor breached any duty to act impartially, merely because they have cast their votes in accordance with the party whip for party political gain.[60] So, councillors are permitted to follow the whip to please their constituents with a view to winning the next election.[61]

iii. Conflicting Professional Duties

7.29 An MP's duty to attend Parliament and vote as instructed by the whip has been held to be subordinate to other professional duties. This is an important consideration in circumstances where many MPs are lawyers by profession, some of whom continue to practise, and a growing number are medical professionals. For example, it was a breach of the Bar Standards Board's Code of Conduct for an MP to return his instructions to appear in a criminal trial without his client's consent on the basis that he had to vote on the Queen's Speech (subject to a three-line whip). In these circumstances an MP may find him or herself between 'a rock and a hard place – his duty to Parliament on the one hand, and his professional duty to his client on the other'.[62] Even so, the dilemma is likely to amount to a significant mitigating factor justifying a lighter sanction from any professional regulatory body.

[56] *R v London Borough of Waltham Forest* [1988] QB 419.

[57] *Bromley London Borough Council Respondents v Greater London Council and Another Appellants* [1983] 1 AC 768 at 829 per Lord Denning.

[58] *R v Local Commissioner for Local Government for North and North East England* [2001] 1 All ER 462, (2000) 2 LGLR 603 at para 29 per Henry LJ.

[59] *Porter v Magill* [2001] UKHL 67, [2002] 2 AC 357 at 394 per Kennedy LJ.

[60] *R (on the application of McClean) v First Secretary of State* [2017] EWHC 3174 (Admin), [2018] 1 Costs LO 37 para 30.

[61] *Porter v Magill* [2001] UKHL 67, [2002] 2 AC 357 at 391–92 per Kennedy LJ.

[62] *Stephen Hesford v General Council of the Bar* (unreported, 22 July 1999), Visitors to the Inns of Court.

iv. Political Inducements

7.30 Confidence and supply agreements,[63] or other similar political deals, may oblige legislators to vote to support particular administrations or policies. These sorts of agreements may promise spending commitments for the benefit of another's constituents, or the enactment of a particular policy. An MP's agreement to vote in return for such spending or policy commitments does not amount to an acceptance of a personal inducement to vote in a particular way in breach of the rules of conduct or standing orders of the House of Commons. Neither the government nor individual MPs will have an illegitimate conflict of interest if they enter into such agreements in return for spending commitments in accordance with it. That is because there is no relevant standard of impartiality or disinterest to apply that can be breached. Rather, all political parties seek to promote their own particular interests and points of view. Such interests are regulated by political standards: the requirements to command majorities in the House of Commons and the Lords on significant votes and to seek re-election at the appropriate time. The principle of parliamentary privilege precludes the courts from questioning proceedings in Parliament, but in any case, the law does not superimpose additional standards which would make the political process unworkable.[64] Thus, in *R (on the application of McClean) v First Secretary of State*, the Divisional Court found that it was legitimate for Democratic Unionist Party MPs to enter into a confidence and supply agreement with the Conservative Party in 2017 in return for spending commitments to Northern Ireland.[65] (Note that there is usually very narrow scope, if any, for councillors to enter into coalition or into supply arrangements with other local authority groups without the agreement of the central party's governing bodies).

v. Contractual Obligations to Vote with the Whip

7.31 Contractual agreements purporting to oblige MPs and other legislators to vote with a particular group in return for a benefit are void for reasons of public policy. They are also contrary to the law of Parliament.[66] The legislators who are parties to such contracts should disregard them.

7.32 The legal principle was set out by the House of Lords (in its judicial capacity) as long ago as 1910 in a case concerning trade unions. In *Amalgamated Society of Railway Servants v Osborne*,[67] a railway workers' union wished to support parliamentary candidates standing for a precursor of the Labour Party to represent the working class. At that time MPs were not paid, which posed a significant barrier to working class representation in Parliament. In 1906 the union amended its constitutional rules and arranged for

[63] ie where one party agrees to support another in votes of confidence or on finance and money Bills.

[64] *R (on the application of McClean) v First Secretary of State* [2017] EWHC 3174 (Admin), [2018] 1 Costs LO 37 para 21.

[65] ibid.

[66] See footnote 46.

[67] *Amalgamated Society of Railway Servants v Osborne* [1910] AC 87.

candidates, when elected, to be paid from its own funds of members' subscriptions. The amended rules included a contractual term that 'all candidates shall sign and accept the conditions of the Labour party and be subject to their "whip"' and 'the executive committee shall make suitable provision for the registration of a constituency represented by a member or members who may be candidates responsible to and paid by this society'. In the judgment of Lord James and Lord Shaw, that particular contractual term was void because it attempted to bind the votes of MPs. The contract presented an unacceptable peril that Parliament would be controlled by secret agreements and bought votes:

> It is no doubt true that a member, although party to such a contract of subjection, would in point of law enter Parliament a free man, because the law would treat as non-enforceable and void the contract which purported to bind him. And it is no doubt true that – parties remaining outside of and making no appeal to the law – this subjection may arise in practice through the operation upon certain natures of various motives, including notably those of sycophancy or fear. But when the law is appealed to, to lend its authority to the recognition and enforcement of a contract to procure subjection of the character described, with the concurrents of money payments and the sanctions of fines or forfeitures, the law will decline such recognition or enforcement because the contract appealed to is contrary to sound public policy. I should be sorry to think that these considerations are not quite elementary. And they apply with equal force not to labour organizations alone, … but with even greater force to individual men, or organizations or trusts of men using capital funds to procure the subjection of members of Parliament to their commands. In this latter case, indeed, adhesion to the principle is of a value all the greater because its violation might be conducted in secret. It needs little imagination to figure the peril in which parliamentary government would stand if, either by the purchase of single votes, or by subsidies for regular support, the public well-being were liable to betrayal at the command and for the advantage of particular individuals or classes.[68]

7.33 In 1980 another union case came before the Court of Appeal on an associated point.[69] USDAW operated a parliamentary representation scheme, requiring candidates who were successfully elected to Parliament to accept the conditions of the Labour Party and be subject to the Labour whip. In return, should the candidate not be selected again thereafter, he was entitled under the scheme to return to employment by the union. Mr Milne was elected for the Blyth constituency under the scheme. In February 1974 a snap general election was called. Unfortunately, Mr Milne had a falling out with the local constituency party; he was not selected and stood – and won – as an independent; he was afterwards expelled from the Labour Party and the Labour whip was removed. He complained that the scheme's contractual obligation on him to follow the Labour whip in return for future employment was void for reasons of public policy. The High Court decided it was not, because the phrase 'accepts the conditions of the Labour Party and be subject to the Whips of that Party' meant little more than Mr Milne was obliged to become a member of the Parliamentary Labour Party, or be subject to the Code of Conduct of the Parliamentary Labour Party. On appeal, the Court of Appeal declined to deal with the point in substance but expressed doubt about

[68] ibid at 111–16 per Lord Shaw.

[69] *Edward Milne v Union of Shop, Distributive and Allied Workers* (unreported, 6 June 1980) (CA), 1975 M No 3454.

the High Court's conclusion. That doubt is well placed. In reality, most political party constitutions in Britain contain terms that require electoral candidates, once elected, to take the party whip. Those terms are an important aspect of political organisation across the country and it would, therefore, be surprising if they were void for reasons of public policy.

D. Challenging the Whip in Court

7.34 The courts are unable either to order or to declare that MPs should do an act within Parliament in their capacity as Members of Parliament. To do so would be to trespass impermissibly on the province of Parliament.[70] It follows that the courts are unable to give effect to instructions from parliamentary whips about how MPs should vote (nor can they declare that members should vote contrary to such instructions).

7.35 Whether withdrawal of the whip from MPs and peers is justiciable in court has not been settled. It is unlikely that parliamentary privilege could be asserted successfully over a decision to remove the whip from an MP or peer so as to preclude the courts from scrutinising it. On one analysis, withdrawal of the whip from a party member may be an act ancillary to the core business of Parliament and non-justiciable. The arrangement of the associations between MPs and between Members of the Lords is a matter integrally connected with collective parliamentary decision making; as the editors of *Erskine May* opine: 'the efficient and smooth running of the Parliamentary machine depends largely on the whips'.[71] Collective deliberation and decision-making in Parliament falls within the scope of parliamentary privilege.[72]

7.36 The difficulty with the forgoing analysis is that, in some instances, the whip will be withdrawn from MPs and peers not because of their voting record but as a response to alleged or actual conduct by them which occurs outside parliamentary business. It is difficult to see why parliamentary privilege should apply to any decision to remove the whip in respect of extra-parliamentary conduct: neither the conduct nor the withdrawal of the whip fall into the category of parliamentary business. The fact that the withdrawal of the whip is an act done by representatives of a private political organisation, rather than a parliamentary body, is also highly relevant. By comparison, the Parliamentary Standards Commissioner has authority to discipline MPs, pursuant to the Commons' Committee on Standards and Privileges, for breaches of the House's rules and standing orders, over which Parliament has exclusive cognisance.[73] The disciplinary actions of the whips are instead acts of the agents of a private political party that exists independently of Parliament's business. On that view, parliamentary privilege is very unlikely to apply.

[70] *R (on the application of Wheeler) v Office of the Prime Minister* [2008] EWHC 1409 (Admin), [2008] ACD 70 at para 79.
[71] *Erskine May: Parliamentary Practice*, 25th edn (LexisNexis, 2019) Part 1, Ch 4, para 4.9.
[72] *R v Chaytor (David)* [2010] UKSC 52, [2011] 1 AC 684.
[73] ibid.

7.37 Notwithstanding questions of privilege, there must be a legal relationship between the party and its elected member that would permit the member to found a claim in law. The party's rules, being a contract between the party and the member, may suffice depending on their terms. The Labour Party's rules contain an express provision that the Parliamentary Labour Party must adhere to the rules of the Labour Party and that members must be treated fairly and afforded procedural fairness by all officers of the party. Its former leader, Mr Corbyn, brought a claim for pre-action disclosure against the Labour Party arising from his suspension from the Parliamentary Labour Party. The court decided that it was at least arguable that Mr Corbyn had a valid claim in contract for a breach of the express term of fairness.[74]

IV. Factions

A. Status

i. Organisation

7.38 A faction is a group of members which supports a particular cause. Informal factions may eventually crystallise into unincorporated (or incorporated) associations with appointed leaders and committees, etc that gain the status of subordinate units of a political party with a legal relationship to the same.[75] For the most part, however, political factions are loose and fluctuating groups of people. These groups have no contractual role in the constitutional affairs of the party, nor do they have any legal status of their own.[76]

7.39 The members of an informal faction may nevertheless assert a representative claim against the party, providing the faction's members have a common interest.[77] If there is a properly maintainable claim in contract, the fact the putative claimants may be described as a 'faction' is not a bar to pursuing the claim.[78] It is, however, an abuse of process to use the courts as a means of settling political rivalries[79] and the courts will not intervene simply 'to give the kiss of life to some faction which is otherwise not viable'.[80]

ii. Power Struggles

7.40 Factionalism becomes especially relevant to the party's internal management by the appearance of 'slates' of candidates in internal elections, for whom members of a

[74] *Corbyn v Evans* [2021] EWHC 130 (QB).

[75] For example, the Conservative Party's 1922 Committee (which has formal constitutional status in the party) or the Conservative Party's European Research Group, or Progressive Britain (formally Progress) and Momentum in the Labour Party (which have no formal constitutional status but are nevertheless unincorporated associations with related companies).

[76] *Hussain and Sattar v Wycombe Islamic Mission and Mosque Trust Ltd and Iqbal* [2011] EWHC 971 (Ch) para 12.

[77] See *John v Rees* [1970] Ch 345.

[78] *Barnett v British National Party* [2020] EWHC 1538 (QB) para 53.

[79] ibid para 41.

[80] *Lewis v Heffer* [1978] 1 WLR 1061 at 1079.

particular faction are encouraged to vote. Party members are not obliged to follow the instructions of a particular faction and the application of pressure to do so in a party election may constitute a disciplinary offence.[81]

7.41 The case of *Lewis v Heffer* concerned a power struggle between self-declared 'moderate' and 'left wing' factions of the Newham East Constituency Labour Party as to whom would be its candidate. Newham East was a safe Labour Party seat. Giving the first judgment of the Court, Lord Denning summarised the relevance of factionalism in a constitutional context:

> The faction which wins will have a representative in Parliament. He will there propagate its ideas. And, if there are other Members of Parliament of like mind, he will, with them, be able to put their objectives into operation. This local struggle may have its counterpart in other constituencies. So the outcome may influence the standing of the Labour Party in Parliament: and thus affect the policies of Parliament itself. Hence its importance.[82]

7.42 Pressures from competing factions may result in a degradation of organisational integrity in local parties or associations, hindering their activities. The party's governing committee will be justified in intervening in subordinate party units' affairs in such circumstances, provided the committee has broad contractual powers entitling it to manage the party generally and there are no relevant express provisions in the rules limiting a power of intervention.[83]

7.43 Where factional disorder is severe enough to require the administrative suspension of local parties or their members, it will not be necessary to provide those members with a hearing before doing so. Nor will it be necessary to undertake a fact-finding investigation first.[84] However, the governing committee should give the members in question notice and a right to be heard if it proposes to proscribe a faction such that those supporting it must inevitably be expelled.[85] An expulsion for adherence to a banned faction must follow the rules of natural justice.[86]

iii. Bad Faith

7.44 The mere fact that factionalism has played a part in the desire to see something done does not mean that the thing has been done in bad faith. So, a claim brought by a group for a court order entitling them to examine their organisation's finances was held to be based on genuine concerns even though factionalism had played a part in their

[81] See, by example, *John v Rees* [1970] Ch 345.

[82] *Lewis v Heffer* [1978] 1 WLR 1061 at 1065.

[83] *Jeffers v Labour Party* [2011] EWHC 529 (QB) para 50; *Lewis v Heffer* ibid.

[84] *Lewis v Heffer*; *Green v Labour Party* (unreported, 27 March 1991) (CA).

[85] *Walsh v McCluskie* [1982] CLY 2509, (1982) Times, 16 December.

[86] *Mackay v Caley* (Ipswich Labour Party) (unreported, 16 September 1986) (CA). See Ch 12, Section III for the content of the duty of natural fairness. The requirements of natural justice in this context are likely to be procedurally minimal, limited to providing a gist of the alleged infraction, the evidence on which the allegation is based and a meaningful opportunity for the member concerned to say something in his defence.

desire to inspect them.[87] A dismissal may be unfair if the reason for it is factional malice or if the dismissal involves inconsistent treatment motivated by factionalism. But the fact that an executive committee is glad to see the back of an employee because of his adherence to a particular faction will not itself render a dismissal unfair.[88]

B. Adherents of Informal Factions

7.45 Being a member of an informal faction does not commit a person to hold particular opinions or act in pursuit of particular aims. A faction's members are under no obligation to stay in the group and they may cease to follow the faction at any time. Members do not require permission from the faction's other adherents to join it. The position of those regarded as the faction's leaders depends entirely on the continued support for them from the other members of the group. Leaders of factions are not formally appointed and they cannot formally be removed, because they have no formal authority. There is no express or implied legal authority between those held out as leaders and their followers. Views expressed by someone who is regarded as a leader of the group may be influential in determining the views of the faction's individual members, but those views cannot oblige followers to take any particular step. Mere membership of, or support for, a faction does not give rise to legal liability among its followers for anything the (perceived) leader has done.[89]

[87] *Garcha v The Charity Commission for England and Wales* [2014] EWHC 2754 (Ch).

[88] Though it may be unfair for other reasons. See *Associated Society of Locomotive Engineers and Firemen v Brady* [2006] IRLR 576, paras 77 and 109.

[89] *Hussain and Sattar v Wycombe Islamic Mission and Mosque Trust Ltd and Iqbal* [2011] EWHC 971 (Ch) paras 10, 11.

8

Organising through Trade Unions and Co-operatives

I. Introduction

8.1 Trade unions and co-operative societies are important secondary vehicles for political organisation. They are independent of political parties but are allowed to be involved in their political work. Trade unions and co-operative societies play a significant role in party politics by funding the Labour Party and the Co-operative Party respectively. Statutory rules regulate the use of trade union money to fund political campaigning: if trade unions wish to do so, they must establish a political fund and abide by the rules governing its operation. Trade unions and co-operative societies also have significant involvement in the organisation and running of the Labour Party and the Co-operative Party by holding designated places on those parties' ruling committees. To stand for Parliament, a Labour Party member must normally be a member of a trade union; nor may a person be a Co-operative Party parliamentary candidate without holding membership of a co-operative society. Section II of this chapter explains the formal relationship between the larger trade unions and the Labour Party, and then sets out the rules governing trade unions' political funds and how trade unions can have their members adopted as Labour Party candidates. The chapter concludes with an explanation of the link between co-operative societies and the Co-operative Party.

8.2 When trade unions and co-operatives spend money to campaign for the Labour Party (or indeed any political party), they will be 'third-party campaigners' (also known as 'non-party campaigners') and subject to rules limiting campaign spending. Those rules are addressed in Chapter 10.

II. Trade Unions

A. Political Influence

8.3 Two statements, made almost 60 years apart, aptly summarise the very great influence the trade union movement has had on the political life of this country. The first was made at a meeting of the Trades Union Congress, after the union movement had built the Labour Party as its political wing and achieved the election of the first Labour government in 1924:

> The phenomenal rise in the influence and importance of the Labour Movement was strikingly demonstrated by the advent in January 1924 of the first British Labour Government. Friends and colleagues who have spent their lives in the ranks of the Trade Unionists are to-day administering the affairs of the nation and displaying a capacity which establishes once and for all Labour's fitness to govern. … Unfortunately there are those who, because of the advent of the Labour Government, minimise the necessity for effective industrial organisation. They take the view of regarding the political Labour Movement as an alternative instead of an auxiliary to the Trade Union Movement. Such an attitude is extremely dangerous … Political organisation, far from being an alternative to the Trade Union Movement, is its natural corollary.[1]

The second statement was made not long before Mrs Thatcher's re-election to serve a second term as Prime Minister in 1983, intent to act on concerns that the Labour movement had too much political power:

> What do we want to see in the year 2000? … A trade union movement whose exclusive relationship with the Labour Party is reduced out of all recognition. Again, it is absurd and unjust that millions of Conservatives, Liberals and Social Democrats should be supporting the Labour Party directly or indirectly. This relationship fossilises the Labour Party and stultifies the whole political dialogue.[2]

[1] Report of the Annual Conference of the Trades Union Congress (1924) 81, available at TUC History Online: www.unionhistory.info.

[2] Memo on trade union reform from Ferdinand Mount to Margaret Thatcher, 21 October 1982 [suggestions on future trade union legislation: 'there is danger of complacency and timidity creeping into our approach to the reform of trade union law'], Prime Ministerial Private Office files, PREM19/1061, The National Archives.

8.4 Trade unions are not registered political parties and they cannot, therefore, stand candidates for public election in their own name. Nevertheless, unions campaign for political parties, support political candidates and donate money to political party campaign coffers. The use of a trade union's members' money on core political activities is regulated by the Trade Union and Labour Relations (Consolidation) Act 1992 (TULRCA 1992). For well over a century trade unions have organised on a political level through, and within, the Labour Party, which they helped establish. The mechanism by which that organisation operates has several key elements:

i. Trade unions operate political funds which they can spend to achieve political objects, including giving support to particular candidates in public elections. The largest trade unions donate money to the Labour Party from their political funds, so that the party can contest and win elections. Donations are made on a national and regional level and are also used to support particular candidates who are members of the union in question.
ii. The largest trade unions[3] are contractually affiliated to the Labour Party. These unions are able to nominate and to support their own members to stand as Labour Party candidates in public elections. A number of seats on the central party's various governing committees are reserved for delegates from the affiliated trade unions and trade unions have voting rights at the Labour Party's Conference. This allows affiliated trade unions to influence the development of Labour Party policy positions, among other things.

B. Affiliation to the Labour Party

8.5 At the time of writing, eleven trade unions are affiliated to the Labour Party. Affiliation is governed by the contractual rules of the Labour Party. To affilliate to the party, unions may apply to the party's National Executive Committee, which has the final say on accepting the application or not.[4] Once affiliated, a union must accept the programme, policy and principles of the party and agree to conform to its rules. The union must also submit its political rules to the Labour Party National Executive Committee.[5] Each affiliated trade union must pay an affiliation fee, calculated as a particular sum multiplied by the number of members the union affiliates to the party. A proportion of the union's affiliation fee is allocated to the Labour Party's national election fund.[6] Affiliated unions have various rights to be involved in the governance of the Labour Party, including sending delegates to the party's governing committees, nominating leadership contenders and affiliating local union branches to local constituency parties. The relationship between the affiliated unions and the Labour Party on a national level is co-ordinated by an internal committee of the Labour Party called the Trade Union Liaison Organisation. The relationship between

[3] At the time of writing (the biggest being the GMB, Unison and Unite).
[4] Labour Party Rule Book 2023, Ch 1, cl II.3.
[5] ibid Ch 1, cl II.4.
[6] ibid Ch 1, cl II.6.

unions and Labour MPs is also co-ordinated by a committee of the Labour Party's parliamentary party.[7]

8.6 The affiliated trade unions and the Labour Party often work in tandem to achieve shared objectives. But that does not mean that the affiliated unions are always in lock-step with the party; trade unions organise politically within the Labour Party and sometimes against the Labour Party leadership and (when in office) a Labour government. Thus the Fire Brigades Union (FBU), which was affiliated to the party, went on strike over a pay dispute when Tony Blair was Prime Minister of a Labour government in 2003. The union and the government fell out significantly, with members of the government calling FBU members 'criminally irresponsible', 'wreckers' and 'criminals' and in 2004 the FBU annual conference voted to disaffiliate from the Labour Party.[8] The union re-affiliated under the leadership of Jeremy Corbyn.[9] The Labour Party National Executive Committee also has the power to disaffiliate or to suspend an affiliated union from its involvement in the party.[10]

C. Political Funds

i. Regulated Political Purposes

8.7 The law regulates how trade unions can spend their members' money on political activities. Trade unions have a significant role in supporting political candidates for public election. The unions are allowed to make payments on the following political activities only if the money is drawn from a valid political fund to which members make political contributions:[11]

i. donating money to a political party;[12]
ii. paying for the union's members to attend political party meetings as delegates; and expending any money on holding meetings by or on behalf of a political party or on any other meeting the main purpose of which is the transaction of business in connection with a political party;[13]
iii. providing 'in kind' support to a political party (eg use of property or premises);[14]
iv. selecting prospective candidates for national and local public political office (eg by spending money on union members' campaigns to win a Labour Party candidate selection);[15]
v. supporting a party candidate's election campaign by encouraging voters to register to vote at public elections and by campaigning for that candidate (ie by producing,

[7] ibid Ch 1, cl II.2.H.
[8] See www.fbu.org.uk/history/fbu-disaffiliates-labour-party-2004.
[9] See www.fbu.org.uk/history/fbu-reaffiliates-labour-party.
[10] Labour Party Rule Book 2023, Ch 1, VIII.3.
[11] TULRCA 1992, s 71.
[12] ibid s 72(1)(a).
[13] ibid s 72(1)(e) and (2).
[14] ibid s 72(1)(b).
[15] ibid s 72(1)(c).

publicising or distributing any literature, document, film, sound recording or advertisement which has as its main purpose persuading people to vote (or not to vote) for a political party or a particular candidate in a public election);[16]

vi. providing financial maintenance to MPs and local councillors or any officer of a political party (eg a General Secretary or director).[17] Maintenance here means maintenance of a person as a politician and includes any expenses reasonably incurred by a MP to perform her parliamentary functions, for example, travelling to and from her constituency, secretarial services and research services.[18]

8.8 The regulation of union spending on these political activities from the political fund applies irrespective of whether the union is undertaking them directly or indirectly, alone or with other unions or political parties.[19] The ordinary administrative expenses of the union do not fall within the scope of spending money on those political activities.[20]

ii. Separation of Union Funds

8.9 The political fund must be separate from the union's general funds, so that payment of sums towards the political objects and activity set out above is made from a separate 'pot' of money.[21] It is impermissible for money to be spent on the regulated political objects by using money in the general fund. For example, one union breached the political fund rules by contributing £42,952 from its general fund towards the purchase of the Labour Party's national headquarters.[22]

iii. Union Rules

8.10 To operate a political fund, a trade union must have rules that govern its use.[23] The rules must provide that:

i. members who are not contributors to the political fund are not under any obligation to contribute to it;[24]
ii. members will not be excluded from any union benefits because they do not contribute to the political fund; and members who do not contribute will not in any way

[16] ibid s 72(1)(f).
[17] ibid s 72(1)(d) and (4).
[18] *Association of Scientific Technical and Managerial Staffs v Parkin* [1983] IRLR 448.
[19] TULRCA 1992, s 71(2).
[20] ibid s 72(3).
[21] ibid ss 71(1)(b) and 82(1)(a). At the beginning of the twentieth century the House of Lords ruled in *Amalgamated Society of Railway Servants v Osborne* [1910] AC 87, that it was unlawful for trade unions to use their funds for political purposes, especially for the maintenance of Labour candidates. The effect of the decision was reversed by the Trade Union Act 1913 which allowed trade unions to use funds for political purposes, if those funds were held in a new 'political fund', separate to the union's general fund, so that members who did not want to contribute to political funding could opt out of doing so.
[22] *Association of Scientific Technical and Managerial Staffs v Parkin* [1983] IRLR 448.
[23] TULRCA 1992, s 71(1).
[24] ibid s 82(1)(b).

be put under a disadvantage or disability compared to other members of the union (except by the fact that non-contributing members will not have any part to play in the management or control of the political fund);[25]

iii. admission as a member of the union is not conditional on contributing to the political fund;[26]

iv. any form (including an electronic form) that a person has to complete to become a union member will include statements to the following effect:[27]

- that the person may opt to be a contributor to the fund;
- that he will not, by reason of not being a contributor, be excluded from any benefits of the union, or be placed in any respect either directly or indirectly under a disability or at a disadvantage as compared with other members of the union (except in relation to the control or management of the political fund).

iv. Political Resolutions

8.11 If the union wants to spend money on political activities and operate a political fund to do so then it must pass a political resolution. A political resolution in this context is a resolution that pursues the political objectives set out in section 72 of the TULRCA 1992 as objects of the union.[28]

8.12 The resolution must be passed by a majority of those voting on a ballot of the trade union's members.[29] The rules for the ballot must be approved by the Certification Officer before the ballot can be held.[30] Once the ballot has been passed the resolution has the same status as a rule in the trade union's rule book. A new resolution must be passed every ten years, as the resolution will lapse on the tenth anniversary of the date of the ballot on which it was passed.[31]

v. Organising against a Proposed Political Resolution

8.13 A union's members can organise *against* a political resolution in several ways. First, they can vote to rescind it using the procedure specified in the union's rule book for repealing union rules.[32] Second, they can pass a new political resolution before the ten-year period lapses.[33] If the union's members pass the new resolution the old one

[25] ibid s 82(1)(c).

[26] ibid s 82(1)(d).

[27] ibid s 82(1)(ca).

[28] ibid s 71(1) and (1)(a).

[29] ibid s 73(1).

[30] ibid s 74. The Certification Officer (a government officer who ensures that trade unions comply with their statutory duties) will not approve the ballot unless he or she is satisfied that the union is following the rules for the conduct of the ballot set out in TULRCA 1992.

[31] ibid s 73(3).

[32] ibid s 73(2). As long as the recission motion is passed by a majority of members voting and the Certification Officer certifies that is so, then the recission (as with any other proposed union rule) will have effect even if not all the procedural requirements for passing it in the union's rule book have been met: ibid s 92.

[33] Note that fresh approval of the rules for the ballot must be obtained from the Certification Officer, even if the rules are no different to those used and previously approved: ibid s 74(2).

shall be treated as rescinded. Third, a new proposed political resolution can be defeated on the membership ballot. The defeat of a proposed political resolution will also cut short the duration of the existing resolution: the latter will cease to have effect two weeks after the date of the ballot (rather than continuing until the end of the usual ten-year period).[34]

vi. Challenging the Political Resolution

8.14 A member can challenge the operation of the political fund by applying to the court or the Certification Officer on the following grounds:

i. the union has spent its funds on political objects without a valid political resolution in breach of section 71 of TULRCA 1992;[35]
ii. the union has undertaken the political ballot using rules that the Certification Officer did not approve;[36]
iii. the union failed to comply with the political ballot rules that the Certification Officer actually approved.[37]

8.15 The application cannot be made to both the court and the Certification Officer so the applicant must pick one or the other.[38] Declarations and enforcement orders made by the Certification Officer have the same effect as those made by the court.[39] Note that a party to the proceedings may appeal against the Certification Officer's decision to the Employment Appeal Tribunal. Only members of the union can bring a challenge and any applicant challenging a political ballot that the union has already held must also have been a member of the union at the time of the ballot.[40] The time limit to make any challenge to the rules of the ballot is within one year after the day on which the union announced the result of the political ballot.[41]

8.16 The Certification Officer has the following powers in respect of an application challenging the rules of the political ballot.

a. Grant the Application and Make a Declaration

8.17 If she grants the application, she must specify the provisions with which the union has failed to comply.[42] If she is satisfied that the union has already taken steps to remedy the deficient ballot or to ensure that a similar mistake does not happen again, or

[34] ibid s 73(4).
[35] ibid s 72A(1).
[36] ibid s 79(1)(a).
[37] ibid s 79(1)(b).
[38] ibid ss 72A(10), (11), 80(10) and 81(8). Where two members or more respectively make applications to the court and to the Certification Officer challenging the rules of the ballot, the court or Certification Officer as the case may be must have due regard to any declarations made by the other.
[39] ibid s 80(8), (9).
[40] ibid s 79(2).
[41] ibid s 79(3).
[42] ibid s 80(3).

that the union has agreed to take remedial steps, the Certification Officer must specify in the declaration what steps the union has taken (or will take).[43]

b. Require the Union to Remedy a Breach

8.18 If the Certification Officer grants the application then she must also make an enforcement order unless it is inappropriate to do so. Where an enforcement order has been made, any member who was a member at the time the order was made is entitled to enforce the order, not just the member who made the application in question.[44] The enforcement order will state the time period within which the union has to comply with it.[45] The order may require the union to do the following things:

i. to hold a fresh ballot in accordance with the union's political ballot rules and any other provisions made in the order;[46]
ii. to take particular steps to remedy the failures in the ballot detailed in the declaration;[47] or
iii. to abstain from particular acts to avoid similar failures in the holding of the ballot in the future.[48]

c. Refuse the Application

8.19 The Certification Officer may refuse the application. If so, she must provide reasons. She may also provide observations about the political ballot or the legal proceedings.[49]

8.20 The Certification Officer may require people to provide information in connection with her enquiries about the application. If the information is not provided by the specified date then the Certification Officer may simply continue to determine the application without it.[50]

8.21 The court has the same powers as the Certification Officer,[51] save that the court may also make an order for interim relief, for example an injunction halting the ballot.[52]

vii. Operating the Political Fund

8.22 There are only two ways in which a union can add sums to the political fund: first, by depositing contributions made to the fund by union members or a person not

[43] ibid s 80(4).
[44] ibid ss 80(5C) and 81(6).
[45] ibid s 80(5A).
[46] ibid s 80(5A)(a) and (5B).
[47] ibid s 80(5A)(b).
[48] ibid s 80(5A)(c).
[49] ibid s 80(5).
[50] ibid s 80(7).
[51] ibid s 81.
[52] ibid s 81(7).

in the union; and second, by adding property or money that accrues to the fund in the course of administering it (eg interest).[53]

8.23 The union must not meet any debts or liabilities owed from the political fund through any of the union's other general funds. This is a strict rule and it applies even where the union has used assets in its general funds as collateral for a financial liability of the political fund (eg a mortgage charge on property belonging to the general funds).[54]

8.24 Unions may not require members to contribute to the political fund without a political resolution in force.[55] The union must not require a member to contribute to the political fund if he has not opted-in to making such contributions by an 'opt-in notice' or if he has withdrawn his opt-in notice. A member may give an opt-in notice to the union (or withdraw it) by delivering it to the union's head office or a branch office himself, by post or by using an agent, or by emailing to a union email address specified for that purpose, or by sending it electronically with an online form. If a member does withdraw his opt-in notice then the withdrawal takes effect at the end of one month after he gave notice.[56] The union must take all reasonable steps to inform all members of their right to give a withdrawal notice.[57]

8.25 The union can take contributions for the political fund in two ways. The first way is by applying a separate political fund levy to any members who have opted-in. The second way is to include the political fund contribution in a single periodical contribution made by members but relieve opted-out members from paying it. If the second method is used then the union must relieve all opted-out members from paying the political fund contribution on the occasion of the same periodical payment so far as possible. The union must also let all its members know what portion of periodical contributions is a contribution to the political fund.[58]

8.26 If the political resolution lapses because members have balloted on a fresh resolution but not passed it, the union may nonetheless continue to make payments out of the political fund for six months from the date of the ballot. However, the union cannot make a payment that causes the fund to be in deficit or increases a deficit in it. The union can add contributions to the fund if the contributions were paid to the union before the political resolution lapsed. The union can also continue to add funds that have accrued in the course of administering the fund's assets.[59]

8.27 Once there is no longer a political resolution in force the union may transfer the whole or part of the political fund to another union fund.[60] The union must also

[53] ibid s 83(1).
[54] ibid s 83(3).
[55] ibid s 83(2).
[56] ibid s 84.
[57] ibid s 84A(1). The information must be provided not later than the end of the period of eight weeks beginning with the day on which the annual return of the union is sent to the Certification Officer.
[58] ibid s 85.
[59] ibid s 89.
[60] ibid.

take necessary steps to ensure that it stops collecting contributions to the political fund as soon as reasonably practicable, but any political fund contributions received after the resolution ceases to have effect may be paid into the union's other funds. However, members may apply for a refund of their contributions to the political fund collected after the political resolution is no longer in force, in which case the union must pay the refund. If the union fails to take reasonable steps to halt collecting contributions to the political fund, any member may apply to the court for a declaration and an enforcement order obliging the union to stop and to take remedial steps.[61]

8.28 Unions rules sometimes allow local branches a portion of their own local members' contributions to the political fund to spend as the branch sees fit. The fact that a union affiliates itself to the Labour Party does not result in an implied obligation in the union's rules that the Labour Party must be the only recipient of political fund money from branches. Affiliation does no more than indicate that the union's policy is to support the Labour Party, so far as the political fund is concerned. Therefore, if individual branches are permitted to receive grants from the political fund to spend as they wish, those branches are entitled to donate the money to a different political party. This is what happened in the case of *Parkin v Association of Scientific, Technical and Managerial Staffs*, in which the court held Mr Parkin, a local union branch chair, was entitled to donate the branch's slice of the political fund to the Conservative Party.[62] Nevertheless, a union's governing committee is entitled to scrutinise any application by its branches to spend portions of the political fund to ensure that the proposed expenditure accords with the union's legitimate political objects.[63]

D. Trade Union Political Candidates

8.29 It has already been observed at paragraph 8.4 above that trade unions are unable to stand candidates for election under the name of the union itself because they are not registered political parties. However, trade unions are able to have their members adopted as Labour Party candidates.

8.30 No person may stand as a Labour Party candidate in any public election unless he is a member of a bona fide trade union (save if he is prevented from being a trade union member by law). With that exception, every Labour MP must be a member of a trade union.[64] Trade union members who do not contribute to their union's respective political funds are ineligible to be a member of the party.[65] This means that all Labour MPs, and most Labour councillors, have a direct link to a particular trade union. It also means that the large unions have a network of legislators across the country.

[61] ibid s 90.
[62] *Parkin v Association of Scientific, Technical and Managerial Staffs* [1980] IRLR 188.
[63] ibid.
[64] Labour Party Rule Book, Ch 5, cl II.3.A.iii.
[65] ibid Ch 2, cl I.9.B.

8.31 The trade unions affiliated to the Labour Party may also affiliate branches of their members to local Constituency Labour Parties (CLPs). That entitles union members to organise within the Labour Party and attend meetings, nominate prospective candidates for selection and, in various circumstances, to vote on local party motions. These local affiliated trade union branches also have a role in voting to remove sitting Labour MPs who are standing for re-selection by means of a 'trigger ballot'. Trigger ballots in the Labour Party are where local members vote on whether to trigger a selection contest for a Westminster seat represented by a sitting Labour MP. The local CLP and its affiliated union and socialist society branches vote in an electoral college whereby a selection contest will be triggered if more than half of affiliated branches (of which trade union branches are most numerous among them) and CLP branch parties vote for one.[66] Affiliated trade union members who pay into the political fund of their unions are also entitled to vote in Labour leadership elections.[67] So long as trade unions operate a legitimate political fund, they may spend money to campaign for their members to be selected within the Labour Party as its candidates, and to campaign for the election of those candidates at the public ballot. In practice, the main affiliated trade unions also provide a great deal of in-kind support to internal Labour Party candidate campaigns and events – for example volunteering premises and IT systems and contributing to conference costs.

III. Co-operative Societies

A. Relationship with the Co-operative Party

8.32 Co-operative societies are another type of organisation active in organised politics, although the activity is not widely publicised and their members generally do not carry out the sort of overt party-political activism that is common in trade unions. The first co-operatives in the UK were founded in the nineteenth century in Lancashire to improve the lives of working class people by providing good quality food at a fair price. There are many small co-operative societies.

8.33 We are principally concerned here with the two largest organisations in the co-operative society family. The Co-operative Group is one of the world's largest consumer co-operatives. It is owned by its members, of which there are millions. The Co-operative Group is a very large food retailer in the UK with more than 2,500 local, convenience and medium-sized stores. The Group also operates community-led social programmes.[68] The Group makes political donations to the Co-operative Party, authorised by motions each year at its annual general meeting. The donations are sizeable: in 2020 and 2021 the Group donated £598,600 each year to the

[66] ibid Ch 5, cl IV.5.B. Affiliated branches have a weight of 50% in this electoral college, as do CLP branches.
[67] ibid Ch 4, cl 2.C.
[68] A summary of The Co-operative Group's activities can be found on its website: www.co-operative.coop/about-us/our-co-op.

Co-operative Party.[69] The Group's Board appoints two people to sit on the Co-operative Party's National Executive Committee (the party's national governing committee).[70]

8.34 Co-operatives UK is an umbrella organisation that represents the interests of co-operative societies and co-operative members and which promotes co-operative values, namely 'self-help, self-responsibility, democracy, equality, equity, and solidarity, honesty, openness, social responsibility and caring for others'.[71] Co-operatives UK is itself a co-operative society and its membership is made up of various co-operative organisations, mutuals, partnerships and other corporate bodies and associates. Its members pay subscription fees. Co-operatives UK's Board is entitled to appoint one person to the National Executive Committee of the Co-operative Party, and the Chief Executive Officer of Co-operatives UK is entitled to attend National Executive Committee Meetings of the party (though he or she is not entitled to vote).[72]

B. Co-operative Party Political Candidates

8.35 The Co-operative Party is a registered political party that operates nationally. It was founded in 1917 as the political wing of the Co-operative movement. Since 1927 the Co-operative Party and the Labour Party have been in an electoral alliance. The parties stand joint candidates under the banner 'Labour and Co-operative Party'. A Co-operative Party individual member is eligible to join that party's parliamentary panel, from which MP candidate selections are drawn, if she is a member of the party and a member of a co-operative society and meets Labour Party eligibility criteria for nomination as a prospective parliamentary candidate.[73]

[69] See Motion 4, Joint Board and Council Motion – Political Donations, Co-operative Party AGM, 2021; and Motion 9, Joint Board and Council Motion – Political Donations, Co-operative Party AGM, 2022.
[70] Co-operative Party Rule Book (2021), r 11.1.4.
[71] Co-operatives UK Rule Book, cl 3 'interpretations'.
[72] Co-operative Party Rule Book (2021), rr 11.1.3 and 11.2.
[73] *Co-operative Party Rule Book* (2021), 'Parliamentary Panel', paras 4–6.

9

Charities, Schools and Lobbyists

I. Introduction

9.1 The regulation of political activity also extends to charities, schools and lobbyists. Section II of this chapter is about charities, including student unions (which are a type of charity); Section III is about schools. Charities and schools are forums in which political debate takes place, but there are important limitations on the extent to which political activities may be undertaken by and within them.

9.2 Charities may undertake political activity, but only if doing so furthers their charitable objects. Charities are not permitted to have political objects or to use their charitable funds to finance partisan political campaigns. Where charities campaign on issues during general elections, they may be caught by the rules about third-party campaign expenditure, explained in detail in Chapter 10. As for schools, there is a total prohibition on state school children under 12 in England and Wales taking part in political activity facilitated by the school and English and Welsh schools must forbid political indoctrination of any pupil. There are also regulations concerning the use of school rooms during elections.

9.3 Lobbying is a practice that regularly elicits concerns from politicians and others about corruption undermining the democratic process. Section IV of this chapter addresses the rules that affect consultant lobbyists, who are regulated (albeit lightly) by statute and who have obligations to report on whose behalf they undertake lobbying services. (Chapter 13 sets out the prohibitions on paid lobbying by parliamentarians contained in the rules of the House of Commons and the House of Lords.)

II. Charities

A. Political Purposes

9.4 Charities often campaign for changes to social and economic policies. Charitable organisations may find themselves involved in the political arena because of their alignment or opposition to policies of the government. The extent to which charities may lawfully undertake political activity is, however, considerably limited. The first major limitation is that a charity's main purpose must not be a political one. The purposes of a charity are known in law as their charitable 'objects', in other words, their charitable aims. A political purpose is not a charitable purpose under the Charities Act 2011 (which governs how charities operate).[1] A 'political object' is one that has as its direct and principal purpose: (i) to further the interests of a particular political party; (ii) to procure changes in the laws of the UK; (iii) to procure changes in the laws of a foreign country; (iv) to procure a reversal of government policy or of particular decisions of

[1] Charities Act 2011, ss 2 and 3.

governmental authorities in the UK; or (v) to procure a reversal of government policy or of particular governmental authorities in a foreign country.[2]

9.5 A fundamental aspect of a charitable aim is that it is for the public benefit. Everyone is free to advocate or promote by lawful means a change in the law. However, the courts have no means of judging whether a proposed change in the law will be for the public benefit or not. That is why a charitable object will be invalid if its principal and direct purpose is to change the law.[3] So, a 'pro-life' organisation established to campaign to change the law to ban abortions would have a political purpose incompatible with charitable status. So too would a body established mainly to oppose a new runway at an airport; the body's main purpose would be to oppose the government's policy on airports. On the other hand, an organisation would not have a political purpose if its main aim was to protect the environment and it carried out some political activity seeking to make the government change its policy on airports.[4]

B. Political Activity

i. Generally

9.6 The fact that a charity is not allowed to have a political purpose does not mean that a charity may not *pursue* a valid, non-political purpose by political means. As long as the charity's main objects are exclusively charitable, the fact that it engages in political activity to further them, including by campaigning to change the law, will not deprive it of its charitable status.[5] The Charity Commission in England and the Office of the Scottish Charity Regulator have both produced guidance about political activity by charities in their respective countries.[6] The Charity Commission's guidance is the more extensive, and is cited where relevant below. Charities operating in Scotland should consult the Office of the Scottish Charity Regulator's guidance; however, common principles are set out by both regulators.

9.7 Political activity here means activity which is aimed at securing or opposing any change in the law or in the policy or decisions of central government, local authorities

[2] *Southwood v Her Majesty's Attorney General* [2000] WTLR 1199, approving *McGovern v Attorney General* [1982] Ch 321, [1982] 2 WLR 222.

[3] See *Bowman v Secular Society Ltd* [1917] AC 406 at 442 per Lord Parker: 'a trust for the attainment of political objects has always been held to be invalid, not because it is illegal, for everyone is at liberty to advocate or promote by any lawful means a change in the law, but because the court has no means of judging whether a proposed change in the law will or will not be for the public benefit'.

[4] 'Campaigning and political activity guidance for charities' (CC9) (Charity Commission, 7 November 2022) para 3.3. It has been held that an organisation established for the promotion and protection of human rights by means of strategic litigation to enforce constitutional rights abroad does not have a political purpose: *The Human Dignity Trust v The Charity Commission for England and Wales* [2015] WTLR 789.

[5] *McGovern v Attorney General* [1982] Ch 321, [1982] 2 WLR 222.

[6] ie 'Campaigning and political activity guidance for charities' (CC9) (Charity Commission, 7 November 2022); and 'Charities and campaigning on political issues: FAQs' (Office of the Scottish Charity Regulator, March 2021).

or other public bodies, in the UK or abroad.[7] It is acceptable for a charity to focus the majority or all of its resources on political activity for a period so long as that activity does not become the reason for the charity's existence,[8] so the charity should keep its political activity under review.

9.8 Nevertheless, a second key limitation prevents charities from engaging too far in political activity: charities must maintain their political independence and the perception that they are politically independent.[9] Support for a political party is not a valid charitable purpose for the reasons above. This means that a charity cannot give general support to a particular political party or the government, nor support a political party financially. For example, a charity's chief executive would not be allowed to sign an open letter, in her capacity as the chief executive, supporting a political candidate or a party: that would be impermissible party political activity.[10] Senior charity employees may decide to support political candidates or parties in a personal capacity, but they should be alive to the risk that by expressing such support they are giving rise to a perception that the charity is not politically independent.

9.9 It is lawful for a charity to support policies advocated by a particular political party (provided that support for the policies pursues the charity's objects).[11] So, while an environmental charity would not be allowed to support the Green Party because the latter proposed a ban on fracking, the charity would be perfectly entitled to express its support for the policies in pursuit of its objects that are also advocated by the Green Party. It is acceptable for charities to participate in policy discussions with political parties and their representatives, including those at annual party conferences. However, the charity must not in so doing take action to assist the party to get elected. Charities should be wary of the risk that political parties may seek to exploit them and their reputations in joint policy activity. The Charity Commission provides the following guidance about what is acceptable:

i. **Events**: it is acceptable to send event invitations to (or accept invitations from) all or several political parties in the course of campaigning for an issue or policy. But if the charity were to accept invitations from or to contact only one political party consistently over time, that could call into question the charity's political neutrality.[12]
ii. **Attending party conferences**: it is acceptable for a charity's chief executive to speak on behalf of the charity at conference fringe events so long as the chief executive

[7] 'Campaigning and political activity guidance for charities' (CC9) (Charity Commission, 7 November 2022) para 2.4 (b).
[8] ibid para 3.8.
[9] Because it is the duty of the charity and its trustees to act only in the interests of the charity or its beneficiaries and to avoid a conflict between the charity's interests and that of another: see for example *Re The French Protestant Hospital* [1951] Ch 567.
[10] 'Campaigning and political activity guidance for charities' (CC9) (Charity Commission, 7 November 2022) para 4.1.
[11] ibid para 4.1.
[12] ibid para 4.2.

and the charity's trustees are clear that doing so supports the charity's charitable purposes and that attendance does not affect the charity's perceived independence.[13]

iii. **Manifestos**: a charity may accept a political party's invitation to comment on the party's draft manifesto, providing that the charity's comments are limited to those aspects that affect its beneficiaries, and that the charity offers to comment on the draft manifestos of all main political parties.[14]

iv. **Charity launches**: it is acceptable for a charity to invite a politician to attend and speak at the opening of a new charity shop, so long as the charity briefs the politician about the event's purpose and has a reasonable expectation the politician will not use the event to promote party political messages.[15] It is also acceptable for a charity to invite politicians to attend a reception to launch a charity report and take photos of the charity's beneficiaries with the politicians, so long as the charity makes it clear that the purpose of taking photos is to promote the charity's work and not that of the politician.[16]

ii. Election Periods

9.10 Charities must make especially clear that they are independent of any political party advocating the same policy during the period of any public election. This is important not only to preserve the charity's political independence, but also to ensure that the charity does not inadvertently and unlawfully spend money in the election period that the Electoral Commission considers to be regulated election campaign expenditure: see Chapter 10 for further detail.

9.11 If the charity produces written material or other publications it should not explicitly compare the charity's views on policy with those of a political party or candidate taking part in the election; and the charity should take care not to appear as though it is engaging in a 'call to action' that influences voters on how to vote. Charities should also, therefore, refuse any request from a political party to appear by reference or otherwise in the party's manifesto or campaign literature.[17]

9.12 Charities must not give publicity to any political party in their own literature, materials or on their websites or publish anything that has the appearance of seeking to influence public support for or against a party or candidate. This is especially important for charities in receipt of local authority funds, as they may lose their funding. The Local Government Act 1986 prohibits a local authority from publishing, or arranging for the publication of, or giving financial assistance to another person to publish, any material which wholly or partly appears to be designed to affect public support for a political party.[18]

[13] ibid para 4.2.
[14] ibid para 4.2.
[15] ibid para 4.3.
[16] ibid para 4.3.
[17] 'Charities, elections, referendums' (The Charity Commission, 7 November 2022).
[18] Local Government Act 1986, s 2(1) and (3).

9.13 Charities that are mainly or wholly funded by public or local authority funds are also banned from campaigning in a referendum, or from publishing any general information (ie information that is not in response to a specific request for information) in the 28 days before the referendum poll is held.[19]

C. University Student Unions

9.14 The main political parties operate political clubs in many universities across the country, in addition to national student and youth organisations. Those clubs are not charities: their political objects preclude charitable status. Whatever formal legal structure they adopt, these clubs are partisan party political entities the aim of which is to promote the interests of the party among the student body. Labour, Conservative and Liberal Democrat student clubs are affiliated to their respective national parties directly or via federated party political organisations.

9.15 Student unions are organisationally quite different from party affiliated political clubs, although it is common that their most active executive members are engaged in party political politics. Student unions normally have charitable status. They are formed, and exist, to further the educational (and social) function of their respective universities. The purposes of the union encompass the need for students to be represented in many areas within the university and outside it, their need to have suitable facilities to cater for interests and activities outside lecture halls and for the promotion of their general welfare.[20] This means, however, that student unions founded as charities are precluded from having political objects and must not expend funds on political activities falling outside their charitable aims, or carry on political activities in furtherance of political aims.

9.16 It is not permissible for student unions to express their collective political views on social issues through a donation, from union funds, to a political campaign. Individual members wishing to express their views financially must do so with their own money. Nor is it permissible for student unions to use their money to contribute to setting up a fund for a political purpose. For example, it was unlawful for Sussex University Student Union to donate money to a fund the purpose of which was to campaign against the government's removal of free school milk for children.[21] Nor may student unions engage in campaigning to influence public opinion on a political issue; so, it was unlawful for the Anglia Student Union to expend its money on a campaign against the Gulf War in 1991.[22]

9.17 None of these rules preclude student unions from involving themselves in political debate and political education. There is nothing wrong with student unions furthering

[19] PPERA 2000, s 125.
[20] *Attorney-General v Ross* [1986] WLR 252.
[21] *Baldry v Feintuck* [1972] WLR 552.
[22] *Webb v O'Doherty and Others* (1991) Times, 11 February, per Hoffmann J, as he then was.

their educational purposes by encouraging students to develop political awareness, or to form and debate political issues, or even to provide facilities for a student party political club, for example, by hosting a Labour or Conservative club activity.[23]

9.18 Many student unions are affiliated to the National Union of Students (NUS). The NUS comprises several different legal bodies. The principal one is National Union of Students UK, which is a company that does not have charitable objects.[24] Its role is to represent, co-ordinate and express student opinion on matters affecting them and on issues of wider national and international significance. The NUS campaigns to change the law and government policy. It is funded in part by affiliation fees paid by university student unions. Student unions may pay subscriptions to affiliate themselves to other external organisations, so long as the purpose of the affiliation is to benefit the student body in their capacity as students.[25] As charities, student unions should not affiliate themselves to political parties, nor to any other organisation as a means to support a political campaign or movement.

III. Schools

A. Political Indoctrination

i. Partisan Political Views and Activities

9.19 Schools in England and Wales have particular duties in respect of political matters. The primary purpose of those duties is to avoid the political indoctrination of pupils. The Department for Education has produced detailed guidance to assist practitioners to fulfil those duties.[26] The requirements of political impartiality apply to all state and independent schools.[27]

9.20 Maintained schools[28] must forbid the pursuit of partisan political activities by junior pupils (ie those under the age of 12) and must forbid the promotion of partisan political views in the teaching of any subject in the school.[29] Similar prohibitions are set out in academy schools' founding documents. Independent schools must not promote partisan political views in the teaching of any subject in the school.[30]

[23] *Attorney-General v Ross* [1986] WLR 252.

[24] The NUS Students' Union Charitable Services is a company with charitable objects which operates as the NUS's charitable arm, charged with promoting student unions for the benefit of the public and supporting the development of student unions to ensure they adequately serve their student membership.

[25] *Webb v O'Doherty and Others* (1991) Times, 11 February, per Hoffmann J.

[26] 'Political impartiality in schools' (Department for Education, 17 February 2022).

[27] ibid 'The law'.

[28] Guidance about the different types of school body can be found on the government's website at www.gov.uk/types-of-school.

[29] Education Act 1996, s 406(1).

[30] The Education (Independent School Standards) Regulations 2014, SI 2014/3283, Sch, Pt 2, para 5.

9.21 The term 'political' in this context is not limited to activities or views that are party political.[31] A political activity here is one that has as its purpose the promotion of a particular political party's interests, or the procurement of changes to the law, or the obtaining of a reversal of government policy or particular governmental decisions in the UK or abroad.[32] Within this broad definition would sit, for example, the promotion of the interests of the Labour or Conservative parties, or the activities of political activist groups like Extinction Rebellion, or trade union and other campaigns to secure changes to the law to benefit workers and other classes of people, or the promotion of particular ideologies like socialism or free-market capitalism. The definition would also include a call to take particular legislative steps in respect of social issues, for example man-made climate change and its attendant dangers. Matters that are subject to intense social debate are not inherently political issues. For example, it has been held that views about sexual orientation and gender are not inherently political, but they are likely to be where they arise in the context of proposals to change the law (for example, proposals to change the law about gay marriage in Northern Ireland or about the self-identification of gender).[33]

9.22 Party political activities and views will by nature be partisan, but the term 'partisan' is wider than that: 'partisan' activities or views in this context means those which are one-sided. A partisan political view might include a superficial treatment of the matter at hand without any indication that the views are subject to legitimate controversy; or the expression of misrepresentations and half-truths about it; or the deployment of material in such a way that prevents pupils testing the truthfulness of it and forming an independent understanding of it and its reliability; or the exaltation of political figures who hold one view and the demonisation of figures who hold the opposing view; or teaching pupils that they must adopt a particular view to do right as opposed to wrong.[34]

9.23 The promotion of partisan political views, as prohibited by the Education Act 1996, does not include simply presenting such views. Teachers are permitted to present films or documents which promote political views in a partisan manner if it is appropriate to do so as part of the syllabus with appropriate context, tuition and debate. Showing an example of Nazi propaganda as part of a history lesson, or an anti-racist film in a citizenship class, or the literature and propaganda of UK political parties in a politics class, would not fall foul of the prohibition.[35]

ii. Junior Pupils

9.24 The Education Act 1996 forbids the pursuit of political activities by junior pupils (ie under the age of 12, which may include many pupils in Year 7, as well as

[31] Assistance can be derived from the law that applies to charitable objects. See *R (on the application of 'L') v Hampshire County Council* [2022] EWHC 49 (Admin) at para 27.

[32] *McGovern v Attorney General* [1982] Ch 321, [1982] 2 WLR 222.

[33] *R (on the application of 'L') v Hampshire County Council* [2022] EWHC 49 (Admin) at para 27.

[34] *Dimmock v Secretary of State for Education and Skills* [2007] EWHC 2288 (Admin), [2008] 1 All ER 367, at para 11.

[35] ibid para 12.

all primary school pupils) on school premises. The prohibition also applies to political activities outside the school if the activities are facilitated by a member of the school's staff acting in that capacity (eg a teacher supervising a school trip) or anyone acting on behalf of the school or its staff in that capacity (eg a charity or company engaged by the school to provide off-site educational or other provision).[36] No equivalent express duty to forbid the pursuit of partisan political activities by junior pupils lies on independent schools, but the Department for Education's guidance suggests that it is unlikely ever to be appropriate for pupils under the age of 12 to engage in political activity at any school.[37]

iii. Scotland

9.25 There is no comparable statutory provision regulating political indoctrination in schools in Scotland. Teachers in Scotland are expected to conduct themselves in accordance with the General Teaching Council for Scotland's (CGTS) Professional Standards, which provide a framework in which political literacy should be taught fairly and without discrimination. The Professional Standards require teachers in Scotland to value and respect social, ecological, cultural and racial diversity and to promote principles of local and global citizenship.[38] The CGTS's Code of Professionalism and Conduct sets out that teachers should help pupils to understand different views; teachers are role models and should therefore be aware of the potentially serious effect which any demonstration of intolerance by them could have on their fitness to teach.[39] In response to a Scottish parliamentary question in 2021, the Scottish Cabinet Secretary for Education and Skills suggested that the existing CGTS framework was sufficient to ensure the political impartiality of all primary and secondary school teachers while they were conducting classes.[40]

B. Political Events and Elections

i. Balanced Presentation of Political Views

9.26 Schools in England and Wales have a duty to teach pupils about democratic values. Schools must also ensure that pupils are offered a balanced presentation of opposing views where political issues are brought to the attention of pupils in school, or during extra-curricular activities organised by or on behalf of the school.[41] Balance here does not require schools to give 'equal air time' to opposing views, nor discussion of every dispute.[42] The law does not require every reference to a subject by a teacher to

[36] Education Act 1996, s 406(2).

[37] 'Political impartiality in schools' (Department for Education, 17 February 2022) 'Political activity by pupils'.

[38] 'The Standard for Full Registration' (General Teaching Council for Scotland, 2 August 2021) para 1.1.

[39] 'Code of Professionalism and Conduct' (General Teaching Council for Scotland) para 5.2.

[40] John Swinney MSP, 17 March 2021, Question Reference: S5W-35837.

[41] Education Act 1996, s 407.

[42] *Dimmock v Secretary of State for Education and Skills* [2007] EWHC 2288 (Admin), [2008] 1 All ER 367.

include a reference to all of the different opinions held in respect of it.[43] What is required is a fair and dispassionate presentation of an opposing view. Where there is a mainstream view and an opposing sceptical view shared by a minority, it will be sufficient to make clear what the mainstream view is and that some people do not accept even the consensus view.[44]

9.27 Schools must be particularly careful to ensure that any discussion of political issues during an election campaign is balanced and non-partisan. Schools are permitted to invite political candidates in public elections, or other politicians or proponents of political parties, to talk to pupils. However, schools should take reasonable steps to ensure that pupils are offered a balanced presentation of opposing views. This can be done by inviting a range of external speakers from different political parties or by teaching pupils about other and opposing political candidates and political parties. If schools fail to do so then a risk will arise that their actions will be interpreted as promoting a partisan political position.[45] The requirements of political impartiality should not prevent pupils over the age of 12 from espousing partisan political views in mock and parallel elections or debates, hustings events or visits from local candidates or political party representatives. Those events must nevertheless be managed so that pupils receive a balanced account of the political issues expressed.[46] The Department for Education's Guidance has the following examples of permitted party political discussion during an election:

> Pupils might be taught about an upcoming general election and key policies in political parties' manifestos. This teaching might cover different partisan political views on specific plans and policies.
>
> Teachers can explore how claims made by supporters and opponents of the policies are supported by evidence, including in economic theory, academic studies, and other sources.
>
> Teachers should not draw pupils to a single conclusion but should correct factual inaccuracies in pupils' understanding. This support can help pupils to form their own reasoned views on the issue, based on the available evidence.[47]

ii. Use of School Resources and Meeting Rooms for Political Activity

9.28 School resources and social media should not be used for partisan political activities. The Department for Education's guidance suggests that it is inadvisable to have a pupil-led society under the banner of a political party because of the high risk that the school's resources would be used for partisan political activity.[48] Local authority maintained schools must not publish material which appears to be designed to affect public support for a political party.[49] This will be especially relevant where the school

[43] *R (on the application of 'L') v Hampshire County Council* [2022] EWHC 49 (Admin).
[44] *Dimmock v Secretary of State for Education and Skills* [2007] EWHC 2288 (Admin), [2008] 1 All ER 367.
[45] 'Political impartiality in schools' (Department for Education, 17 February 2022) 'During political events'.
[46] ibid 'Balance in teaching'.
[47] ibid 'Scenario E'.
[48] ibid 'political activity by pupils'.
[49] Local Government Act 1986, s 2.

produces written material using local authority funds to publicise talks given by political candidates to the school. In general, it is permissible for local authorities to publish factual information which identifies the names, electoral wards and parties of candidates at elections but local authorities should not issue any publicity which seeks to influence voters.[50]

iii. Providing School Rooms to Candidates During Elections

9.29 Candidates standing for election to the House of Commons or local government have a legal right to hold political meetings in a local school room or other publicly funded meeting rooms, at reasonable times and free of charge during an election period.[51] The right applies only to public meetings the purpose of which is to advance the candidate's candidature. The room must be situated in the constituency or electoral area in which the candidate is standing, or if none is available there, in an adjoining constituency or electoral area.[52] A list of suitable school rooms must be compiled and revised by the relevant local authority in which the room is situated.[53] The candidate or his agent is entitled to consult a copy of the list at all reasonable times during the election period.[54] The candidate must give reasonable notice to use the room for the meeting and may not override the room's usual users who have already booked it, nor interfere with its use during school hours (in the case of a school room) or with any other prior bookings.[55] Arrangements for using a school room should be made with the local authority in the case of a maintained school, or with the school's governing body in the case of a voluntary aided or foundation school.[56]

C. Attending Political Protests

9.30 There is nothing to stop pupils or teachers attending a political protest outside the school's premises at an event that is neither organised by the school nor by a person on behalf of the school. It is acceptable for teachers to support discussion, in school, about the issue underlying the protests so long as teachers do not encourage pupils to join the protests or promote partisan political views that are expressed by the protest movement (or by its political opponents).[57] The Department for Education's guidance suggests that it would not be appropriate for a teacher to suggest that pupils should join a particular campaigning group or engage in a particular upcoming protest. That does not preclude teachers from explaining to pupils how they can engage more actively in political activities outside of school; for example, by telling them where they can find

[50] Code of Recommended Practice on Local Authority Publicity (Department for Communities and Local Government, 31 March 2011.

[51] Representation of the People Act 1983, ss 95 and 96; *Ettridge v Frances Morrell* [1987] CLY 2378.

[52] Representation of the People Act 1983, ss 95(2) and 96(2).

[53] ibid Sch 5, para 2.

[54] ie on dissolution or when a vacancy for a seat in a constituency occurs: ibid Sch 5, para 5.

[55] ibid s 95(5).

[56] ibid Sch 5, para 1.

[57] 'Political impartiality in schools' (Department for Education, 17 February 2022) 'Scenario Q'.

out more information or by explaining the different partisan political views advocated by protest groups.[58]

IV. Lobbying

> The lunches, the hospitality, the quiet word in your ear, the ex-ministers and ex-advisors for hire, helping big business find the right way to get its way. … The Hansard Society has estimated that some MPs are approached over one hundred times a week by lobbyists. Much of the time this happens covertly. We don't know who is meeting whom. We don't know whether any favours are being exchanged. We don't know which outside interests are wielding unhealthy influence. This isn't a minor issue with minor consequences. Commercial interests – not to mention government contracts – worth hundreds of billions of pounds are potentially at stake. I believe that secret corporate lobbying, like the expenses scandal, goes to the heart of why people are so fed up with politics. It arouses people's worst fears and suspicions about how our political system works, with money buying power, power fishing for money and a cosy club at the top making decisions in their own interest.[59]

A. Paid Lobbying

9.31 Lobbying is another method of pursuing political aims. We are concerned here with the practice of influencing members of the legislature in the exercise of their legislative functions or the government in the exercise of its executive functions. Lobbyists come in many forms: pressure groups; businesses; foreign governments; international organisations; charities; trade unions; and individual constituents. An important part of good democratic government involves legislators and ministers listening to the voices of all who are affected by particular policies and decisions. It is the moral duty of the government and the legislature to consider all the conflicting arguments and relevant facts put before them before making laws. To that end, lobbying by special interest groups and others can be beneficial and contribute to good governance so long as the lobbying is transparent and open.

9.32 Rather different is paid lobbying,[60] where money changes hands in return for advocating a particular interest or position in Parliament. In *Cruddas v Calvert* the

[58] ibid 'Political activity by pupils'.

[59] David Cameron MP (now Lord Cameron), 'Rebuilding trust in politics', 8 February 2010, available at web.archive.org/web/20100212012031/https://www.conservatives.com/News/Speeches/2010/02/David_Cameron_Rebuilding_trust_in_politics.aspx. Nevertheless, the problems posed by lobbying have not been resolved. In 2021 the House of Common's Treasury Committee published a report addressing allegations that Lord Cameron had broken lobbying rules by lobbying senior members of government, including the then Chancellor, Rishi Sunak MP, for Greensill Capital. The Treasury Committee found that Lord Cameron had acted as a representative of Greensill Capital, with a very significant personal economic interest in the firm; and further found that Lord Cameron had demonstrated a significant lack of judgement. The Treasury Committee concluded that Lord Cameron had not broken the rules governing lobbying by former Ministers, which reflected on the insufficient strength of the rules. See 'Lessons from Greensill Capital' (House of Commons, Treasury Committee, 20 July 2021) para 147.

[60] The rules about public procurement also have relevance for lobbying practices. See the Government's Guidance on Public Procurement Policy (2023) and the associated legislative regime (the Public Contracts

Court of Appeal determined a defamation appeal. Journalists from *The Sunday Times* had arranged a meeting with Lord Cruddas, a former treasurer of the Conservative Party. The journalists pretended to be agents for foreign financiers seeking to make donations to the Conservative Party. They covertly recorded the meeting and *The Sunday Times* published articles based on the recording, variously entitled 'Tory Treasurer charges £250,000 to meet PM', 'Cash for Cameron: cosy club buys the PM's ear', 'Pay the money this way and the party won't pry'; and 'Rotten to the Core'. *The Sunday Times* carried an editorial entitled 'Sack the Treasurer and clean up lobbying'. The High Court found in favour of Mr Cruddas and awarded him damages of £180,000. On appeal the Court of Appeal had to decide, for the purposes of meaning in the defamation claim, whether it was 'inappropriate, unacceptable and wrong' for major donors to the Conservative Party to use their access to senior ministers in order to obtain confidential information, enhanced influence over policy making, or unfair commercial advantage. The Court concluded that it is unacceptable for politicians to provide donors with confidential information or any form of unfair commercial advantage or preference during or after socialising with them.[61] It is unacceptable for people to pay sums to politicians and thereby gain enhanced influence over the democratic decision-making process or preferential access to information or benefits to profit their own businesses.[62] It is not acceptable for politicians to place greater weight on the views of donors about policy issues simply because such people donate money to them. A core element of every MP's role is to act as an intermediary between the government and all his constituents,[63] not just a wealthy few.

9.33 We are concerned, below, with the rules about lobbying that apply to the Parliament at Westminster and the UK government and civil service. Two sets of rules directly regulate the practice of lobbying. The first set forbids MPs and Members of the Lords from undertaking their parliamentary duties in return for financial rewards from extra-parliamentary organisations or individuals. (Exceptions exist for the payment to MPs of maintenance by their respective political parties and associated bodies.) Lobbying by MPs and Members of the Lords in return for payment amounts to a serious breach of the parliamentary standards regime for which their respective Houses may suspend them. The rules against paid lobbying operated by each House are addressed in Chapter 13.

9.34 The second set of rules regulate the business of paid lobbyists, otherwise known as 'lobbying consultants': those people who carry on business by lobbying ministers and civil servants for profit on behalf of other wealthy people or organisations. The rules about consultant lobbying are found in the Transparency of Lobbying, Non-Party Campaigning and Trade Union Administration Act 2014. The rest of this chapter is about that regulatory regime. Note that similar legislative provisions apply to consultant

Regulations 2015, the Utilities Contracts Regulations 2016, the Concession Contracts Regulations 2016 and the Public Procurement (Amendments, Repeals and Revocations) Regulations 2016).

[61] See *Cruddas v Calvert* [2015] EMLR 16 (CA) at paras 28 and 63 per Jackson LJ.

[62] ibid.

[63] See eg *R v Rule* [1937] 2 KB 375 (CA); *De Buse and Others v McCarthy* [1942] 1 KB 156 (CA).

lobbying of Members of the Scottish Parliament and the Scottish government; those are set out in the Lobbying (Scotland) Act 2016 (and further guidance can be found on the Scottish Parliament's website).[64]

B. Lobbying Consultants

i. The Register of Consultant Lobbyists

9.35 The Transparency of Lobbying, Non-Party Campaigning and Trade Union Administration Act 2014 regulates lobbying by people carrying on business as lobbying consultants. The Act establishes a regulator – the Registrar of Consultant Lobbyists – who must maintain a register of consultant lobbyists which records the identity of their clients. By 2023 there were 3,976 clients recorded on the register for whom lobbying has been done since the register was established. The Registrar may also issue guidance.[65] A person who carries on business as a consultant lobbyist will commit a criminal offence or be liable to pay a penalty if he carries on business lobbying without being registered or if he fails to provide the information required by the Registrar in quarterly returns.

ii. Lobbying Activities

9.36 A person carries on the business of consultant lobbying if he makes oral or written communications personally to a minister or permanent secretary in the civil service[66] on behalf of another person, and is paid in return for doing so, about the following matters:[67]

i. the development, adoption or modification of any government proposal to make or amend legislation, or of government policies;
ii. the making, giving, issuing by the government, or any other government steps related to government licenses, contracts, grants, financial assistance or government authorisation; or
iii. the exercise of any of the government's functions (eg prerogative powers[68]).[69]

9.37 The legislation binds any communications that fall into those categories, even if both parties to the communication are outside the UK when the communication is made. Communications that must be made by law are excluded from the definition of

[64] See www.parliament.scot/get-involved/lobbying/guidance-on-lobbying. No equivalent legislative regime applies to consultant lobbying in the Welsh Senedd at the time of writing.

[65] See 'Guidance on registration and quarterly information returns' (Office of the Registrar of Consultant Lobbyists, July 2023).

[66] Included in this category of people are: the Cabinet Secretary; Chief Executive of Her Majesty's Revenue and Customs; Chief Medical Officer; Director of Public Prosecutions; First Parliamentary Counsel; Government Chief Scientific Adviser; Head of the Civil Service; Prime Minister's Adviser for Europe and Global Issues. See the Transparency of Lobbying, Non-Party Campaigning and Trade Union Administration Act 2014, Sch 1, para 11(1).

[67] ibid s 2(1).

[68] ibid Explanatory Notes, para 19.

[69] ibid s 2(3).

communication under the Act.[70] An individual who makes a communication in the course of somebody else's business is treated as making the communication alongside the other person or business. If that individual is an employee then he is treated as making the communication on behalf of the employer's client and not the employer.[71]

iii. Persons Excluded from the Scope of the Act

9.38 Various exclusions permit the individuals who actually do the lobbying to avoid having to register or being named on the register. A person is not in the business of consultant lobbying under the Act if he is not VAT registered.[72] This essentially has the effect of removing small businesses from the scope of the Act. Any business with a turnover below the VAT registration threshold (£85,000 in 2024) does not have to be on the register of lobbyists (unless they are voluntarily VAT-registered). It also means that the person actually undertaking the lobbying can avoid being named on the register if they are an employee of a company or firm that carries on the business of lobbying: in those circumstances the company or firm will be VAT registered but the individual will not.[73] Further, under the Act an employee does not *himself* carry on the business of consultant lobbying by making communications as an employee in the course of a business carried on by his employer,[74] even though the reality of lobbying is that it relies precisely on personal contacts between individuals and minsters or legislators – and those relationships are exactly what could be made more transparent.

9.39 A person does not fall within the 2014 Act's scope if their business mostly consists of activities other than lobbying the government (including the devolved and local governments) and the lobbying is incidental to those other activities;[75] nor if the person acts generally as a representative of a particular class or description of people and the lobbying is incidental to his representative functions.[76] The Act does not apply to lobbying done by foreign governments and their employees or to international organisations (and their employees) of which the UK (or UK government) is a member.[77]

iv. 'In Return for Payment'

9.40 The definition of payment under the 2014 Act includes payments of any kind, including indirect payments, and including where the lobbyist is paid by a third party rather than his client, or where he is paid on retainer rather than for a particular communication.[78] Note that MPs and peers carrying out their usual parliamentary business are not caught by the Act because the Act excludes their public remuneration from

[70] ibid Sch 1, para 9.
[71] ibid Sch 1, para 10.
[72] ibid s 2(1)(b).
[73] ibid, Explanatory Notes, para 20.
[74] ibid Sch 1, para 4.
[75] ibid Sch 1, para 1.
[76] ibid Sch 1, para 2.
[77] ibid Sch 1, para 3.
[78] ibid Sch 1, para 6.

the definition of payment.[79] Pro-bono lobbying and lobbying for which no payment is received from the client is not within scope of the Act.[80]

v. Duty to Register

9.41 A person who falls within the 2014 Act's scope must register with the Office of the Registrar of Consultant Lobbyists to carry out regulated lobbying lawfully, and must provide the following information on registration:

i. **Companies** must provide their name, company number, the address of their registered office, the names of any directors, secretaries and shadow directors;
ii. **Partnerships** must supply the names of all partners and the address of the partnership's main office or place of business;
iii. **Individuals** who are VAT registered must provide their name and the address of their main place of business or, if there is no such place, their home or business address where they may be contacted.

9.42 Companies, partnerships and individuals must all supply their VAT registration numbers and any other name or names under which the person or organisation carries on business as a consultant lobbyist.[81]

vi. Lobbying Code of Conduct

9.43 Those under a duty to register must state whether they have made an undertaking to comply with a relevant lobbying code of conduct, and, if so, where the code may be inspected.[82] The Registrar's guidance states that a 'relevant' code of conduct is one which:

i. goes 'beyond setting out general, good professional behaviour and must contain provisions that are of particular relevance to the way that consultant lobbying activity is carried out';
ii. recognises 'a consultant lobbyist's responsibilities to those to whom representations are made. A code that fails in this is unlikely to be "relevant"';
iii. provides:

> a process for anyone affected by the registrant's consultant lobbying activities to complain about an alleged breach of the code of conduct. This process must include oversight or control of the complaints process which is not carried out by the registrant themselves. This might be provided in a number of ways, including, for example, by an external adjudication or arbitration process defined in the code, or by the mechanisms of a professional body.[83]

[79] ibid Sch 1, para 5.

[80] ibid Sch 1, para 7.

[81] If the consultant lobbying activity is carried out by a trading division of a parent company, the directors of the parent company should be declared unless the trading division is itself a company and has its own legal personality. See 'Guidance on registration and quarterly information returns' (Office of the Registrar of Consultant Lobbyists, 20 May 2022).

[82] Transparency of Lobbying, Non-Party Campaigning and Trade Union Administration Act 2014, s 4.

[83] 'Guidance on registration and quarterly information returns' (Office of the Registrar of Consultant Lobbyists, 20 May 2022) para 3.5.2.

vii. Duty to Submit Returns

9.44 Once a person is registered he must submit to the Registrar a quarterly return within 14 days after the end of each quarter. The return must specify:

i. the name of the clients on whose behalf lobbying was done in return for payment during the relevant quarter; and
ii. the name of the clients on whose behalf lobbying is or was to be done if the consultant received payment for the lobbying during the relevant quarter;[84] or
iii. if no lobbying was done and no payments were received in the quarter in question, a statement that the registered person neither engaged in lobbying in return for payment nor received payment to engage in lobbying; and
iv. details of any change in that quarter in the consultant's registered details.[85]

9.45 Clients' names should be provided in full, without acronyms, unless the acronym is the registered name of the client. A single act of consultant lobbying on behalf of a client triggers the requirement to submit the name of that client in the return, but it is not necessary to list how many individual communications were made on behalf of a client.[86] Given that there is an obligation to provide the accurate names of clients, it is good practice for lobbyists to inform their clients that their identities may be made public.

viii. Offences

9.46 The 2014 Act creates several criminal offences for a failure to comply with its provisions and a liability to pay a civil penalty. The civil and criminal regimes are mutually exclusive, so that if a person is convicted of an offence he is not also liable to pay a civil penalty; and if he pays a civil penalty he may not be convicted of an offence for the same conduct.[87] (In this respect the 2014 Act is similar to the penalty regime that operates in respect of election campaign spending under PPERA 2000).

9.47 A person will commit a criminal offence if he is required to be registered and carries on the business of consultant lobbying while he is unregistered. Both the person who should be registered and the individual person who actually carries out the lobbying will commit the offence. It is also an offence for a registered person to engage in lobbying if the person's entry in the register is incomplete or inaccurate, or if the person has failed to provide sufficient information in respect of an information return to enable the Registrar to rectify the error or omission on the register.[88] So too will a person commit an offence if he fails to comply with an information notice served on him by the

[84] Thus, the same client may be declared in two different quarters for the same lobbying activity. However, a retainer payment does not trigger the need for a client declaration unless relevant communication has taken place: ibid para 4.1.
[85] Transparency of Lobbying, Non-Party Campaigning and Trade Union Administration Act 2014, s 5.
[86] Guidance on registration and quarterly information returns' (Office of the Registrar of Consultant Lobbyists, 20 May 2022) para 4.1.
[87] Transparency of Lobbying, Non-Party Campaigning and Trade Union Administration Act 2014, s 18.
[88] ibid s 12(1)–(3).

Registrar, requiring him to supply further information. If the recipient of the notice fails to supply the information on or before the deadline to do so, or he provides inaccurate or incomplete information, he will commit an offence.[89]

9.48 There is a statutory defence to those criminal offences if the person can show that he exercised all due diligence to avoid committing them.[90] If convicted, the person is liable on summary conviction to a fine.[91] If the person is a corporate body, for example a company, then its individual directors, managers, secretaries or officers may also be liable if it is proven that they consented to or connived in the commission of the offence or the offence arose from their negligence. The same is the case for partners of Scottish partnerships.[92]

9.49 The Registrar may also impose a civil penalty on a person if he is satisfied that the person's conduct amounts to an offence under the Act. There is no due diligence defence in such cases.[93] Before imposing any penalty the Registrar must give the person notice complying with section 15 of the 2014 Act and consider any written representations received within a defined period set out in the notice.[94] The Registrar must then, if he or she so decides, serve the person with a penalty notice setting out the impugned conduct, the reason why the Registrar is satisfied the person has engaged in that conduct, the amount of the penalty (which may not be more than £7,500[95]), specify the period and the form in which the person must pay and inform the person of their right to appeal to the First Tier Tribunal.[96] If the person decides to appeal they do not have to pay the penalty until the appeal is determined.

[89] ibid s 12(4).
[90] ibid s 12(5).
[91] ibid s 12(7), (8).
[92] ibid s 13.
[93] ibid s 14.
[94] ibid s 15.
[95] Though all the penalties issued to date have been very small and in the region of a couple of hundred pounds. See the Registrar's record of statutory notices.
[96] Transparency of Lobbying, Non-Party Campaigning and Trade Union Administration Act 2014, ss 16 and 17.

10

Election Campaign Expenditure: Bodies other than Political Parties

I. Introduction

10.1 This chapter is about how much money may be spent on campaigning during a general election by organisations and individuals that are *not* political parties fielding candidates. The rules about this are intricate, though it is vital that organisations wishing to campaign in a general election understand them: criminal penalties apply if the rules are breached.

10.2 Organisations that campaign during a general election period about specific issues, or for or against particular parties or candidates, must comply with rules regulating their expenditure.[1] Trade unions, political clubs and pressure groups are examples of bodies that regularly undertake this sort of involvement in election campaigning. Charities may also campaign on particular issues (but not for or against political parties or candidates, as they are precluded from doing so). Rarely, registered political parties decide not to field candidates in particular constituencies, but to take part in campaigning to support or oppose the candidates of other political parties. All these organisations and individuals are known interchangeably as 'third-party campaigners' or 'non-party campaigners' because they are not registered political parties campaigning in support of their own candidates. In this chapter we refer to them as 'third party campaigners' or 'third parties'.

10.3 The Political Parties, Elections and Referendums Act 2000 (PPERA 2000) sets out the rules regulating third-party campaigning expenditure. The PPERA 2000 imposes spending caps that have been amended on various occasions by legislation, recently in 2014, 2022 and 2023. The legislative provisions are detailed and the Electoral Commission has issued a statutory Code of Practice called the 'Non-party Campaigner Code of Practice' (2023), to which it must have regard when exercising its functions.[2]

10.4 Organisations that are eligible to register with the Electoral Commission as third-party campaigners (see paragraph 10.18 below), and which do register, are able to spend much greater sums on general election campaigns than unregistered eligible organisations. The maximum sum that registered third parties may spend on controlled expenditure is a percentage of the maximum sum that registered political parties would be able to spend if they contested all available seats in a general election. In 2023 the government increased the maximum expenditure cap for registered political parties: it is now £35,106,500. Table 1, below, sets out a summary of PPERA-controlled campaign expenditure limits.

[1] No limits, as such, are imposed on controlled expenditure by third parties in connection with local government elections under PPERA 2000, although any such expenditure incurred during the relevant campaign period for a general election would count towards the expenditure limit for that election. See PPERA 2000, Explanatory Notes, para 186.

[2] The Code is subject to revision from time to time. The latest version of the Code at the time of writing is that released in 2023. The Code is issued pursuant to PPERA 2000, s 100B. Compliance with the Code of Practice provides a defence to some offences under PPERA 2000 in certain circumstances set out in the statute.

Table 1 PPERA-controlled campaign expenditure limits

	Registered political party*	Registered third party	Unregistered third party	'Targeted' expenditure
England	£29,327,430	£586,548	£20,000	£58,654
Scotland	£3,078,570	£81,571	£10,000	£6,157
Wales	£1,728,320	£54,566	£10,000	£3,456
Northern Ireland	£972,180	£39,443	£10,000	£1,944
UK-wide campaign	£35,106,500	£702,130	£10,000	N/A
In one constituency	N/A	£17,553	£17,553**	N/A

Source: see paragraphs 10.18–10.27 below.

* Based on a party standing a candidate in every constituency.

** See paragraphs 10.26–10.30 below.

10.5 Third-party organisations that wish to campaign in local elections are also subject to rules about spending limits. The Electoral Commission does not oversee compliance with those rules. The limit for a third-party campaigner campaigning for or against a candidate in a ward is £50 + 0.5p for each elector in the ward. Any spending over that limit must be authorised by a candidate's election agent; the spending above the limit will count towards the candidate's own spending limit.[3]

10.6 Spending rules apply to organisations that campaign in referenda. There have been various referenda in the UK which have determined significant constitutional issues (on membership of the European Economic Community, on the voting system for parliamentary elections, Scottish independence and Brexit), but they happen infrequently. The rules about campaign spending in referenda may be found in Part VII of PPERA 2000. A notable exercise of the Electoral Commission's regulatory powers in respect of referenda rules was when it fined the campaign group Vote Leave for overspending by hundreds of thousands of pounds, and submitting an inaccurate spending return, in respect of the Brexit referendum.[4]

II. The Regulated Period

10.7 The rules about controlled expenditure do not apply all the time. They apply during a specific regulated period for general elections under PPERA 2000, being one of the following:

i. the period of 365 days ending with the date of polling day for the general election; or

[3] Representation of the People Act 1983, s 75(1), (1ZZB) and (1ZA)(b).

[4] For further information about the case, see the Electoral Commission's summary, 'Vote Leave fined and referred to the police for breaking electoral law', 17 July 2018 (as amended on 25 July 2019, 14 August 2019 and 7 May 2020): www.electoralcommission.org.uk/media-centre/vote-leave-fined-and-referred-police-breaking-electoral-law.

ii. where the election in question shortly follows another general election that was held less than a year before, the relevant period begins with the day after polling day for the prior election and ends on polling day for the subsequent election. This means that where two general elections are held within one year, the period will extend from a year before the date of the first election to the date of the second election.[5]

10.8 In practice, the regulated period may well apply retrospectively to a third-party campaigner's spending. We return to the retrospective effect of the regulated period, below in paragraph 10.17.

III. 'Controlled Expenditure'

A. What Does it Include?

10.9 A third-party's normal expenditure on existing campaigns or projects during the election period is unlikely to be caught by the regulatory regime. The spending limits apply to money spent to influence policies, parties or candidates in the election. This is called 'controlled expenditure'. Expenditure is 'controlled expenditure' if it meets two tests: a test of qualification and a test known as 'the purpose test', which are set out below.

B. Qualifying Expenditure

10.10 To count as 'qualifying expenditure',[6] the expenditure must be associated with any of the following:[7]

i. the production or publication of material which is made available to the public at large or any section of the public (in whatever form and by whatever means);
ii. canvassing, or market research seeking views or information from, members of the public;
iii. press conferences, or other media events, organised by or on behalf of the third party;
iv. transport (by any means) of persons to any place or places with a view to obtaining publicity (expenses in respect of the transport of such persons include the costs of hiring a particular means of transport);

[5] PPERA 2000, Sch 10, para 3(3).

[6] Note that expenditure is not third-party qualifying expenditure if it should instead fall to be recorded as the regulated expenditure of registered political parties, or a candidate's expenditure under the Representation of the People Act 1983, s 75, or expenditure that falls to be recorded in respect of the Recall of MPs Act 2015 (ie associated with a recall petition): PPERA 2000, s 87.

[7] PPERA 2000, Sch 8A, para 1.

v. public rallies or other public events (but expenses in respect of the third-party's annual conferences do not fall into the definition of controlled expenditure).[8] Qualifying expenses associated with public events include costs incurred in connection with people's attendance at such events, the hire of premises for the purposes of such events or the provision of goods, services or facilities at them. The costs of providing protection or security for people or property do not count as qualifying expenditure and therefore fall outside 'controlled expenditure'.

10.11 There are some necessary, incidental costs associated with the matters above that are nonetheless excluded from the definition of qualifying expenditure. These are:

i. expenses that are associated with or in consequence of the translation of anything from English into Welsh or Welsh into English;
ii. reasonable personal expenses incurred by an *individual* in travelling or in providing for their accommodation or other personal needs;
iii. reasonable expenses incurred that are reasonably attributable to an individual's disability.[9]

10.12 Any costs associated with the publication of any matter relating to an election in a newspaper or a periodical (other than an advertisement) are excluded from the definition of qualifying expenses. This is commonly known as the 'newspaper exception'.[10] The scope of the newspaper exception – and whether it includes online as well as traditional paper content – has not yet been tested in the courts. It has been held in a different context that whether something can properly be defined as a newspaper depends not so much on the medium on which the publication was printed, nor indeed its shape or size, but upon its content and whether it contains news.[11] The Electoral Commission seems to consider that the newspaper exception includes online newspapers,[12] though it has not stated so in its 2023 Code of Practice.

[8] Note that in Northern Ireland there is an exemption from this list for any public procession or protest meeting, within the meaning of the Public Processions (Northern Ireland) Act 1998, in respect of which notice is given in accordance with s 6 or 7 of that Act.

[9] PPERA 2000, Sch 8A, para 2(1). The definition of disability for these purposes is that in the Equality Act 2010, s 6, namely, a mental or physical impairment that has a substantial adverse effect on a person's ability to carry out day-to-day activities and such effect is long-term (ie it has lasted, or is likely to last, at least 12 months or where it may not last that long but may well reoccur). Some conditions are automatically disabilities within the meaning of that Act: HIV infection, cancer and multiple sclerosis.

[10] PPERA 2000, Sch 8A, para 2(1)(a).

[11] *Davis v Westminster City Council* [2012] EWHC 2303 (Admin) per Moses LJ; *cf News Corpn UK & Ireland Ltd v Revenue and Customs Commissioners* [2023] UKSC 7, in which the Supreme Court considered whether the definition of 'newspaper' in tax legislation from the 1970s and 1990s could include online newspapers for the purposes of VAT and determined that it could not. That judgment concerned a narrow question in a very different area of law that had to be construed according to limitations set out by European Union legislation. The judgment is unlikely to have application to the definition of newspaper in electoral law and in the electoral context Art 10 ECHR would very likely require the definition of 'newspaper' to be construed much more broadly.

[12] 'The production or publication of any content – other than an advertisement – in a newspaper or periodical (including online versions of newspapers and periodicals) is not regulated campaign activity)': 'Overview of regulated non-party campaigning' (Electoral Commission, 2021).

C. The Purpose Test

10.13 If the expenditure is qualifying expenditure, it will only be 'controlled expenditure' if it meets 'the purpose test'. That is, the expenditure must reasonably be seen to intend to promote or to procure the electoral success of:

i. one or more registered political parties; or
ii. registered political parties which advocate or oppose particular policies (eg a particular environmental policy); or
iii. candidates who support or oppose (or are neutral on) particular opinions or policies (eg candidates who support the nationalisation of the water industry) or otherwise fall within a particular category of candidates.[13]

10.14 Electoral success is defined for these purposes as the return of candidates to the legislature. Promoting or procuring electoral success includes doing so by prejudicing the electoral prospects of a rival party or candidate as well as supporting the prospects of a preferred candidate. The provisions of this part of PPERA 2000 are broad and catch in their scope activities that do not expressly mention the name of the candidate or party in question, as well as activities that are intended to achieve another, non-regulated purpose.[14] The Electoral Commission's Code of Practice identifies particular factors that are relevant to the purpose test:

i. A call to action to voters to vote in a particular way. The call to action may be explicit or implicit, but it is unlikely that a public campaign without an explicit or implicit call to action to voters will meet the purpose test.
ii. A campaign that has a positive or negative tone towards a particular party or candidate or policy closely and publicly associated with a party or a candidate. A campaign that leads voters to think of a particular party or category of candidates is likely to meet the purpose test.
iii. The context and timing of the campaigning activity. A campaign is more likely to meet the purpose test if it is about something that is a prominent issue at the time of the relevant election and which also contains a call to action or has a particular tone towards a party or candidate. An ongoing campaign is unlikely to be reasonably regarded as intending to influence voters to vote in a particular way at the election.[15]

10.15 According to the Electoral Commission's Code of Practice 'a campaign that explicitly promotes particular parties or candidates, or implicitly promotes certain political parties or candidates over others, is likely to meet the purpose test'. So far as tone is concerned, the Code explains:

> A campaign that is positive or negative towards a political party or parties, a category of candidates or a policy closely and publicly associated with a party or category of candidate is

[13] PPERA 2000, s 85(2).
[14] ibid s 85(4) and (4A).
[15] Non-party Campaigner Code of Practice (Electoral Commission, 2023).

likely to be reasonably regarded as intending to influence voters to vote in a particular way and so meet the purpose test.

10.16 The key point here is that the purpose test is determined objectively, not on the subjective basis of whether the third party intends to meet it or not. The Code states that: 'Campaign activity will only meet the purpose test if a reasonable person would regard the activity as intending to influence voters to vote in a particular way at an upcoming election'. In other words, it is not the campaigner's intention which counts, but what an objective reasonable person would see as (at least part of) the intention, from the context and content of the campaigning.

D. The Retrospective Regulated Period

10.17 The Electoral Commission's Code of Practice provides guidance about the retrospective application of the regulated period. Activity that took place before the announcement of the relevant period should only be regulated if it could reasonably be regarded as meeting the political purpose test at the time it was carried out. An ongoing campaign on a particular issue that was in force during the retrospective regulated period would be unlikely to meet the purpose test. Nor would activity that was focused on an issue rather than how an elector should vote where there were no upcoming relevant elections at the time of the activity.[16] But campaign activity *will* be regulated retrospectively if the activity meets the purpose test for *any* relevant election that was taking place at the time of the activity, even if the election was not a UK parliamentary election. Campaign spending will also be retrospectively regulated if it was incurred in respect of a scheduled election, regardless of what election that was (for example, a previous local election). So, by way of general illustration:

i. A charity has an ongoing campaign to stop the deportation of asylum seekers for which it held a rally and produced campaign literature that was disseminated to the public. A general election is called nine months after the rally. The rally therefore took place during the retrospective regulated period. The deportation of asylum seekers becomes a key issue in the general election. The rally is nevertheless unlikely to be regulated activity because it was part of an ongoing campaign and did not address how voters should vote.
ii. A union undertook a series of public meetings to campaign for a new living wage in the run up to a local election in May. The union spent money holding events to support candidates advocating a living wage for all local authority employees. A general election is called for the following December and policies on the living wage are a point of difference between the main parties. The union's expenditure on the events was not related to the general election. Nevertheless, the expenditure may well be regulated retrospectively: it was related to a local election, which is a relevant election, the campaigning is about an issue that is relevant at the time of the general election and the campaigning falls within the retrospective regulated period.

[16] ibid.

IV. The Spending Limits

A. Eligible and Unregistered Third Parties

10.18 Not all organisations are eligible to register as third-party campaigners. Most ubiquitous types of organisation are eligible, though, including trade unions, companies, charities and registered political parties, as well as individuals registered on the electoral registers.[17] Unincorporated associations (eg political clubs) are eligible if they carry on business or other activities wholly or mainly in the UK and their main office is there.[18] Only organisations which are eligible to be third parties can lawfully incur controlled expenditure above £700 in the regulated period.[19] Eligible third parties that do not register as third-party campaigners with the Electoral Commission are called 'unregistered' third parties (also referred to in the legal framework as 'unrecognised'). They are subject to the following maximum spending limits exceeding which constitutes a criminal offence: £10,000 nationally; or £20,000 in England; or £10,000 in each of Scotland, Wales and Northern Ireland;[20] £17,553 in any particular constituency (but see paragraph 10.30 below).[21] (Table 1 above sets out a summary of relevant spending limits).

B. Registered Third Parties

i. *Registration*

10.19 Registered third parties are those that have registered as such with the Electoral Commission. The requirements of registration are detailed but formulaic; PPERA 2000, section 88 and guidance on the Electoral Commission's website sets out details of the information to be provided. The administrative effect of registration is that a third-party campaigner must submit controlled expenditure returns as well as weekly and quarterly donation reports in the regulated general election period.[22] Third-party campaigners spending more than £250,000 on controlled expenditure must also provide the Electoral Commission with a statement of accounts accompanied by an auditor's report.[23] The third-party must also nominate a 'responsible person' to comply with those administrative requirements and to be in charge of authorising the incurring and payment of controlled expenditure. A failure to comply with those requirements amounts to a criminal offence, though there is a defence in some cases of reasonable excuse.

[17] PPERA 2000, ss 88(2) and 54(2).
[18] ibid s 54(2)(h).
[19] ibid s 89A(2).
[20] ibid s 94(3) and (5).
[21] ibid s 94(3)(a)(i) and (5ZA).
[22] Permissible donors for third parties and political parties are set out in PPERA 2000, s 54(2). It suffices for these purposes to note that foreign donors are generally not permissible donors. There is an obligation to return donations that come from an impermissible source or if the source cannot be ascertained. If third parties breach these rules the donations can be forfeited and there are criminal penalties for non-compliance. Third parties must also report a permissible donation of an amount above £500. See PPERA 2000, ss 96 and 98.
[23] ibid s 97.

ii. Spending Limits

10.20 Registered third parties are subject to higher expenditure limits during the relevant period of a general election. The expenditure limits are calculated with reference to the maximum campaign expenditure limit for registered political parties,[24] as follows:

i. England: £586,548.60;[25]
ii. Scotland: £81,571.40;[26]
iii. Wales: £54,566.40;[27]
iv. Northern Ireland: £39,442.60;[28]
v. the UK-wide limit, for campaigns that are UK wide, is £702,130;[29]
vi. the expenditure limit for campaigning in a particular constituency is £17,553 (but see paragraphs 10.27–10.31 below).[30]

iii. Allocation of Spending to Regions and Constituencies

10.21 PPERA 2000 allocates incurred spending to the regions and constituencies which the expenditure primarily affects. The practical effect of this is that a third party's incurring of controlled expenditure must be proportional.

i. Expenditure will be attributed solely to a particular region if the expenditure is confined wholly or substantially to that region so that the expenditure has no significant effects in any other part of the UK. The example given in the legislation is 'expenditure on an advertisement in a newspaper circulating in Wales is to be attributed solely to Wales if the newspaper does not circulate to any significant extent in any other part of the United Kingdom'.[31] The expenditure limit in such a case will be the regional limit above (eg £54,566.40 in the case of Wales).
ii. Where expenditure is wholly or substantially attributed to more than one region (for example, England and Scotland), then the expenses are attributed to those

[24] The campaign expenditure limits for registered political parties were increased significantly in November 2023 by the Representation of the People (Variation of Election Expenses, Expenditure Limits and Donation etc Thresholds) Order 2023, SI 2023/1235. In 2024 the maximum expenditure limit for registered political parties in England is £29,327,430 and £3,078,570 in Scotland, £1,728,320 in Wales and £972,180 in Northern Ireland.

[25] Formula: 2% (PPERA 2000, Sch 10, para 3(2)(a)) of £54,010 x 543 (constituencies) (ibid Sch 9, para 3(2)(a)).

[26] Formula: £20,000 + 2% (ibid Sch 10, para 3(2)(b)) of £54,010 x 57 (constituencies) (ibid Sch 9, para 3(2)(a)).

[27] Formula: £20,000 + 2% (ibid Sch 10, para 3(2)(c)) of £54,010 x 32 (constituencies) (ibid Sch 9, para 3(2)(a)).

[28] Formula: £20,000 + 2% (ibid Sch 10, para 3(2)(d)) of £54,010 x 18 (constituencies) (ibid Sch 9, para 3(4)).

[29] The UK-wide limit is not simply the sum of the limits for the constituent countries of the UK. That is because ibid Sch 10, para 2(1) requires UK-wide campaign spending to be apportioned to each of England, Scotland, Wales and Northern Ireland in proportion to the number of parliamentary constituencies situated in each part. However, the individual country expenditure limits cited above still apply. Because the number of constituencies in England account for 83.54 percent of the total, 83.54 percent of spending in a UK-wide campaign must be apportioned to England. If anything more than £702,130 were spent across the UK then the apportionment of 83.54 percent of that amount would exceed the maximum spending cap for England.

[30] ibid s 94(5ZA).

[31] ibid Sch 10, para 2(2)(b) and (3).

regions in proportion to the number of parliamentary constituencies for the time being situated in them.[32] In the example of England and Scotland (600 constituencies in total), 90.5 per cent of the expenditure would be attributed to England and 9.5 per cent to Scotland.

10.22 Similar rules apply to expenditure in particular constituencies. Expenditure in one constituency that has no significant effects in any other will be allocated to that constituency alone; the expenses limit would be £17,553. Where controlled expenditure is incurred in a multi-constituency campaign, the expenditure will be attributed to each constituency in equal proportions.[33] This means that a third party cannot aggregate the total spending cap in different constituencies during a multi-constituency campaign and spend more than the cap in one and less in another.

iv. 'Targeted' Expenditure

10.23 PPERA 2000 also imposes limits for 'targeted' controlled expenditure by third parties, within the maximum overall limit. Controlled expenditure is 'targeted' at a particular registered party if it can reasonably be regarded as intended to benefit that party or any of its candidates, and not intended to benefit any other registered party or any of its candidates. A limit applies to targeted controlled expenditure that is incurred during the relevant period before a general election and is targeted at a particular registered party.[34] The targeted expenditure limit is:

i. England: £58,654;
ii. Scotland: £6,157;
iii. Wales: £3,456;
iv. Northern Ireland: £1,944.[35]

10.24 Where a third party is not authorised by the registered political party to incur targeted controlled expenditure it is an offence for the third party to incur controlled expenditure in excess of the cap.[36]

v. Lower-tier Expenditure Limits

10.25 On registration a third party may declare that it shall be subject to the 'lower-tier expenditure limits'. The lower tier limits are the same as those that apply to non-registered third-party campaigners, above.[37] The effect of registering as a third-party campaigner subject to the lower-tier limits is that the third party is excused from the

[32] ibid Sch 10, para 2(2)(a).
[33] ibid Sch 10, para 2A(2) and (3).
[34] ibid s 94D.
[35] ie 0.2% of the maximum campaign expenditure limit for political parties in that part of the UK: ibid s 94D(4).
[36] ibid s 94E.
[37] ibid ss 88(3D), 85(5B) and 94(5).

administrative financial reporting burden imposed by PPERA 2000. The third party does not have to submit expenditure reports, nor weekly or quarterly donation reports to the Electoral Commission as it otherwise would.[38] Nor may the third-party campaigner notify the Commission that it is a lead campaigner in a joint campaign with other third-party campaigners.[39] If the third-party breaches those lower tier limits then it will commit a criminal offence. It will also stop being subject to the lower-tier limits and instead be subject to the higher-tier expenditure limits and the financial administration that goes with them.[40]

C. Spending on Constituency Candidates

10.26 There are two different spending limits that apply to third-party campaign expenditure in individual constituencies: one under PPERA 2000 and the other under the Representation of the People Act 1983 (RPA 1983). The relationship between the two is not entirely clear. It has been complicated further by the changes to political party spending limits in 2023.

10.27 The RPA imposes spending limits by third parties on particular candidates in particular constituencies during a general election campaign. A person who is not the candidate or her election agent may not spend more than £700 without the written authorisation of the election agent.[41] The limit applies to spending on any of the following:[42]

i. advertising of any description, including costs of agency fees, design costs and other costs in connection with preparing, producing, distributing or otherwise disseminating such advertising or anything incorporating such advertising and intended to be distributed for the purpose of disseminating it;
ii. unsolicited material addressed to electors (whether addressed to them by name or intended for delivery to households within any particular area);
iii. expenses in respect of such material include design costs and other costs in connection with preparing, producing or distributing such material (including the cost of postage);
iv. the costs of transporting people, including the costs of hiring a means of transport for a particular period;
v. the costs of public meetings, including costs incurred in connection with the attendance of persons at such meetings, the hire of premises for the purposes of such meetings or the provision of goods, services or facilities at them;
vi. accommodation and administrative costs.

[38] ibid ss 95A(10A), 95B(10A) and 96(9).
[39] ibid s 94A(5A).
[40] ibid s 94(10A).
[41] RPA 1983, s 75.
[42] ibid Sch 4A, paras 1–6.

10.28 A breach of the £700 limit amounts to a corrupt practice under the RPA 1983 and carries a potential penalty of an unlimited fine or up to one year imprisonment (see paragraph 10.37 below). Those individuals who aided, counselled or connived to breach the limit can be liable individually for those penalties.

10.29 As set out above, PPERA 2000 appears to provide that a registered third party can spend up to £17,553 in a constituency. However, the statutory provision is not entirely clear in respect of unregistered third-party campaigners. The effect of section 94(3)(a)(ii) and (5Z) is that an unregistered third party must not spend more than £17,553 in a constituency. However, section 94(3)(ai) provides a limit of £10,000 for the incurring of '*any* controlled expenditure' by an unregistered third-party campaigner. It is difficult to reconcile those two provisions. Before 2023 the difficulty did not arise because the constituency limit was less than £10,000. The explanatory notes to the Act which introduced the constituency limit described the limit as a 'further limit'.[43] That is, an unregistered third-party campaigner would have to register with the Commission upon reaching the lower constituency threshold. That made logical sense, as it allowed the Commission to have more careful oversight of spending in the constituencies than across the country as a whole. The position as it now stands does not make logical sense, as on a literal reading of PPERA 2000 it appears that an unregistered third-party campaigner would have to register before exceeding expenditure of £10,000, even though the constituency spending cap is considerably greater than £10,000. It may be that the drafters of the secondary legislation that amended the spending limits in 2023 simply did not realise the effect that the new legislation would have on the third-party constituency limits.

10.30 A further confusion arises in how the PPERA 2000 limit relates to the RPA 1983 limit. When would a third party campaigner be caught by the much lower expenditure ceiling of £700 under the RPA 1983 rather than PPERA 2000's cap of £17,553? First, the RPA 1983 limit applies only from the time that a person officially becomes a candidate in the election,[44] whereas the PPERA 2000 limit applies throughout the regulated period of 365 days before a general election. Second, it is probable that if a third party were to campaign for a particular candidate in a particular constituency, then it would be subject to the £700 cap. But if the third party supported a particular category of candidates, for example, Labour candidates in the Midlands, or candidates who had signed up to a particular pledge, rather than a particular named candidate, then it is likely the PPERA 2000 cap would apply instead. That would be concordant with the explanatory notes to PPERA 2000 which describe the purpose of the third-party campaigning regime as regulating *national* expenditure that is to *generally* promote or procure the election of a registered party and its candidates.[45]

[43] Transparency of Lobbying, Non-Party Campaigning and Trade Union Administration Act 2014, Explanatory Notes.

[44] RPA 1983, ss 75(1) and 90ZA(1). See also ibid, s 118A for the time at which a person becomes a candidate.

[45] PPERA 2000, Explanatory Notes, para 184.

V. Penalties for Breach

A. Stop Notices

10.31 The Commission may issue a stop notice to a person if it believes she is actually carrying on, or is likely to carry on, an activity that involves or is likely to involve the commission of an offence under PPERA 2000 or a contravention of a restriction set out in that Act.[46] The effect of the stop notice is to prohibit the person carrying on the activity until they have taken the steps specified in the notice.[47] A person commits an offence if he is served with a stop notice and fails to comply with it. The penalty for failing to comply is a fine of £20,000 or imprisonment of not more than 12 months on summary conviction in England and Wales, Scotland and Northern Ireland (save that the term of imprisonment on summary conviction in Northern Ireland is not more than six months); and on conviction on indictment, an unlimited fine and a term of imprisonment of not more than two years.[48]

B. Penalties for Excess Spending under PPERA 2000

10.32 It is a criminal offence for a third party to incur controlled expenditure in the relevant period in excess of the statutory limits set out by PPERA 2000.[49] The offence is triable either summarily or by indictment and the penalty is a fine of unlimited amount. It is a defence that the party complied with the Non-party Campaigner Code of Practice in determining whether the expenditure was controlled, and that the offence would not have been committed on the basis of the controlled expenditure as determined in accordance with the code.[50] Liability for these offences is potentially wide ranging and the following people may be found guilty of them:

i. the responsible person notified as such with the Commission who authorised the expenditure to be incurred, if he or she knew or ought to have known the expenditure incurred would exceed the limit;
ii. the third-party body itself (eg the company incurring the expenditure);
iii. any director, manager, secretary or officer of the organisation if that person consented to or connived in the incurring of the excess expenditure, or if the incurring of that expenditure was attributable to any neglect on the part of him or her.[51]

10.33 It is also an offence for an individual person to incur or to pay controlled expenditure in the regulated period without proper authorisation from a third-party campaigner's 'responsible person'[52] or the person to whom the responsible person has

[46] ibid Sch 19C, para 10(1), (2) and (3).
[47] ibid Sch 19C, para 10(1).
[48] ibid Sch 20.
[49] ibid s 94(2)(a)(i)), (2)(a)(ii), (4)(a)(i), (4)(a)(ii).
[50] ibid s 94(4A).
[51] ibid s 152(1).
[52] ie the person within the third party who is responsible for compliance with PPERA 2000's financial regime (this is usually the treasurer or the financial officer of the organisation).

delegated a power of authorisation.[53] So too is it an offence for the person exercising a power of delegated authorisation to fail to notify the responsible person that payment of controlled expenditure has been made and provide the relevant invoice for payment. The penalty for those offences is an unlimited fine.

10.34 The following also amount to criminal offences:

i. Incurring expenditure targeted at a particular registered political party (ie in support of that political party) without the authority of the political party and the expenditure exceeds the statutory targeted expenditure limit.[54] The offence is triable either summarily or by indictment and the penalty is an unlimited fine. It is a defence that the third party complied with a relevant statutory code of practice promulgated under the Act in determining whether the expenditure was controlled and the offence would otherwise not have been committed on the basis of controlled expenditure as determined in accordance with the code.[55]
ii. Failing to provide donation reports to the Commission during the general election period.[56] The responsible person is liable for this. There is a defence of reasonable excuse.[57] The penalty is an unlimited fine.
iii. Failing to declare that donations recorded in reports to the Commission are from permissible donors in compliance with PPERA 2000, sections 95A(9) and 95B(8). The responsible person is liable if a false declaration was made knowingly or recklessly.[58] The penalty on conviction by indictment is an unlimited fine or not more than one year's imprisonment or an unlimited fine on summary conviction.
iv. Failing to submit valid expenditure returns compliant with PPERA 2000, section 96. The responsible person is liable if he fails to submit compliant reports. There is a defence of reasonable excuse.[59] The penalty on indictment is an unlimited fine or not more than one year's imprisonment, or an unlimited fine on summary conviction.

C. Fixed Monetary Penalties from the Commission

10.35 The Commission may issue fixed monetary penalties on any person or third party if it is satisfied beyond reasonable doubt that the person has committed an offence under PPERA 2000, or has otherwise contravened a restriction or requirement imposed by the Act.[60] The fine may be of unlimited amount. The Commission may also in the same circumstances impose a variable monetary penalty of an amount which it decides, called 'a discretionary requirement'.[61] A person on whom a fixed monetary penalty or

[53] PPERA 2000, ss 90 and 91(1).
[54] ibid s 94E.
[55] ibid s 94E(4).
[56] ibid ss 95A and 95B.
[57] ibid s 95C(1).
[58] ibid s 95C(2).
[59] ibid s 98(4).
[60] ibid Sch 19C, para 1.
[61] ibid Sch 19C, para 5.

a discretionary requirement is imposed cannot at any time be convicted of an offence under PPERA 2000 in respect of the act or omission giving rise to that penalty.[62]

D. Penalty for Excess Spending under the Representation of the People Act 1983

10.36 In relation to breaches of the constituency spending limit imposed by section 75 of the RPA 1983, it is an offence for a person to incur, or to aid, abet, counsel or procure the incurring of, unauthorised expenditure. A person who does so will be guilty of a corrupt practice[63] and be liable to a term of imprisonment not exceeding one year or to a fine (or both) on indictment; and on summary conviction, to imprisonment for a term not exceeding six months or to a fine of unlimited amount.[64] Where a corporate body or association is guilty of the offence, any person who at the time the offence was committed was a director, general manager, secretary or other similar officer or purporting to act in that capacity shall be deemed guilty of the offence unless he proves that the offence took place without his consent or connivance and that he exercised all such diligence to prevent the commission of the offence.[65]

VI. Joint Campaigns with Other Organisations

A. Definition of 'Joint Campaign'

10.37 There are complex rules about acting in concert on a joint campaign during an election period. Primarily these rules control which organisations in the joint campaign are deemed to have incurred controlled expenditure and which are responsible for reporting it to the Commission. The rules on joint campaigning apply to registered *and* unregistered third-party campaigners.[66] Joint campaigning is where more than one third-party organisation:

i. enters into a plan or other arrangement;
ii. they all intend to incur controlled expenditure in pursuance of that plan or arrangement;
iii. one or more of them actually incurs controlled expenditure in pursuance of the plan or arrangement; and
iv. that plan or arrangement can reasonably be regarded as intending to achieve a common purpose.[67]

[62] ibid Sch 19C, paras 4(2) and 8(1).
[63] RPA 1983, s 75(5).
[64] ibid s 168(1).
[65] ibid s 75(6).
[66] PPERA 2000, s 94(7).
[67] ibid s 94(6).

10.38 The Commission's Non-Party Campaigner Code of Practice addresses joint campaigning. It states that: 'Non-party campaigners who happen to campaign about similar or related issues are not joint campaigners'. Activities likely to fall within the scope of joint campaigning include a joint advertising campaign, a co-ordinated campaign where it is agreed which areas are to be covered, which issues raised or which voters targeted, or where one party has the power of veto or the power to approve the other's campaign materials. For example:

> Campaigner A and campaigner B agree to run a campaign encouraging voters to vote for a particular political party. Both intend to incur controlled expenditure as part of the joint campaign. Campaigner A incurs expenditure on the joint campaign, but campaigner B never spends their intended share. This is joint campaigning, and the spending should be treated as such by both campaigner A and campaigner B.[68]

B. Deemed Expenditure and the Lead Campaigner Exception

10.39 If there is a joint campaign then all the spending on the joint campaign counts towards each of its members' spending limits. So, if A and B are in a joint campaign and A incurs controlled expenditure in pursuance of the campaign, B will be deemed to have incurred it too and each member of the campaign will be required to report it as expenditure.[69]

10.40 The exception to this is where one member of the joint campaign agrees to be a 'lead campaigner'. In that case, the other parties to the joint campaign are 'minor campaigners'. The controlled expenditure incurred by the minor campaigners pursuant to the campaign is instead attributed to the lead campaigner and counts towards the lead campaigner's spending limits, so long as the minor campaigner has not generally incurred more than £10,000 of controlled expenditure outside the joint campaign in the regulated period.[70] The lead campaigner is responsible for reporting all the incurred expenditure on the joint campaign, including by the minor parties, to the Commission.[71] Parties to a joint campaign can only benefit from the 'lead campaigner' provisions if the designated lead campaigner is itself a recognised third party campaigner and gives notice to the Commission complying with PPERA 2000, section 94A that it is a lead campaigner, identifying the minor campaigners in the campaign.

[68] Non-party Campaigner Code of Practice (Electoral Commission, April 2023).
[69] PPERA 2000, s 94(6)(b).
[70] ibid s 94B.
[71] ibid s 94B(2).

11

Equality and Discrimination

I. Introduction

11.1 This chapter is about the rules and laws that protect people's right to vote and to stand for public election, and that forbid discrimination in the political sphere. The underlying principles are enumerated in many foundational human rights instruments, especially in the Preamble and Article 2 of the Universal Declaration of Human Rights and the Preamble to the European Convention on Human Rights (ECHR). The European Court of Human Rights has observed that:

> according to the Preamble to the Convention, fundamental human rights and freedoms are best maintained by 'an effective political democracy'. Since it enshrines a characteristic principle of democracy, Article 3 of Protocol No 1 [ie the right to vote and stand in elections] is accordingly of prime importance in the Convention system.[1]

The Council of Europe's advisory body on political parties and other constitutional matters is the European Commission for Democracy through Law, also known as the Venice Commission. A guiding principle of the Venice Commission's Code of Good Practice in the Field of Political Parties is that 'Political parties should not act against the values of the ECHR and the principle of equality. Parties must not discriminate against individuals on the basis of any ground prohibited by the ECHR'.[2] Domestic jurisprudence also confirms a public interest in political parties properly addressing allegations of discrimination.[3] The Equality and Human Rights Commission (EHRC) has set out that

> participation in the democratic process matters. It gives people a say in the type of society they want and how they want to be governed … If our democratic institutions fully reflect the people they serve and the society in which we live, they can be more inclusive and make more informed decisions that work for everyone.[4]

II. The Right to Vote

A. The Franchise

11.2 The franchise is the right to vote in public elections. There is no common law right to vote.[5] The legal source of the present franchise is the Representation of the People Act 1983 (RPA 1983). British citizens, qualifying Commonwealth citizens[6] and Irish citizens who are at least 18 years old have the franchise in the UK if they are registered to vote. The RPA 1983 also sets out rules about voter registration.[7]

[1] *Mathieu-Mohin and Clerfayt v Belgium* (1988) 10 EHRR 1 para 47.

[2] As adopted by the Venice Commission at its 78th Plenary Session, 2009, at para 18.

[3] *Neslen v Evans* [2021] EWHC 1909 (QB) and also see by analogy *Unite the Union v McFadden* [2021] IRLR 354.

[4] 'The Equality Act 2010: A Guide for Political Parties' (EHRC, February 2018) Introduction.

[5] *Moohan v Lord Advocate* [2014] UKSC 67, [2015] AC 901 at [37], [56]. See Ch 1.

[6] ie those Commonwealth citizens who have the requisite immigration status in the UK.

[7] Representation of the People Act 1983, ss 8–18.

Various categories of people are legally incapacitated from voting: convicted offenders during their detention in prison or a mental institution;[8] peers who are members of the House of Lords;[9] and those people who have been convicted of an electoral offence.[10] The Lords Spiritual (ie 26 archbishops and bishops) are entitled to vote but by convention do not do so.

B. The Right to Vote in National Legislative Elections

11.3 The right to vote in national legislative elections is secured by Article 3 of Protocol 1 of the ECHR: there is an 'active' right to vote and a 'passive' right to stand for election. Article 3 of Protocol 1 requires the state 'to hold free elections at reasonable intervals by secret ballot, under conditions which will ensure the free expression of the opinion of the people in the choice of the legislature'.[11] The article is effective in UK law through the Human Rights Act 1998.[12]

11.4 The scope of Article 3 of Protocol 1 is limited. The active right to vote therein does not extend to referenda or local elections and there is wide room for manoeuvre in how the state decides to organise its electoral arrangements to comply with the article.[13] The active right to vote under Article 3 of Protocol 1 implies the principle of equality of treatment of all citizens in the exercise of their right to vote. The article's protection lies against restrictions on the right to vote (or to stand for election) that impair the very essence of the right to vote and deprive it of its effectiveness.[14] This is, in practice, a high threshold. An interference with the right to vote is likely to be disproportionate if it runs

[8] ibid ss 3 and 3A. Note that in *Hirst v UK (No 2)* (2006) 42 EHRR 41 the ECtHR determined that an indiscriminate disqualification of convicted prisoners from the franchise in the UK contravened Art 3 of Protocol 1.

[9] The case of *Earl of Beauchamp v Overseers of Madresfield* (1872) LR 8 CP 245 is precedent for the proposition that peers do not have the right to vote in parliamentary elections (decided at a time when hereditary peers were entitled to sit as Members of the House of Lords). Peers who are not Members of the House of Lords are nevertheless entitled to vote in parliamentary elections: House of Lords Act 1999, s 3(1) (hereditary peers); House of Lords Reform Act 2014, s 4(5) (peers who resign or who lose their membership through non-attendance for an entire parliamentary session or because they are convicted of serious criminal offence); House of Lords (Expulsion and Suspension) Act 2015, s 3 (peers who are expelled by the House of Lords).

[10] People convicted of a corrupt practice are ineligible to register to vote, and are therefore ineligible to vote, for five years after the date of their conviction; for those convicted of an illegal practice the period of ineligibility is three years: Representation of the People Act 1983, ss 160 and 173.

[11] Note that, where it applies, Art 3 of Protocol 1 prevails over the general provisions of the ECHR, including Art 10, which cannot be relied upon: *Zdanoka v Latvia* (2007) 45 EHRR 17 para 141.

[12] See Ch 1.

[13] *Mathieu-Mohin v Belgium* (1988) 10 EHRR 1 para 52. The standards to be applied for establishing compliance with Art 3 of Protocol 1 are less stringent than those applied under Arts 8–11 of the ECHR: *Zdanoka*, para 115(a). As for justifying measures limiting the right, the court must satisfy itself that the electoral measures under scrutiny pursue a legitimate aim and that they are proportionate. In practice, proportionality here entails an assessment of two criteria taken as one: whether there has been arbitrariness or a lack of proportionality; and whether the restriction has interfered with the free expression of the opinion of the people. See *Mathieu-Mohin*, *Zdanoka*. See also *Aziz v Cyprus* (2005) 41 EHRR 11 and *Hirst v UK (No 2)* (2006) 42 EHRR 41.

[14] *Mathieu-Mohin* at para 52; *Aziz* at para 30.

counter to maintaining the integrity and effectiveness of an electoral procedure aimed at identifying the will of the people through universal suffrage.[15] So too would a measure be disproportionate if it excluded groups or categories of the general population from the franchise and was not reconcilable with the underlying purposes of Article 3 of Protocol 1: the principle of universal suffrage maintaining the democratic validity of the legislature thus elected, as well as the democratic validity of the laws the legislature promulgates.[16]

11.5 A generally applied regime of voter identification at polling stations is unlikely to amount to a disproportionate interference with Article 3 of Protocol 1, though voter identification arrangements that prevent particular groups from voting may well do so. Voters in Great Britain must now provide documentary identification to vote, as has been required in Northern Ireland for many years. Voters must present a form of identification at their respective polling stations to obtain a ballot paper.[17] The requirement for voter identification, introduced in 2023, is a prerequisite to exercise the right to vote. The stated aim of this new requirement is to reduce voter fraud. That may, in itself, be a good thing: if people have confidence in the electoral system by a reduction in voter fraud then they might be encouraged to vote by virtue of their increased confidence in the electoral process.[18] Various European democracies operate a voter identification regime and the Venice Commission has expounded that a system of voter identification is 'of paramount importance for the overall integrity of the electoral process'.[19] Nevertheless, there are concerns that the voter identification regime may disadvantage minority groups, especially minority ethnic groups, who may lack appropriate forms of identification or who may be deterred from voting by the requirement to present identification. The new regime may be unnecessary given the vanishingly small amount of reported voter fraud but there is no reliable evidence at present that the requirement restricts the franchise on discriminatory grounds such that it would contravene Article 3 of Protocol 1.

[15] *Hirst* at para 62; *Zdanoka* at para 104.

[16] *Hirst* at para 62. See for example the ECtHR case of *Aziz v Cyprus* (2005) 41 EHRR 11, in which the electoral measure under scrutiny effectively denied the right to vote to Turkish Cypriots in Cyprus. After the Turkish invasion of Cyprus the Greek state continued to use the electoral system on the island that predated the invasion: Greek Cypriots were only entitled to vote for a Greek list of candidates to Parliament and Turkish Cypriots only for a Turkish list. However, following the invasion the Turkish list became defunct. Thus, the ECtHR found that: 'Consequently, the applicant, as a member of the Turkish-Cypriot community living in the government-controlled area of Cyprus, was completely deprived of any opportunity to express his opinion in the choice of the members of the House of Representatives of the country of which he is a national and where he has always lived. The Court considers that, in the light of the above circumstances, the very essence of the applicant's right to vote, as guaranteed by Art 3 of Protocol No. 1, was impaired. It follows that there has been a violation of that provision' (at paras 29–30).

[17] Elections Act 2022.

[18] See the comments of Lord Stephens with which the rest of the Supreme Court agreed in *R (on the application of Coughlan) v Minister for the Cabinet Office* [2022] UKSC 11 at para 51. That case was concerned with a challenge to the pilot voter identification scheme that preceded the new national requirement for voter identification.

[19] M Kennerich, *Report on Electoral Law and Electoral Administration in Europe* (Venice Commission, 2020) para 196.

C. The Right to Stand for Election

11.6 Any person who is not disqualified has the right to stand for election. (Those disqualified are listed in paragraph 6.16 above). In practice very few people are elected who are not endorsed as the candidate of a political party. Therefore, it is important that the law forbids discrimination by parties in the selection of their candidates. Paragraphs 11.18–11.21 below provide further detail about discriminatory selection procedures. Chapter 6 deals with selection arrangements generally, including forms of positive action that the law permits, for example, all women shortlists.

III. Discrimination in the Political Sphere

A. The Equality Act 2010

11.7 Discrimination in British politics is not an abstract matter. Colour bars, racism, sexual harassment and the underrepresentation of women and minority groups have all arisen and, in some cases, persist. The Equality Act 2010 bans political parties from engaging in unlawful discrimination against prospective and actual members. The 2010 Act also provides for positive action to promote underrepresented groups' access to legislative bodies (see Chapter 6).

11.8 The Equality Act 2010 defines several concepts of discrimination and renders them unlawful in particular relationships.[20] There are special provisions in the 2010 Act that affect people engaged in political activity. The paragraphs that follow set out the law so far as it is relevant to the political sphere.

B. Enforcement of Rights under the Equality Act 2010

i. Protected Characteristics and Individual Rights

11.9 Political parties are associations. The Equality Act 2010 prohibits discrimination by associations against members and guests on the grounds of age, disability, gender reassignment, pregnancy and maternity, race, religion or belief, sex or sexual orientation.[21] Nascent parties, or minor ones operating on the parish council level, with fewer than 25 members, are not subject to the 2010 Act's provisions prohibiting discrimination by associations.[22] Nevertheless, the prohibitions on discrimination in employment apply to them. Political parties are prohibited from discriminating against their employees, workers or corporate office holders by Part 5 of the Equality Act 2010.

[20] A detailed discussion of discrimination law and its fundamental concepts can be found in K Monaghan, *Monaghan on Equality Law*, 2nd edn (Oxford University Press, 2013).

[21] Equality Act 2010, s 101. The Act excludes the protected characteristic of marriage and civil partnership from the protections held by an association's members and guests: ibid s 100.

[22] ibid s 107.

11.10 Members, associates and guests (actual or prospective) may bring claims for breaches of the Equality Act 2010 by a political party in the county court. The time limit to do so is six months from the date of the discriminatory act or omission, though that primary limitation period may be extended by the court if it decides it is just and equitable to do so.[23] Employees may bring claims against their employers (whether individual MPs or peers or political organisations) in the employment tribunal. The time limit to do so in the employment tribunal is only three months, though that too can be extended on the same basis.[24]

ii. Enforcement by the Equality and Human Rights Commission

11.11 The EHRC has powers to take action to remedy discrimination. It is also responsible for issuing statutory codes of practice that must be taken into account by the courts when interpreting the Equality Act 2010.[25] To date, three statutory codes have been issued: a Code of Practice on Employment;[26] a Code of Practice on Equal Pay;[27] and a Code of Practice on Services, Public Functions and Associations.[28] The EHRC issued non-statutory guidance for political parties in 2018, 'The Equality Act 2010: A Guide for Political Parties'.

11.12 The EHRC's powers to enforce the 2010 Act include powers to undertake statutory investigations and inquiries into individuals and organisations, including political parties.[29] To date the EHRC has taken enforcement action against the British National Party (by litigation) and the Labour Party (through a statutory investigation).

11.13 How should statutory investigations into political parties be carried out in practice? The EHRC must have a reasonable suspicion that a breach of the 2010 Act has occurred, without which it will have no power to launch investigation proceedings.[30] The terms of reference for the investigation must be carefully drafted so that the reasonable suspicion, the allegations and the persons under investigation are all clearly and precisely framed.[31] The terms of reference should set out expressly the different units

[23] ibid s 118. The limitation period may also be extended to hear otherwise time-barred allegations which form part of a continuing act of discrimination, the last incident of which is within the statutory limitation period.

[24] ibid s 123. Note that claimants who wish to bring claims in the employment tribunal must (save for a few specific exceptions) take part in mandatory 'early conciliation' with Acas and obtain a certificate confirming they have done so before any claim is lodged. That means that a claimant must begin early conciliation before the three-month statutory time-limit has elapsed.

[25] Equality Act 2006, ss 14 and 15.

[26] Employment Statutory Code of Practice (EHRC, 2011).

[27] Equal Pay Statutory Code of Practice (EHRC, 2011).

[28] Services, Public Functions and Associations Statutory Code of Practice (EHRC, 2011).

[29] Pursuant to the Equality Act 2006.

[30] ibid s 20(2).

[31] See *R v Commission for Racial Equality, ex p Hillingdon LBC* [1982] AC 779 per Lord Diplock: '... the commission cannot "throw the book at him"; they cannot, without further particularisation of the kinds of acts of which he is suspected, tell him no more than that they believe that he may have done or may be doing some acts that are capable of amounting to unlawful discrimination under the Act ... or under some very broadly drafted sections of it ... if their real belief (which is a condition precedent to embarking upon a belief

and associations of the party that fall within the investigation's scope, as well as any officers of the party that are deemed to represent the party's interests as a whole (for example, the General Secretary or Chairman). The EHRC is required to give the person or entity under investigation two opportunities to make representations: first, during the course of the investigation; and,[32] second, on receipt of the EHRC's final report.[33] The EHRC has the power to compel people to provide information; if those people do not comply, it has the power to seek penal action against them in court.[34]

11.14 At the conclusion of the investigation the EHRC may decide to issue an unlawful act notice stating that the person or organisation under investigation has committed an act in contravention of the Equality Act 2010.[35] The unlawful act notice may require the person or organisation under investigation to draw up an action plan to avoid the sort of discrimination set out by the unlawful act notice.[36] The action plan must be approved by the EHRC. The EHRC is an organ of the state and any action it recommends must not interfere disproportionately with a political party's right to autonomy under Article 11 of the Convention.[37] The EHRC has the power to take further action in court to compel the party to comply with the action plan.

C. Prohibited Discrimination by Political Parties

i. *Admission to Membership*

11.15 Political parties must not decline to admit people as members on discriminatory grounds. A line of legal cases in the last century permitted Conservative Associations and Labour Clubs (and other political associations by analogy) to operate a 'colour bar' and exclude non-white people from membership. Mr Shah was born in India. He moved to London and worked in the Post Office. In 1966 he applied to join the East Ham South Conservative Club. But the club's committee did not want him. 'Is colour relevant?' asked one committee member. The chairman said: 'I regard it as relevant'. The committee was split: five against Mr Shah, five for him. The chairman had the casting vote. The club would not accept Mr Shah as a member. The Race Relations Board took his case to court. Eventually it reached the highest court: the House of Lords. There, the Law Lords decided that nothing in the law prohibited the club from discriminating against Mr Shah because of the colour of his skin.[38]

investigation at all) is confined to a belief that he may have done or may be doing only acts of one or more particular kinds that fall within the general definition of unlawful acts contained in some broadly drafted section'.

[32] Equality Act 2006, Sch 2, para 6(2).

[33] ibid s 20(4).

[34] ibid Sch 2, paras 9–14.

[35] ibid s 21.

[36] ibid s 22.

[37] See Ch 1 for further detail on the application of Art 11 ECHR to political parties.

[38] *Charter v Race Relations Board* [1973] AC 868 (HL). See, as other examples, *Dockers' Labour Club* [1976] AC 285 and *Hector v Smethwick Labour Club* (unreported, 29 November 1988) (CA).

11.16 The Equality Act 2010 forbids a political party from discriminating in the arrangements it makes for deciding whom to admit to membership, as to the terms on which it admits them, or by refusing applications for membership.[39] Registered political parties, unlike other types of association, are not allowed to restrict membership to people who share a particular protected characteristic.[40] For example, the ninth Constitution of the British National Party (BNP) restricted its membership strictly to 'a defined "racial group" this being "Indigenous Caucasian" and defined "ethnic groups" emanating from that race'. That was unlawful. Thus, parties that have as their principal aim the promotion of a particular protected group's rights must not restrict membership to that group alone (eg a party established to campaign for the rights of women cannot exclude men from membership).

11.17 The prohibition against discrimination in membership admissions also encompasses indirect discrimination. Generally applied admissions criteria that disadvantage protected groups will be unlawful unless the criteria can be objectively justified. It is not unlawful for a party merely to espouse discriminatory views, but the party may not require members to subscribe to those views as a condition of membership. The BNP's constitution included a rule barring 'non-indigenous' British people from that party's membership. The EHRC took enforcement action against the BNP. By the time the case reached a final hearing, the BNP had removed the offending rule from its constitution.[41] However, the party retained rules requiring members to pledge to reverse immigration to the UK and to restore and maintain by legal changes 'the Indigenous British as the overwhelming majority in the make-up of the population of and expression of culture in each part of our British Homeland'. The Court found that the BNP was likely to commit unlawful indirect discrimination by the operation of those pledge requirements and ordered the party to remove them from its constitution.[42]

ii. Discriminatory Selection Procedures

11.18 A party must not discriminate against its members by refusing to select them as candidates for election because of a protected characteristic (save in some exceptional circumstances provided for under the 2010 Act addressed in Chapter 6). That prohibition applies to all stages of a selection process from arranging a longlist to the party giving its final approval to a member's candidature.[43]

11.19 Political convenience provides no lawful justification for discriminatory candidate selections. A party must not decline to select a member to be its candidate on the basis that it perceives that another member, holding a different protected characteristic, might have a greater chance of securing the trust of voters and winning an election.

[39] Equality Act 2010, s 101(1).
[40] ibid Sch 16, para 1(5).
[41] 'The Equality Act 2010: A Guide for Political Parties' (EHRC, February 2018) at 17.
[42] *The Commission for Equality & Human Rights v Nicholas John Griffin* [2010] EWHC 3343 (Admin).
[43] Equality Act 2010, s 101. Note that a political party's selection of a candidate is not a conferment of an approval which is needed for, or which facilitates engagement in, a profession. Political parties are not

11.20 In the 1990s the Labour Party suspended several local party branches for three years following articles in the press alleging that local councillors of Pakistani origin, or associated with the Pakistani community, were helping Pakistani residents to jump the queue for housing grants. Mr Ahsan was Pakistani. He was an aspiring candidate for the 1997 general election. The Labour Party undertook a selection process in which the claimant was interviewed but not selected. The party instead selected a white man. The claimant brought a claim for race discrimination against the Labour Party, which was upheld in the employment tribunal and the Employment Appeal Tribunal.

11.21 When the case reached the Court of Appeal, Buxton LJ held that the Labour Party's wish not to have a candidate who would be seen to identify with the Pakistani community was a 'legitimate objective … provided that the perception that the problem was predominantly a Pakistani one was itself legitimate'; an objective would have been illegitimate if 'the judgment that the problems were particularly associated with the Pakistani community had been influenced at least in part by the racial make-up of that community'.[44] The House of Lords disagreed and overturned the judgment of the Court of Appeal. Lord Hoffmann, with whom all other Law Lords agreed, doubted that it was possible to form a view that a problem is 'associated with the Pakistani community' but reach that view uninfluenced by 'the racial make-up of that community'. The only meaning that could be ascribed to the Court of Appeal's distinction was that it would be acceptable for a political party to discriminate against a Pakistani candidate if it held no racist views about Pakistanis but thought that it was better not to have a Pakistani candidate because the electorate would identify 'the problem' with the Pakistani community. That was unacceptable and nothing more than an attempt to justify race discrimination with political expediency.[45]

iii. Expulsion and Access to Membership Benefits

11.22 It is unlawful for a political party to discriminate against a member or to victimise him[46] by refusing him access to a benefit, facility or service, by removing his membership or varying the terms of membership, or by subjecting him to any other detriment.[47] This prevents parties from expelling or suspending members on discriminatory grounds, or from refusing members entry to party meetings and annual conferences on such grounds.

qualification bodies certifying candidates to be politicians. That means that members wishing to challenge a discriminatory selection decision must do so in the county court and not the employment tribunal. See *Watt (formerly Carter) v Ahsan* [2007] UKHL 51, [2008] 1 AC 696, which considered materially similar antecedent legislation.

[44] *Carter v Ahsan* [2005] ICR 1817 (CA), para 93.

[45] *Watt (formerly Carter) v Ahsan* [2007] UKHL 51, [2008] 1 AC 696 at para 47.

[46] Victimisation has a particular legal meaning here: it is where person A subjects person B to a detriment because person B has made an allegation of discrimination, brought or given evidence in legal proceedings under the Equality Act 2010 or done anything else in connection with the Equality Act 2010, or because person A thinks person B has done so: Equality Act 2010, s 27.

[47] ibid s 101(2).

iv. *Harassment and Political Debate*

11.23 Parties, their employees and officers must not harass members.[48] Harassment is unwanted conduct related to a protected characteristic that has the purpose or effect of violating the target's dignity or creating an intimidating, hostile, degrading, humiliating or offensive environment for the target.[49] But harassment will only be established if it is objectively reasonable for the unwanted conduct to have created the forbidden environment, taking into account all the circumstances and the target's perception.[50] The words 'intimidating, hostile, degrading, humiliating or offensive' in the Equality Act 2010 are an important control to prevent trivial acts causing minor upsets being caught by the concept of harassment.[51] Democracy relies on pluralism.[52] Pluralism is a practical necessity where people hold inconsistent views about important matters;[53] and political parties are private organisations with 'an essential role in ensuring pluralism and the proper functioning of democracy'.[54]

11.24 *Fraser v UCU* provides an example of a claim for harassment failing in the context of political debate. The claimant complained that various anti-zionist motions at the University and College Union's annual congress amounted to unwanted conduct related to race that created the proscribed effect for him. Dismissing the claim for various reasons, the employment tribunal found that:

> we are quite clear that it would not be reasonable for it to have had such an effect ... the Claimant is a campaigner. He chooses to engage in the politics of the union in support of Israel and in opposition to activists for the Palestinian cause. When a rugby player takes the field he must accept his fair share of minor injuries ... Similarly, a political activist accepts the risk of being offended or hurt on occasions by things said or done by his opponents (who themselves take on a corresponding risk). These activities are not for everyone. Given his election to engage in, and persist with, a political debate which by its nature is bound to excite strong emotions, it would, we think, require special circumstances to justify a finding that such involvement had resulted in harassment.[55]

11.25 There is no prohibition against political associations committing harassment of their *members* related to the protected characteristics of religion or belief or sexual orientation (see paragraph 11.59 below).[56] The prohibition *does* apply when political parties are acting as employers, service providers or companies.

[48] ibid s 101(4), (5), (6), (7).
[49] ibid s 26.
[50] ibid s 26(4).
[51] *Grant v HM Land Registry* [2011] EWCA Civ 769 at para 47. See, by analogy, *Richmond Pharmacology Ltd v Dhaliwal* [2009] ICR 724 at para 22; it is important not to encourage a culture of hypersensitivity in political parties in respect of every unfortunate phrase.
[52] See, inter alia, *United Communist Party of Turkey v Turkey* (1998) 26 EHRR 121; *Handyside v United Kingdom* (1979–80) 1 EHRR 737; *Castells v Spain* (1992) 14 EHRR 445.
[53] eg *Trimingham v Associated Newspapers* [2012] 4 All ER 717 at para 265.
[54] eg *United Communist Party of Turkey* (1998) 26 EHRR 121.
[55] *Fraser v UCU* Employment Tribunal Case 2203290/2011.
[56] Equality Act 2010, s 103.

v. *Sexual Harassment*

11.26 The prohibition against sexual harassment applies to political parties in their role as membership associations and employers. Reports of sexual harassment in political life are common.[57] Sexual harassment is defined in two ways under the 2010 Act and applies irrespective of the sex of the perpetrator or target (the following examples refer to a female target):

i. A engages in unwanted conduct of a sexual nature that has the forbidden purpose or effect on B, described at paragraph 11.23 above. This protects a person from suffering unwanted sexual advances; but it also protects her from unwanted conduct of a sexual nature that is not targeted at her, for example, the putting up of salacious calendars in her place of work or sexual advances to another person in her presence.
ii. The second definition protects person B from being subjected to retaliation for rebuffing or accepting a sexual advance. The definition is: where A or another person engages in unwanted conduct of a sexual nature or that is related to gender reassignment or sex, and that conduct has the forbidden purpose described above and because of B's rejection of or submission to the conduct, A treats B less favourably than A would treat B if B had not rejected or submitted to the conduct.

11.27 The prohibition against sexual harassment also applies to any individual politician who employs his or her own staff. In 2021 an employment tribunal sitting in London ordered a (now former) MP to pay over £400,000 in compensation for sexual harassment of his employee that comprised serious findings of physical and emotional unwanted conduct related to her sex, and of a sexual nature.[58]

vi. *Non-members*

11.28 The Equality Act 2010's prohibitions apply similarly to the treatment of associates and guests.[59] In the case of the latter, the most obvious area of practical application will be at annual party conferences or at ordinary party meetings where guests are invited to speak.

vii. *Disciplinary Processes and Complaints Handling*

11.29 Unlawful indirect discrimination may arise in a political party's handling of disciplinary complaints. (Chapter 12, Section III addresses disciplinary procedures in

[57] 'The nature and extent of the sexual harassment of staff alleged to be happening in the House of Commons, together with descriptions of the lack of support for those affected and of the inadequate procedures in place to deal with it, paint a bleak picture': per Dame Laura Cox DBE, 'The Bullying and Harassment of House of Commons Staff: Independent Inquiry Report' (15 October 2018) at para 190. See Chapter 13 for further detail about the standards and rules of conduct that apply to Members of Parliament and Members of the House of Lords.

[58] *Ms A v Mr Hill* Employment Tribunal Case 2203040/2019.

[59] Equality Act 2010, s 102.

political parties generally.) The EHRC identified two apparently discriminatory practices in its Final Report into alleged antisemitism in the Labour Party. One was a lack of specific training for staff on handling antisemitism complaints. The EHRC concluded that the lack of such specific training amounted to indirect discrimination because:

> the failure to provide adequate training to those involved in antisemitism complaints is relevant to every antisemitism complaint, whether or not the complainant is Jewish. However, the practice of allowing untrained individuals to make important decisions in, and decide the outcome of, antisemitism complaints puts Jewish members at a particular disadvantage because they are more likely to experience antisemitism and complain about it. As we explain above, this is bound to have had a negative effect on the quality of antisemitism complaints handling.[60]

The EHRC's conclusion in this case (that a lack of training amounts to indirect discrimination) appears to contradict the terms of its own public guidance: that equality training is a means to avoid discrimination but a failure to supply it is not in itself discriminatory.[61] Its conclusions about the Labour Party's lack of complaint-specific training suggest that most political parties are likely to be practising unlawful indirect discrimination, as they typically do not have specific training about handling particular types of discrimination complaints. If correct, the EHRC's finding implicitly requires that political parties devote more resources to providing complaints handling training.

11.30 Another apparently discriminatory practice identified by the EHRC relates to political interference in disciplinary cases amounting to unjustified (and therefore unlawful) indirect discrimination. The EHRC defined political interference as 'people influencing decision-making or taking decisions in complaints outside of established processes'.[62] The EHRC concluded that this constituted unlawful indirect discrimination because

> these practices or policies put the person making an antisemitism complaint at a disadvantage, because they gave rise to a reasonable perception of different and detrimental treatment ... Jewish members are proportionately more likely than non-Jewish members to make a complaint about antisemitism. Consequently, the practice of political interference in antisemitism complaints and in 'politically sensitive' complaints generally put Jewish members at a particular disadvantage compared to non-Jewish members.[63]

This finding by the EHRC is not foreshadowed in any relevant jurisprudence. Political parties are by their nature political organisations. The EHRC's finding here appears to ignore the overlapping disciplinary regimes of party membership and of the party whip, the latter being the exclusive preserve of politicians and the leadership. Due respect should be afforded to the EHRC's important work. Yet the findings described in this and the previous paragraph are difficult to square with the current state of the law. Political parties would be wise to focus on the current terms of the law set out in jurisprudence and the Equality Act 2010 itself until these matters receive judicial analysis.

[60] EHRC, 'Final Report: Investigation into antisemitism in the Labour Party' at 95.

[61] See by way of example 'The Equality Act 2010: A Guide for Political Parties' (EHRC, February 2018): 'Political parties can take steps to avoid discrimination by ... providing equality and diversity training to anyone who acts on behalf of the party'.

[62] EHRC, 'Final Report: Investigation into antisemitism in the Labour Party' at 42.

[63] ibid 55.

viii. Reasonable Adjustments for Disabled People

11.31 Political parties are under a duty to make reasonable adjustments for disabled members, guests and prospective members and guests. A failure to comply with that duty will constitute unlawful discrimination under the Equality Act 2010.[64] The duty is anticipatory, which means that political parties must anticipate the needs of those disabled people and make appropriate reasonable adjustments for them.[65] That requires parties to consider in advance barriers that preclude disabled members from enjoying their membership rights and to take positive steps to remove those barriers. The duty is only to take *reasonable* steps; parties are not under an obligation to take all steps or even steps preferred by those who need them. Nor is the party required to take a step that would fundamentally alter its nature as a political party or the nature of the benefits associated with membership.[66] What constitutes a reasonable step will depend on the circumstances and context at hand. Parties must not place the costs of making reasonable adjustments on the disabled person(s) who require them.[67] The EHRC's 'The Equality Act 2010: A Guide for Political Parties' suggests that the following factors will affect the reasonableness of any adjustment a party may need to make:

i. whether particular steps would be effective in overcoming the disadvantage that disabled people face;
ii. the extent to which it is practicable for the political party to make changes;
iii. the financial and other costs of making the adjustment;
iv. the extent of any disruption making the changes would cause;
v. the extent of the political party's financial and other resources;
vi. the amount of resources already spent on making adjustments;
vii. the availability of financial or other assistance.

a. General Policies and Practices

11.32 The duty to make adjustments has three 'requirements'. The first requirement is to make adjustments to a provision, criterion or practice that puts disabled people at a substantial disadvantage compared to non-disabled people in relation to accessing a benefit, facility or service; retaining membership rights (or avoiding having them varied); and being admitted to membership or being invited as a guest.[68] Once the duty has been triggered, the duty is to make reasonable adjustments to the provision, criterion or practice. This first requirement would apply, among other things, to arrangements made for selection meetings and voting. Some examples:

i. A local party has a practice that members must be present in person at a candidate selection meeting and vote in writing by secret ballot to cast their votes. This is likely to disadvantage disabled members who are unable to attend the meeting in person or who are unable to write without difficulty. The party has a duty to

[64] Equality Act 2010, ss 21 and 103(1).
[65] ibid Sch 15, para 2; Explanatory Notes, para 902.
[66] ibid Sch 15, para 7.
[67] ibid s 20(7).
[68] ibid Sch 15, para 4.

consider how to adjust the policy so that those disadvantages are alleviated (eg by letting a disabled member vote by proxy or online).

ii. The EHRC's 'The Equality Act 2010: A Guide for Political Parties' has the following example: 'a political party normally allows each prospective candidate five minutes to speak at selection meetings. One of the candidates has a speech impairment and is allowed extra time'.

iii. A party has a policy that members must be suspended if they use profane or abusive language online. A member suffers from severe depression and anxiety that means he is unable to regulate his emotions well. He uses offensive and profane language on social media during an argument with another social media user. The party should consider whether to adjust the disciplinary policy so that a less severe sanction is imposed for his conduct.

b. Physical Features

11.33 The second requirement is to make adjustments to physical features that put disabled people at a substantial disadvantage (compared to non-disabled people) in relation to accessing a benefit, facility or service, or being admitted to membership or invited as a guest. Where there is such a physical feature, the party has a duty to do one of two things.[69] It must take reasonable steps either to avoid the disadvantage, or to adopt a reasonable *alternative* method of affording access to the benefit, facility or service or of admitting persons to membership or inviting persons as guests.[70]

11.34 This second requirement of the duty to make reasonable adjustments is especially relevant to disabled members and guests who want to access party meetings. The steps that it is reasonable for a party to take will depend on the type and the location of the meeting:

i. **National and regional party meetings**: where meetings are held on the party's own premises (for example, the national party's headquarters), the party will be expected to have anticipated any barriers to access and to have removed them, or to have changed the location of the meeting to an accessible location. The EHRC's 'The Equality Act 2010: A Guide for Political Parties' sets out the following example, which reflects the nature of the duty and the control a party will have over its own premises: 'A regional branch meets every month in the party HQ building. There are stairs at the entrance and despite the reasonable adjustment duty being anticipatory, no ramp has been installed. A new member who is a wheelchair user wants to become active in the branch and attend the meetings. The branch arranges for a ramp to be built at the entrance to the building so the new member can attend branch meetings. They also undertake an audit of the whole building to ensure any other reasonable adjustments are made. As a result they also install an accessible toilet and improve the building's signage'.[71]

[69] ibid s 20(4).
[70] ibid Sch 15, para 3.
[71] 'The Equality Act 2010: A Guide for Political Parties' (EHRC, February 2018) at 21.

ii. **Local party meetings**: local parties, by contrast, will frequently meet in premises that are not their own which they have hired for several hours. Local parties should ensure that these meetings take place in locations that are accessible to disabled people with mobility impairments. For example, it is likely to be reasonable to hold meetings on the ground floor of a local church rather than on an upper floor requiring the use of stairs.[72]

iii. **Meetings in private homes**: sometimes, local party meetings may take place in members' own homes; this is a common practice for small executive committees of local parties, as well as members canvassing on polling day when members often volunteer their homes to be a base for local canvassers. The Equality Act 2010 expressly does *not* require a member or associate in whose house meetings of the party take place to make adjustments to a physical feature of the house.[73] (Nevertheless, local parties will want to make sure that meetings are held in accessible locations for when disabled members wish to attend.)

c. Physical Aids

11.35 The third requirement of the duty to make reasonable adjustments concerns the provision of physical aids. Where a disabled person would, but for the provision of an auxiliary aid, be put at a substantial disadvantage in relation to a relevant matter[74] in comparison with persons who are not disabled, the party must take reasonable steps to provide the auxiliary aid. The EHRC's 'The Equality Act 2010: A Guide for Political Parties' provides the following example in respect of party conferences:

> the venue where the party holds its annual conference is inaccessible to some disabled people. When members register to attend the conference they are asked if they require any additional support or assistance. A disabled member asks for assistance to help them move around the conference venue and fringe meetings. Staff are allocated to provide assistance with guiding. This would be an additional service.[75]

11.36 Parties must ensure that information is provided to members, guests and associates (and prospective members and guests) in an accessible format as reasonable in the circumstances. This requires parties to provide information, for example in large print to members who cannot read normal sized text easily.

11.37 Candidates for public elections are subject to limits imposed by the Representation of the People Act 1983 on the amounts of money they may spend in their election campaigns. Expenditure that is reasonably attributable to a candidate's disability does not count towards the expenditure limit, to the extent that those expenses are reasonably incurred.[76]

[72] See by analogy the Explanatory Notes to the Equality Act 2010 at para 902.

[73] Equality Act 2010, Sch 15, para 8. Nevertheless, a party that consistently held meetings in a house that was inaccessible would risk committing indirect discrimination against its disabled members.

[74] The relevant matters are: accessing a benefit, facility or service; retaining membership rights or avoiding having them varied; and being admitted to membership or being invited as a guest.

[75] 'The Equality Act 2010: A Guide for Political Parties' (EHRC, February 2018) at 20.

[76] Representation of the People Act 1983, Sch 4, para 7A. For PPERA's similar provision, see 10.11 iii.

D. Discrimination against Political Office Holders

i. Political Offices

11.38 The Equality Act 2010's protections do not extend to the *election* of a person to a personal office.[77] So the appointment by election of a General Secretary, Chairman, President or Board/Executive Committee officer falls outside the scope of the Equality Act 2010. If party officers are employed in those positions then their recruitment will instead fall within the Act's protections for employees.[78]

11.39 The 2010 Act's prohibitions against discrimination do not apply to the election or appointment of a political office, for example, the leader of a political party, nor to the Leader of the Opposition's appointment of the Opposition Chief Whip, nor to the elevation of a person to the House of Lords. The Act defines political offices exhaustively: it includes 'an office of a registered political party',[79] as well as a multitude of political posts including various ministerial, mayoral and devolved government offices.[80] The Act does not define further the term 'office' of a registered political party, but it is presumably referring to party officers registered pursuant to the Political Parties, Elections and Referendums Act 2000, ie the party leader and party treasurers, nominating and campaigning officers.[81] A life peerage is not an office protected by the Equality Act 2010 either. The appointment of a life peer falls outside the Act's scope.[82] Whether a party's decision not to recommend a member for a life peerage for discriminatory reasons would attract the Act's protection is unclear, given the difficulties inherent in obtaining judicial scrutiny of purely political acts. In principle, though, such a decision, taken on prohibited grounds, would constitute unlawful conduct under Part 7 of the Equality Act 2010.

ii. Discrimination against Councillors and Mayors by Local Authorities

11.40 A local authority must not discriminate against, or harass, its local councillors in relation to their official business, either in the way the authority gives them access (or refuses access) to training or receiving any other facility or by subjecting them to any other detriment.[83] Local authorities have a duty to make reasonable adjustments for disabled council members.[84]

11.41 Local councils have the power to appoint councillors to committees and other official posts, including by nominating them to bodies associated with the local authority (eg a maintained school's board of governors). A mere failure to appoint

[77] Equality Act 2010, s 52(5).
[78] ibid Sch 6, para 1.
[79] ibid Sch 6, para 2.
[80] ibid Sch 6, para 2.
[81] PPERA 2000, ss 24 and 25.
[82] Equality Act 2010, Sch 6, para 3.
[83] ibid s 58(1) and (3).
[84] ibid s 58(6).

a council member to an office or committee of the local council will not amount to discrimination.[85] Nor will a failure to appoint, or to nominate for appointment, a council member to a body over which the local authority has a power of appointment.

E. Positive Action

11.42 The Equality Act 2010 allows for positive action to reduce inequality in prescribed circumstances. Those statutory provisions are particularly important for attempts to increase the representation of minority groups in political activity. Before 1979, female parliamentary candidates accounted for, at the very most, 10 per cent of candidates fielded in any general election. By the 2005 general election men still accounted for 80 per cent of parliamentary candidates.[86] By 2023 only a third of MPs were women. Specific provisions in the Equality Act 2010 permit political parties to use all-female shortlists, and reserve places for members from other protected groups, when selecting who should be the party's candidates in public elections. Those provisions apply only in certain circumstances, which are addressed in detail in Chapter 6. In short: (i) those protected groups must be underrepresented among the party's cohort of legislators in the legislative body concerned; and (ii) it must be proportionate to use 'positive action' selection arrangements to reduce inequality in the party's representation in that particular legislative body.[87] (This second requirement of proportionality is not relevant to all-women shortlists.)

11.43 The Equality Act 2010 also has general provisions about positive action. The provisions apply if an organisation reasonably thinks that people who share a protected characteristic suffer disadvantage connected to the characteristic, or people of a particular protected characteristic have different needs to people without the characteristic, or participation in an activity by people sharing a protected characteristic is disproportionately low.[88] In that case, a political party will be allowed to take any action to enable or encourage such people to overcome or minimise that disadvantage, to meet those needs or to enable them to participate in the relevant activity, so long as the means the party uses to do so are proportionate.[89] Whether the means are proportionate depends, among other things, on the seriousness of the relevant disadvantage, the extremity of need or under-representation and the availability of other means to counter them.[90] A party must consider whether the action it proposes to take is reasonably necessary to achieve the relevant aims and whether the aims could be achieved effectively by other means that do not entail treating one protected group more favourably than another.

[85] ibid s 58(4).

[86] C Watson, 'House of Commons trends: How many women candidates become MPs?' (House of Commons Library, 30 October 2020).

[87] For an example of sex discrimination arising from the use of an all-women shortlist that predates the Equality Act 2010, see *Jepson v The Labour Party* [1996] IRLR 116.

[88] A 'reasonable belief' requires some indication or evidence to show that one of the statutory conditions applies. But it does not require sophisticated statistical data or research: see the Services, Public Functions and Associations Statutory Code of Practice (EHRC, 2011) at para 10.12.

[89] Equality Act 2010, s 158.

[90] ibid Explanatory Notes, para 512.

Note that these general positive action provisions do not apply to candidate shortlisting and selection arrangements, positive action in respect of which is only permitted by the Equality Act 2010, section 104.[91]

11.44 The general positive action provisions will be especially useful to parties that wish to encourage underrepresented groups to take part in campaigning for the party or to manage its affairs. The Act would permit parties to hold additional training for protected groups or to set up forums or committees for them, among other things. The EHRC statutory Code of Practice sets out that positive action can include providing additional or bespoke services, separate facilities, accelerated access to services, targeting resources or induction or training opportunities to benefit a particular disadvantaged group.[92] The EHRC's 'The Equality Act 2010: A Guide for Political Parties' gives the following example of what the provisions permit:

> A party carried out a survey of the diversity of their members and interviewed party officials and equality organisations about how to improve diversity. The research identified more limited participation of LGBT members in the party structures compared to other groups. The party decided to take positive action to encourage and support LGBT members to get involved in committees, groups, campaigning activities and conferences. The action was specifically directed at LGBT members and included: training, mentoring schemes, targeted invitations to become active in the party structures and paid internships.[93]

F. Liability of Political Parties for Discrimination by Members

11.45 Political parties operate by delegating management and campaigning activities to employees, members and elected representatives. That means that a great number of volunteer activists may be carrying out the party's functions. The Equality Act 2010 renders employers liable for discriminatory acts carried out by their employees done in the course of employment. The Act also renders political parties responsible for unlawful discrimination done by members (who are not also employees) acting as their legal agents.

i. Legal Agency

11.46 Legal agency arises from an agreement that one person (the agent) should act on behalf of another (the principal). A long-standing and essential element of agency is that the agent has the power to affect the principal's relationship with third parties.[94] Generally, two crucial elements must be present to establish an agency relationship: a person must be carrying out authorised functions; and they must have some authority to represent the principal in relation to third parties. The starting point for the purposes

[91] ibid s 158(4)(b), (5).
[92] Services, Public Functions and Associations Statutory Code of Practice (EHRC, 2011) para 10.5.
[93] 'The Equality Act 2010: A Guide for Political Parties' (EHRC, February 2018) at 12–13.
[94] *Bowstead and Reynolds on Agency*, 23rd edn (Sweet & Maxwell, 2024) Ch 1, Art 1, para 1-001; *Chitty on Contracts*, 33rd edn (Sweet & Maxwell, 2018) Vol II, Ch 31 'Agency', para 31-001.

of the Equality Act 2010 is that 'the principal will be liable wherever the agent discriminates in the course of carrying out the functions he is authorised to do'.[95] The Court of Appeal agreed in *Nailard v Unite the Union* that 'it is inherent in the principal/agent relationship that the agent be in a position to affect the principal's legal relationship with third parties'.[96] The agent must, therefore, be 'standing in the shoes of [the principal] in relation to independent third parties' for the principal to be bound.[97] The EHRC has produced guidance about the Equality Act which reflects this basic meaning of agency. The guidance states that an agent is someone the organisation has instructed to do something on its behalf.[98] The guidance makes clear that a person will not be acting as an agent where they have:

> acted outside the scope of their authority (in other words, that they did something so different from what the service provider asked them to do that they could no longer be thought of as acting on the service provider's behalf).[99]

ii. Social Media Posts by Party Members

11.47 It would be unfair and impractical for a political party to be responsible in law for the social media posts of ordinary members made in a personal capacity. It is equally plain that responsibility for posts made by an elected representative of the party, in the course of his authorised functions on behalf of the party, should fall at the party's door. A grey area arises in respect of elected party representatives who make discriminatory social media posts in their own time. The EHRC has had cause to consider that scenario in its investigation into alleged antisemitism in the Labour Party. The EHRC found a local councillor guilty of race-related harassment on social media, for which it held the Labour Party legally responsible. The EHRC concluded that her conduct amounted to discrimination by the Labour Party because she was a legal agent of the party such that the party was legally responsible for her Facebook posts. The basis for that conclusion about legal agency was that her Facebook 'profile identified her as a "Labour Party member/councillor for Corbyn" and her profile picture, at least for part of the period covered by the posts above, included the words "Jeremy Corbyn Keep the Faith"'. To make at least one of the posts above, the councillor had used a Facebook page named after herself.

11.48 Some of the EHRC's conclusions about legal agency in this area appear contrary to the state of the law set out by the senior courts (and indeed by the EHRC's own published guidance in some respects). The EHRC's analysis disproportionately focuses on the contents of the social media publication itself (for example, a councillor's profile photo or description) rather than asking and answering the question that is in fact

[95] *Ministry of Defence v Kemeh* [2014] IRLR 377 at para 11, *Unite the Union v Nailard* [2018] EWCA Civ 1203, [2018] IRLR 730 at para 42.

[96] *Unite the Union v Nailard* [2018] EWCA Civ 1203, [2018] IRLR 730 at para 43.

[97] *Ministry of Defence v Kemeh* [2014] IRLR 377 at para 44.

[98] 'Your rights to equality as a member, associate member or guest of an association, club or society' (EHRC, 2015) at 35.

[99] ibid at 36.

determinative: whether the councillor can properly be held to be standing in the shoes of the political party in respect of others when the post was made. If the EHRC's conclusion about legal agency were correct it would inevitably increase the risk of a party being held liable for a councillor's discriminatory social media posts. It would also mean that parties must take much greater steps to control the discourse of many thousands of members online, placing political parties in the position of regulating political discourse on social media. That, however, is neither achievable nor the proper role of a political party in our democratic and parliamentary system.

IV. Political Belief

A. Protected Beliefs

11.49 The Equality Act 2010 prohibits discrimination on the ground of philosophical belief in the context of employment, in the provision of services and in the context of associations (among other circumstances). A political belief may be a species of philosophical belief for the purposes of Article 9 ECHR and section 10 of the Equality Act 2010. Not all political beliefs qualify for protection. The protections against detriment for holding a protected belief are especially important to prevent:

i. the abuse or exclusion by political parties of their members of prospective members because of those members' beliefs;
ii. the dismissal or detrimental treatment of employees and workers by their employers because of their political belief or political affiliation.

11.50 A protected belief under section 10 of the Equality Act 2010 is to be broadly construed in line with Article 9 ECHR[100] and, for expediency, the two are taken together here. In summary, a belief will only fall within the scope of the Equality Act 2010's protection if it satisfies the following criteria (which have come to be known widely as the Grainger criteria):

i. The belief must be genuinely held;
ii. It must be a belief and not an opinion or viewpoint based on the present state of information available;
iii. It must be a belief as to a weighty and substantial aspect of human life and behaviour.
iv. It must attain a certain level of cogency, seriousness, cohesion and importance.
v. It must be worthy of respect in a democratic society, be not incompatible with human dignity and not conflict with the fundamental rights of others.[101]

11.51 Whether a belief meets the Grainger criteria is a question for the courts. The question whether a belief is 'valid' or 'correct' has no part to play in the test

[100] See the Equality Act 2010, Explanatory Notes, paras 51–53.
[101] *Grainger plc & Others v Nicholson* [2010] IRLR 4 at para 24.

the courts must apply.[102] The state must maintain neutrality between competing beliefs and refrain from expressing any view as to whether a particular belief is more acceptable than another, while ensuring that groups opposed to one another tolerate each other.[103] The bar for a belief to come within the scope of protection is a low one.[104]

11.52 That a belief is deeply offensive to many, or shocking, does not alone deprive it of legal protection. A free and plural society 'must expect to tolerate all sorts of views which many, even most, find completely unacceptable'.[105] The fifth limb of the Grainger criteria has received a great deal of attention in jurisprudence, especially in respect of beliefs about political issues. Its limits were reviewed by the Employment Appeal Tribunal in the case of *Forstater v CGI Europe and Others*.[106] That case addressed whether a gender critical belief – that sex is biologically immutable, a material reality and cannot change – was protected. The EAT noted that 'to maintain the plurality that is the hallmark of a functioning democracy, the range of beliefs and convictions that must be tolerated is very broad'.[107]

11.53 Examples of political beliefs that judges have decided are protected under Article 9 ECHR/section 10 of the Equality Act 2010 include: a belief in left-wing democratic socialism,[108] socialism, Marxism and communism; anti-zionism, free-market capitalism;[109] a belief in anthropogenic climate change,[110] and pacifism.[111] Mere support for a particular political party does not in itself satisfy the Grainger criteria and does not amount to a protected belief.

11.54 Issue-based political beliefs that fall for protection include a belief that sex is immutable and a material reality,[112] a fervent belief against fox-hunting,[113] the belief that public service broadcasting has a higher purpose of promoting cultural interchange and social cohesion;[114] a belief that same-sex relationships are sinful;[115] a belief that abortion is wrong;[116] and principled opposition to military service.[117]

[102] eg *R (Williamson) v Secretary of State for Education and Employment* [2005] 2 AC 246; *Forstater v CGD Europe and Others* [2022] ICR 1 (EAT) at para 55.

[103] See *Metropolitan Church of Bessarabia v Moldova* (2002) 35 EHRR 13 at paras 115 and 116; *Forstater v CGD Europe* at para 55(c).

[104] *R (Williamson) v Secretary of State of Education and Employment; Harron v Chief Constable of Dorset Police* [2016] IRLR 481 (EAT); *Gray v Mulberry Co (Design) Ltd* [2020] ICR 715 (CA).

[105] eg *R (Williamson)* at para 77.

[106] *Forstater v CGD Europe and Others* [2022] ICR 1 (EAT).

[107] At para 59.

[108] *General Municipal and Boilermakers Union v Henderson* [2015] IRLR 451.

[109] *Grainger plc v Nicholson* [2010] 2 All ER 253, [2010] ICR 360.

[110] ibid.

[111] *Arrowsmith v the United Kingdom* (1981) 3 EHRR 218 para 69.

[112] *Forstater v CGD Europe* [2022] ICR 1.

[113] *Hashman v Milton Park (Dorset) Ltd t/a Orchard Park* Employment Tribunal Case 3105555/09.

[114] *Maistry v BBC* Employment Tribunal Case 1313142/10.

[115] *Eweida and Others v UK* (2013) 57 EHRR 8.

[116] *Grimmark v Sweden* (2020) Application no 43726/17.

[117] *Bayatyan v Armenia* (2012) 54 EHRR 15.

11.55 Examples of beliefs that have fallen outside protection include those that are not worthy of respect in a democratic society, for example Nazism or beliefs akin to totalitarianism;[118] or those that involve hate towards a protected group of people, for example, fundamental antipathy towards gay people.[119] Other beliefs have fallen outside protection because they are properly not philosophical beliefs but opinions, for example, a belief in poppy-wearing associated with Remembrance Sunday;[120] an emotional attachment to Israel.[121]

B. Discrimination within Political Parties

11.56 A party is prohibited from discriminating against a person by refusing their application for membership.[122] Political parties will not fall foul of that prohibition if they refuse admission to a person because of his previous support for a rival political party. Mere support for a political party does not amount to a protected belief under section 10 of the Equality Act 2010. So, the Green Party would not contravene the Act by refusing to admit a person because he had previously supported the Conservative Party.

11.57 A core aspect of the representative democratic system is political parties winning elections on shared political manifestos. The prohibition against discrimination under the Equality Act 2010 must be construed concordantly with a political party's right of freedom of association under Article 11 ECHR;[123] a political party must have the right to exclude people from membership who do not share its core political philosophy. To find otherwise would serve to permit political entryism – for instance, if the Conservative Party was obliged by the operation of the Equality Act 2010 to accept members who were committed communists. The degree to which Article 11 may modify section 101(c) of the Equality Act 2010 will depend on the values of the political party concerned and the belief in question. For example, it is very unlikely that a mainstream party would act lawfully if it were to reject an application for membership because the person applying holds a belief in ethical veganism, or gender-critical beliefs. But some single-issue beliefs may offend a party's core values to such an extent that the refusal to admit a person because he holds that belief will be lawful.

11.58 The prohibition against harassment under the Equality Act 2010 does not apply to the protected characteristic of religion or philosophical belief (or sexual

[118] eg *Forstater*.

[119] *Ellis v Parmagan Ltd* Employment Tribunal Case 1603027/13. In that case the claimant described his belief to be that homosexuality is contrary to nature and the teaching of the Bible and is a corrosive force in society. The employment tribunal found that his true belief was actually simply antipathy towards gay people per se, so the belief was not protected. This must be contrasted with truly held religious beliefs that homosexual relationships are sinful and should not be promoted; however offensive that belief may be to many, it appears to be protected: see, for example, *Lee v Ashers Baking Co Ltd and Others* [2018] UKSC 49, [2020] AC 413 (SC).

[120] *Lisk v Shield Guardian Co Ltd and Others* Employment Tribunal Case 3300873/11.

[121] *Fraser v University & College Union* Employment Tribunal Case 2203290/2011.

[122] Equality Act 2010, s 101(1)(c).

[123] Human Rights Act 1998, ss 3 and 6.

orientation).[124] In many scenarios this exception will be irrelevant; detrimental treatment otherwise capable of meeting the legal definition of harassment may well also amount to direct discrimination. The effect of the exemption does have the curious consequence, however, that unwanted conduct related to a political belief is permitted in political parties. Thus, by way of example, the 2010 Act would not prohibit a local party chair from making derogatory or exclusionary comments about those of a political ideology generally (eg 'I hate Trots'[125] or 'we need to get the Terfs[126] out') though if the party developed a repeated practice of accepting such slurs that may amount to unjustified indirect discrimination. Nor would the 2010 Act prohibit a party chair from making derogatory comments about gay people in general at a party meeting. Many people will consider this exception to be entirely unjustified and inexplicable. Derogatory comments made to or about a specific gay person are nevertheless likely to amount to direct discrimination in contravention of section 13 of the Equality Act 2010.[127]

C. Dismissal from Employment

i. Discrimination under the Equality Act 2010

11.59 Discrimination by employers against employees because of the latter's political beliefs is prohibited by Part 5 of the Equality Act 2010.[128] The prohibition encapsulates direct discrimination, indirect discrimination, harassment and victimisation. A dismissal will be unlawful under the Equality Act 2010 if it amounts to discrimination because of philosophical belief. So far as direct discrimination is concerned, the key question (as ever) will be whether the belief has had a material influence on the mind of the person dismissing the employee in question. Where the reason for the dismissal is predicated on misconduct arising from holding the protected belief, the usual less favourable treatment comparison exercise is likely to be redundant and the question will be what the reason for the treatment was, bearing in mind there may be more than one reason. This is because, where a tribunal has identified a misconduct reason for the dismissal, to ask whether another person with the same unmanageable conduct would have been dismissed in the circumstances suggested involves a meaningless comparison that risks producing the wrong answer. Further, one must take care not to fall into the trap of confusing the employer's reasons for treating the employee as it did with the employee's reasons for acting as he did.[129]

[124] Equality Act 2010, s 103(2)(a).

[125] A derogatory term used for leftists (ie 'Trotskyists').

[126] A term used to describe gender-critical feminists which is considered by many to be a slur (ie 'trans-exclusionary radical feminists').

[127] Note that the exemption does not apply to the protected characteristic of gender reassignment or sex, only sexual orientation. This is (curiously) an example of the legal protections for gay people being less stringent than for transgender people. One explanation for the Equality Act 2010's exemption of sexual orientation from harassment under Part 7 of the Act is that, at the time the Bill was introduced in Parliament, same-sex marriage was not yet legal. It is possible that the drafters of the Act did not want to attract opposition to the Bill from those who opposed same-sex marriage, the prospect of which was controversial at the time. The subsequent legalisation of same-sex marriage removes that rationale for the Act's exemption of sexual orientation.

[128] Equality Act 2010, ss 39, 40.

[129] See *GMB Union v Henderson* UKEAT/0073/14/DM, citing *London Borough of Islington v Ladele* [2009] IRLR 154.

11.60 In *Forstater v CGD Europe and Others*, Ms Forstater complained that her employer had failed to renew her contract because of her gender-critical beliefs that she had expressed in various tweets. The employment tribunal concluded that her tweets were part of the reason why she was not offered employment and, therefore, her protected belief was a substantial (ie more than trivial) part of the reason for the failure to employ her.[130]

11.61 In *Henderson v The General Municipal and Boilermakers Union*,[131] Mr Henderson, a regional organiser for his employer trade union, claimed the union had committed discrimination by dismissing him for holding left-wing, democratic socialist beliefs. Mr Henderson's job included undertaking political work as part of the trade union's political efforts on behalf of the Labour Party. The history of the case starts with a strike by House of Commons staff in 2011. The striking staff were GMB members. The strike vote included a provision that Labour MPs should not cross the picket line. The tribunal found that the claimant publicised the strike to the media, stating that Labour MPs were expected to avoid crossing the picket line. The picket was publicised by journalists including on *Sky News*. The Leader of the Labour Party, then Ed Miliband, was given a hard time in the House of Commons chamber during Prime Minister's Questions by David Cameron who suggested that he was controlled by the trade unions. The claimant complained that, after that, Mr Miliband's office complained to the GMB general secretary, who phoned him up and shouted at him, telling him that he was too left wing. Thereafter, the claimant complained that he was subjected to a campaign of bullying by people within the union and the Labour Party. The tribunal identified a lengthy series of events during which the claimant's relationship with his employer and the local Labour Party became fraught. During the course of those events the claimant was not permitted to stand as a Labour Party council candidate. The claimant complained of collusion between Labour Party politicians and his employer, alleging that 'extreme right-wing elements' in both the union and the Labour Party colluded to prevent a 'left-wing unionist and a Labour Party activist from a working-class background' from progressing in the Labour movement. Eventually, the claimant was dismissed from his employment for gross misconduct, namely, for challenging the authority of his line management and the trade union's regional secretary and making serious allegations of collusion between the GMB and the Labour Party.

11.62 At trial, the employment tribunal found that Mr Henderson had been treated less favourably by the GMB and that a substantial part of the reason for his dismissal was because of his philosophical belief in left-wing democratic socialism. On appeal to the Employment Appeal Tribunal, Mrs Justice Simler (as she then was) overturned the employment tribunal's decision. The EAT concluded that neither challenging the authority of line management in an employment context, nor making unsubstantiated allegations of collusion, had anything to do with left-wing democratic socialism. The employment tribunal had concluded that the reason for the dismissal was

[130] *Forstater v CGD Europe and Others* Case No 2200909/2019.
[131] *Henderson v The General Municipal and Boilermakers Union* UKEAT/0073/14/DM.

Mr Henderson's protected belief in the absence of any findings of fact or evidential basis to support that conclusion and had impermissibly drawn unsupported factual and legal assumptions. Mr Henderson's case was dismissed.

ii. Unfair Dismissal

11.63 The right not to be unfairly dismissed is protected by the Employment Rights Act 1996; it is a right distinct from the rights contained in the Equality Act 2010. Some dismissals are 'automatically' unfair, because the main or principal reason for the dismissal is a proscribed reason under the Employment Rights Act 1996 (for example, a dismissal for raising health and safety concerns). It is not automatically unfair to dismiss employees for their political opinions or beliefs.

11.64 Usually, employees may only bring an unfair dismissal claim if they have had two years' continuous service with their employer. Where the main or principal reason for a dismissal is an employee's political opinions or affiliation (including party-political affiliation), there is no requirement for an employee to have two years' continuous service to bring a claim of unfair dismissal.[132] Where the employee's political opinions or affiliation are merely a subsidiary reason for dismissal this extension to the employment tribunal's jurisdiction will not apply. Nor does it apply to employees who are dismissed merely because they lack political neutrality: neutrality has nothing to do with the content of the political opinion or the identity of the affiliation. So, a housing officer who proposed to depart from political neutrality by standing as a candidate for the Scottish Labour Party in the 2019 general election was unable to bring an unfair dismissal claim without two years' continuous service: her dismissal arose from her lack of political neutrality, not from her affiliation with Scottish Labour.[133]

11.65 *Greenwich London Borough v Dell* was a case in which an employee was dismissed for holding racist political beliefs. The tribunal found that the claimant was dismissed unfairly; however, the case demonstrates that, while a dismissal for prejudiced beliefs is capable of being unfair, the content of such beliefs may affect whether the claimant can obtain reinstatement to his former post or not. The claimant was a caretaker employed by the local council. He was caught waving a BNP paper while attending a BNP demonstration. The council dismissed him after a disciplinary procedure. After holding at trial that his dismissal was unfair, an employment tribunal determined that it was reasonably practicable for the council to reinstate the claimant, but that would mean he would need to be kept away from direct or indirect contact with racial minorities. On

[132] Employment Rights Act 1996, s 108(4). The law was introduced to give effect to the ECtHR's judgment in *Redfearn v United Kingdom* [2013] IRLR 51 (in fact an Art 11 freedom of association case). Redfearn concerned a claimant who was a bus driver and BNP member. His work entailed driving passengers to whom his political opinions and party political affiliation were offensive. His employer dismissed him because of the damage to its reputation posed by his affiliation with the BNP and its views. He was unable to claim unfair dismissal because he had not worked for two or more years with the employer. The ECtHR concluded that the lack of a remedy was a breach of his right to freedom of association under Art 11 of the ECHR.

[133] *Scottish Federation of Housing Associations v Jones* [2022] EAT 114.

appeal the EAT disagreed and overturned the tribunal's decision on reinstatement. The notion that the re-engagement should be to a post which would not bring the applicant into any sort of contact, direct or indirect with racial minorities was offensive to the practice of racial equality, with which the council had built a reputation of complying.[134]

D. Northern Ireland

11.66 The law as it relates to Northern Ireland is materially different to the law of the rest of the UK in this area. The Fair Employment and Treatment (Northern Ireland) Order 1998 prohibits discrimination in employment and in the provision of services (among other areas) on the ground of political opinion (and religious belief).[135] Political opinion is not defined in the Order. Jurisprudence has defined it as an opinion relating to the policy of government and matters touching the government of the state,[136] or matters relating to public policy.[137] An association with a particular political party or ideology would also count.[138] An opinion that favours the use of violence is a political opinion for the purposes of the Order[139] (though the actual commission of violence would not be something protected by the legislation). An opinion held in the past also falls within the scope of the Order's protection.[140] The protections of the Order do not, however, compel employers or providers of goods, facilities and services to express a message with which they disagree, unless justification is shown for doing so.[141] Note that the Northern Ireland Act 1998 prohibits the Northern Ireland Assembly and a Minister or Northern Ireland department from making any legislation or doing any act that discriminates on the ground of political opinion or religious belief.[142]

[134] *Greenwich London Borough v Dell* EAT/1166/94.
[135] Arts 2(2) and 3(1)(a).
[136] *McKay v Northern Ireland Public Service Alliance* [1994] NI 103 at 117.
[137] *Ryder v Northern Ireland Policing Board* [2007] NICA 43 at para 15.
[138] *Lee v Ashers Baking Co Ltd and Others* [2018] UKSC 49, [2020] AC 413 (SC) at para 41.
[139] *McConkey v Simon Community* [2009] UKHL 24, [2009] NI 297.
[140] ibid.
[141] *Lee v Ashers Baking Co Ltd and Others* [2020] AC 413 (SC) at para 56.
[142] Northern Ireland Act 1998, ss 6(2)(e) and 24(1)(c).

12

Conduct in Political Parties

I. Introduction

12.1 This chapter sets out the standards of conduct to which political parties and their activists and officers are expected to adhere. The essentially private status of political parties means that their conduct is subject to far fewer agreed standards and rules than that of their members elected to public office. Nevertheless, broad principles of good governance for political parties emerge from case law and various international instruments, notably those produced by the Venice Commission,[1] which is an advisory body of the Council of Europe that works in the field of constitutional law. Section II of this chapter addresses those broad principles of good governance for political parties. Section III deals with misconduct by party members, tracing standards of conduct that are common to all main parties in section A, and then setting out in sections B–E the legal rules about disciplining members for misconduct, the requirements of natural justice, and how party members may remedy unfairness that arises in disciplinary proceedings, including through the court's intervention.

II. Principles of Good Governance

12.2 In the European human rights context, the Venice Commission has acknowledged how too much regulation can stifle political participation, but an absence of regulation can generate ruthless politics.[2] In any case, whatever the level of external regulation, political parties' internal organisation and functioning should abide by the principles of democracy and legality.[3] The commentary commissioned by the Committee on Standards in Public Life, *Public Ethics and Political Judgment* enumerates a similar principle in the domestic context:

> The relationship between political ethics and modern politics more widely has several dimensions that are not always easy to reconcile. For example, politics is partly about winning – nominations, candidacies, elections, offices, debates, votes. But winning cannot be achieved at any price: not least participants should respect the rules and procedures of the process. Moreover, while many political systems are vulnerable to winners altering the rules to make it more likely that they will keep winning, the legitimacy of the political system depends on a high degree of consensus on the character of the political game and the rules for contesting political office.[4]

The following broad principles of good governance arise from case law and non-binding guidance about political activity.

[1] Formally known as the European Commission for Democracy through Law. See para 11.1.

[2] 'Explanatory Report to the Code of Good Practice in the Field of Political Parties', adopted by the Venice Commission at its 78th Plenary Session (Venice, 13–14 March 2009): 'the lack of regulation risks ruthless politics and jeopardises public accountability but strict laws can discourage political participation. Considering this trade-off, the Council of Europe member states have developed political parties' regulation to a variable degree, implying different approaches to legal micromanagement of political parties by the state' (at para 91).

[3] 'The basic tenets of democracy are not satisfied with mere formal adherence or lip-service paid by the statutes of the party but require substantial application of them': ibid at para 100.

[4] M Philip, *Public Ethics and Political Judgment* (Committee on Standards in Public Life, 2014) para 5.3.

A. The Proceedings of Political Parties Should be Free from Corruption

12.3 That public elections should be free from corruption is a firmly established and important principle. It has had a legislative basis since the nineteenth century[5] and today has statutory force by the Representation of the People Act 1983, which outlaws corrupt practices in the course of local and parliamentary elections. The Political Parties, Elections and Referendums Act 2000 (PPERA 2000) safeguards election campaign expenditure, and party funding, against corruption. The principle against corruption in political finance is recognised by Article 7(3) of the United Nations Convention against Corruption, which obliges signatory states to strive to improve transparency in the funding of political parties. This fundamental principle against corruption in public elections also extends to the internal affairs of political parties outside public election campaigns. The corrosive effect of corruption on democracy means that all elements of the democratic system should be free from it, including the affairs of private political entities that participate in democratic engagement. There is, therefore, a strong public interest that the internal affairs of political parties should be free from corruption; that interest has been acknowledged by domestic courts[6] and by the European Court of Human Rights.[7]

B. Decision-making Ought to be Transparent

12.4 Transparency in political parties' affairs bolsters public confidence in the political process.[8] The Code of Good Practice in the Field of Political Parties adopted by the Venice Commission provides that 'parties should offer access to their programmatic and ideological documents and discussions, to decision-making procedures and to party accounts in order to enhance transparency and to be consistent with sound principles of good governance'.[9] A similar principle is expressed by the concept of 'openness' in 'The Seven Principles of Public Life': 'holders of public office should act and take decisions in an open and transparent manner. Information should not be withheld from the public unless there are clear and lawful reasons for so doing'.[10] The statutory regulation of political spending and donations in the UK through a system of registration and reporting introduces an important degree of transparency in political parties' financial affairs. UK Supreme Court justices, sitting as the Privy Council, have made non-binding comments that decision-making by politicians ought to be transparent: 'sunlight is said

[5] eg the Corrupt Practices Prevention Act 1854 and the Corrupt and Illegal Practices Prevention Act 1883.

[6] *Choudhry v Treisman* [2003] EWHC 1203 (Comm) para 82.

[7] *Cumhuriyet Halk Partisi v Turkey* (2016) Application No 19920/13, para 69.

[8] *Cumhuriyet Halk Partisi v Turkey* (ECtHR) (Second Section) (2016) Application No 19920/13, para 69.

[9] Code of Good Practice in the Field of Political Parties, adopted by the Venice Commission at its 77th Plenary Session (Venice, 12–13 December 2008), para 19.

[10] 'Guidance: The Seven Principles of Public Life' (Committee on Standards in Public Life, May 1995) para 1.5. See Ch 3 paras 13.4 and 13.5.

to be the best of disinfectants'.[11] Transparency has its limits, both legal (for example, data protection legislation that precludes the dissemination of personal membership data without consent) and practical: parties will want to keep politically sensitive or embarrassing information private when it is lawful to do so. Nevertheless, appropriate systems of transparent decision-making about party members will often assist parties to show that they have complied with the implied obligations of fairness and good faith to which they are subject when exercising powers under the party constitution.

C. Decision-making Should be Democratic and, Where Possible, it Should Promote Democratic Engagement

12.5 Political parties are necessarily concerned with promoting democratic engagement because their primary function is to provide candidates for election to public office. The Venice Commission's Code of Good Practice for Political Parties emphasises that democratic decision-making in political parties is important for a well-functioning democracy generally.[12] The principle that party decision-making ought to promote democratic engagement has been recognised by the courts in various contexts, for example, as providing a legitimate basis for processing personal data under data protection legislation.[13]

D. Access to and Participation in Party Politics Should be Free from Unlawful Discrimination

12.6 Chapter 11 addresses how this fundamentally important principle is established in law.

III. Party Membership Disciplinary Procedures

A. Standards of Conduct

i. Common Standards

12.7 Party members are subject to the general provisions of the law and, where they undertake a statutory office in a political party, to the financial and accounting

[11] *Ramadhar v Ramadhar and Others* [2020] UKPC 7, [2020] EMLR 16 paras 36–40.

[12] Code of Good Practice in the Field of Political Parties, adopted by the Venice Commission at its 77th Plenary Session (Venice, 12–13 December 2008) para 17: 'Parties are an integral part of a democracy, and their activities should ensure its good functioning. Hence, a commitment to internal democratic functioning reinforces this general function'. See also para 28: 'applied within a party, these principles mean that the structure of the party and its procedures should represent the opinion of the members and they should be receptive towards these. Although this commitment may not entail a legally expressed obligation, their breach runs against the basic intuitive concept of democratic organisation'.

[13] *Ramsay v Hacket Pain* [2020] EWHC 3655 (Ch) para 10; *Gardner v Newstead* (unreported, 18 February 1997) (ChD).

requirements set out in the PPERA 2000. Party members who hold public office are subject to 'The Seven Principles of Public Life' (which are addressed in further detail in Chapter 13) and, where relevant, the Ministerial Code and other codes of conduct applicable to publicly elected representatives, when they exercise the powers of their office. But there are no universally accepted codes of behavioural standards to which volunteer political party members should adhere akin to 'The Seven Principles of Public Life'. Political parties' constitutions do, however, provide for how their members are expected to act in relation to the party. The following principles are common to most political parties.

a. Disrepute

12.8 Members should not do anything that is detrimental to the party or which brings it into disrepute. It is this principle which permits political parties to discipline members for conduct that is embarrassing or politically prejudicial. Thus, members must not engage in 'conduct that has brought, or is likely to bring the party into disrepute' (Liberal Democrats);[14] or 'that is likely to bring an Association or the Party into disrepute' (Conservative Party);[15] or that is 'prejudicial or grossly detrimental to the Party' (the Labour Party);[16] or 'conduct likely to cause damage to or hinder the Party's proper pursuit of its aims in accordance with its constitutionally laid down policy and direction' (Scottish National Party);[17] or 'whose behaviour is otherwise damaging to the party' (Plaid Cymru);[18] or 'not bring the Party into disrepute by engaging in unethical conduct' (Green Party).[19] Parties generally expect their elected representatives to conform to higher standards of conduct than other classes of member.

b. Prejudice

12.9 Members should not treat other people prejudicially in respect of[20] a protected characteristic (race, sex etc).[21]

[14] The Federal Constitution of the Liberal Democrats 2022, cl 3.8(B).

[15] Constitution of the Conservative Party (as amended), cl 17.22.

[16] Labour Party Rule Book 2023, Ch 2, cl I.11.

[17] Constitution of the Scottish National Party, Code of Conduct for Members, rule 2, para 1.

[18] Plaid Cymru Cyfansoddiad/Constitution 2017, cl 5.1.

[19] Green Party Members Code of Conduct, Part B, cl 7.3.

[20] The principle echoes the core definitions of discrimination in the Equality Act 2010 but it is not phrased in party rule books with the precision of that Act; and for that reason the legal causative tests relevant to the 2010 Act 'because of' and 'related to' are avoided here. Note, too, that some party rule books go further than the Act by introducing the characteristic of 'gender identity', which is not one protected under the Act.

[21] eg Labour Party Rule Book 2023, Ch 2, cl I.11; The Federal Constitution of the Liberal Democrats 2022, cl 3.8(F); Constitution of the Scottish National Party, Code of Conduct for Members, rule 2, paras 5 and 6; Green Party Members Code of Conduct, Part B, cl 11.3; Conservative Party Code of Conduct for Members and Representatives of the Conservative Party, Part 1, s 1.

c. Rivals

12.10 Nor should members stand against the party in an election or support a rival political party.[22] Members must comply with the fundamental political values and aims of the party.[23]

ii. Codes of Conduct

12.11 The main parties all have relatively detailed codes of conduct for members that complement their constitutional rules. These codes of conduct set out the standards expected of each party's members and usually also set out the party's disciplinary procedures. The establishment of detailed codes of conduct about expected behavioural standards within parties is a relatively new phenomenon that arose between 2010 and 2022. The codes of conduct are not terms of the membership contract unless the constitution states otherwise. The codes may nevertheless have contractual effect because the party's constitution requires officers to have regard to them in any disciplinary case. Even if the codes do not amount to contractual terms, they are likely to form part of the framework of the party's constitution and provide legitimate factors that are relevant to the party's exercise of its disciplinary powers.[24]

iii. Intimidation: Joint Statement on Conduct of Political Party Members

12.12 The Labour Party, the Liberal Democrats, the Green Party of England and Wales and the Scottish National Party are all signatories to a statement of principle that prohibits intimidation and violence, and advocates dignity and respect, in the activities of party members.[25] This 'Joint statement on conduct of political party members' was produced by the Jo Cox Foundation in collaboration with the Committee on Standards in Public Life, which undertook a review of some political parties' codes of conduct.[26] The statement aspires to set out a minimum standard of behaviour expected from political party members at all times. The statement prohibits intimidation by using or threatening violence or other unlawful force; damaging property or making threats to damage property; engaging in bullying, harassment or victimisation, or unlawfully discriminating against another person or group; using abusive or threatening words or behaviour,

[22] The Federal Constitution of the Liberal Democrats 2022, cl 3.8(C) and (D); Labour Party Rule Book, Ch 2, cl 5.I.B; Constitution of the Scottish National Party, cl 4.3(b) and (c); Cyfansoddiad/Constitution 2017, cl 4.2.ii; Conservative Party Code of Conduct for Members and Representatives of the Conservative Party, Part 1, s 1 ('helping political opponents').

[23] The Federal Constitution of the Liberal Democrats 2022, para 3.8; Labour Party Rule Book, Ch 2, cl I.9.A; Constitution of the Conservative Party (as amended), cl 17.22; Constitution of the Scottish National Party, cl 4.2(b) and Code of Conduct for Members, rule 2, para 2.

[24] eg *Evangelou v McNicol* [2016] EWCA Civ 817 at 44. In that case, the Court of Appeal reviewed The Labour Party's codes of conduct (in that case, relating to leadership elections) which were set out in appendices to the contractual rules. The court held that the appendices formed part of the scheme of the rules, were legitimate internal aids to the construction of the membership contract and provided indications as to what factors were relevant to the exercise of the powers conferred under the rules.

[25] 'Joint Statement on conduct of political party members' (Jo Cox Foundation, 2019) www.jocoxfoundation.org/joint_statement.

[26] 'Review of Political Parties' Codes of Conduct' (CSPL Secretariat, 2019).

including the use of hateful or sexualised language or imagery; making vexatious or malicious allegations of illegal or improper conduct; or using violent metaphors or allusions to violence. The statement has no legal or contractual force because it creates no new contractual obligations within parties' constitutions. Nevertheless, the prohibitions that the statement enumerates should serve as a useful guide for party officers as to the sort of conduct that amounts to intimidation in a political context.

iv. Conduct on Social Media

12.13 A consequence of the advent of social media is that political party members can publish their views more regularly and widely than before. Before the widespread use of social media, political parties had a certain degree of supervision over the views expressed by their adherents under the banner of party membership, for example in leaflets or party newspapers. Party literature requires authorisation by the local or central party before its dissemination, and damaging speeches or arguments in party meetings can be halted or disrupted by the chair (see Chapter 4 for the chair's powers to adjourn meetings). Now, however, party officers have little – if any – control over what is being published publicly online by people associated with the party. Parties must frequently deal with politically embarrassing or ill-advised forays into online political debates by members, councillors and MPs who may post without much forethought, let alone deference to the party's communications strategy. This reality has sometimes given rise to an expectation that parties will, or should, regulate the online behaviour of their members generally. That is an unachievable objective and parties are not responsible in law for the online conduct of ordinary party members outside of party activities (see Chapter 3 for further detail about parties' responsibility for their members generally, and Chapter 11 for responsibility for discriminatory acts).

12.14 The main parties have taken steps to establish guidelines for party members' online conduct. Most of those guidelines capture not only conduct online that is overtly political, but also that which may be politically embarrassing due to the party's public association with the member in question. Most of the guidelines apply the expectations of members' face-to-face conduct to their conduct online, but there are nuances in the parties' approaches to social media. The Liberal Democrats emphasise the additional risk posed to the party's reputation by public online exchanges and provide advice about how members should act online; for example by encouraging members with influential social media profiles to be particularly cautious of facilitating the harassment or bullying of other people and by suggesting that members apologise for any offence given online.[27] The Conservative Party's guidelines define 'misuse' of social media, comprising seven different categories of misconduct, chiefly amounting to a breach of the law or the party's rules and other codes of conduct (eg committing a criminal offence or an unlawful act under the Equality Act 2010 or the Data Protection Acts).[28]

[27] 'Code of Conduct for Members and Registered Supporters' (Liberal Democrats, 2023) 'Online conduct'.

[28] 'Code of Conduct for Members and Representatives of the Conservative Party', 'Behaviour on Social Media'.

The Conservative Party's guidelines do not concern themselves with advice about how social media should be used. The Labour Party's guidelines provide general principles for Labour Party members' use of social media (eg 'we make legitimate criticisms based on policy and political actions, never making personal attacks' and 'we use accessible language and avoid jargon that could exclude or alienate') and emphasises that members have a responsibility to stand in solidarity with those who receive online abuse, and to report it.[29]

B. Procedural Fairness: Disciplinary Proceedings

12.15 An obligation to treat members fairly is implied into the constitutions of political parties by common law. Fairness in this context means procedural fairness, also referred to interchangeably with the term 'natural justice'.[30] The requirements of natural justice vary depending on the context of the decision being taken: the standards of fairness are not immutable and principles of fairness should not be applied identically in every situation.[31] Nevertheless, the requirements of fairness in political party disciplinary proceedings are not particularly onerous. The principles of fairness to which parties must adhere are the following. First, the party must give the member sufficient notice of the allegations against him. This is necessary so that, second, he may set out his position in respect of those allegations. Those requirements are correlative: the key is that a member must be given a fair opportunity to correct or contradict any relevant statement prejudicial to his position.[32] Third, the party must consider any representations from him in good faith, rationally and without bias.

12.16 The standard of fairness imposed by those principles is close to the basic minimum standard of natural justice. That is because the most severe disciplinary sanction that a party can impose on a member is the removal of his membership. Save in the case of sitting, elected public representatives, the removal of membership will have no effect on a person's livelihood, his liberty or his status in society. That is not to say that expulsion from a political party is not a serious event for the member in question, given that it may render the member politically homeless and remove access to social circles and activities. But expulsion is, nonetheless, on the lower end of severity when compared to the consequences of disciplinary sanctions in other legal contexts, for example, termination of employment or removal of a registration required to practise a profession. Another reason not to adopt more elaborate disciplinary procedures is that political parties' procedures are often operated by volunteers (or a mix of volunteers

[29] 'NEC Codes of Conduct', 'Code of Conduct: Social Media Policy', Labour Party Rule Book 2023 App 8.

[30] *O'Reilly v Mackman* [1983] 2 AC 237 at 275 per Lord Diplock; *Secretary of State for Communities and Local Government v Hopkins Developments* [2014] EWCA Civ 470 at para 85 per Beatson LJ.

[31] See *R v Secretary of State for the Home Department, ex p Doody* [1994] 1 AC 531 at 560D–561B per Lord Mustill.

[32] See *Board of Education v Rice* [1911] AC 179 at 182 per Lord Lordburn LC; *Ridge v Baldwin* [1964] AC 40 at 79 per Lord Reid; *Russell v Duke of Norfolk* [1949] 1 All ER 109 at 118 per Lord Denning; *Manning v Ramjohn* [2011] UKPC 20 at para 39 per Lord Brown.

and employees). Those people are typically not lawyers, and their primary aim is to win (or at least be competitive in) elections rather than to regulate the conduct of other party members. The procedural rights of individual members must be protected properly, but a balance needs to be struck that enables the party to function and to achieve its core aims.[33]

i. Charges and Evidence

12.17 Various High Court authorities have addressed what fairness demands of charges in party membership disciplinary proceedings. The cases have often been about the Labour Party, but also the Liberal Democrats and UKIP. There is no obvious reason why the standard set out in those cases should not apply to all political parties, given their broad similarities in nature, purpose and structure. Each party has its own procedural rules. Where those rules impose other or greater procedural requirements than the basic requirements set out in jurisprudence, those additional standards must be adhered to, otherwise the party will act in breach of its constitution.

12.18 It is sufficient for the charge to be written in such a way that it gives the gist of the allegations against the member concerned rather than the complete detail;[34] though the charges ought to be framed so that a member can understand which rule in the constitution he is said to have breached,[35] and how. This entails the party setting out its concerns in a way that is sufficient for the member to address the allegations made against him if he wishes to do so;[36] especially by stating the substance of the allegations and by providing particulars of the evidence said to be relevant. It is also good practice for the party to state explicitly the internal guidance or rules (and their relevant terms) on which it is relying to frame the charges, and that they will be taken into account in assessing whether there has been a breach of the party's constitution.[37]

12.19 The member must be sent the evidence on which the charge is based. The requirement is to provide sufficient evidence to enable the member to know adequately the allegations against him and to be in a position to answer the allegations.[38] The person must be able to know the important parts in support of the case against him, particularly so that he is able to adduce his own evidence and argue his own case. The evidence sent to the member must, therefore, be relevant and in such a form that he has a fair opportunity to deal with it.[39]

[33] *Brian Green v Labour Party* (unreported, 27 March 1991) (CA) per Neill LJ.

[34] *R v Secretary of State for the Home Department, ex p Doody* [1994] 1 AC 531 at 560 per Lord Mustill; *Hussain v Elonex plc* [1999] IRLR 420 per Mummery LJ.

[35] *John v Rees* [1970] Ch 345.

[36] *Choudhry v Treisman* [2003] EWHC 1203 (Comm) at para 77.

[37] *Neslen v Evans* [2021] EWHC 1909 (QB).

[38] ibid; *Walsh v McCluskie* (1983) Times, 16 December (ChD).

[39] See eg *Spink v Express Foods Ltd* [1990] IRLR 320; *R (on the application of O) v Tower Hamlets LBC Independent Appeal Panel* [2007] EWHC 1455 (Admin).

ii. Opportunity to Make Representations

12.20 Once charges have been framed and presented to a member he must be afforded an opportunity to make meaningful representations in answer to the allegations. There is no obligation on him to do so. The party's rules may limit the period in which the member may make representations but an unreasonably short period in which to do so is likely to render the process unfair. There is no common law obligation to hold a hearing; however, where the matter is complex or the evidence depends mainly on oral testimony, a party is likely to act unfairly if it determines the proceedings without a hearing. The party's rules may make particular provision for holding one; if so, those must be adhered to as a matter of contract law. It is doubtful that a member who is a respondent to disciplinary proceedings has a right to cross-examine witnesses at a membership disciplinary hearing unless the rules expressly afford him such a right.[40] It may be that fairness in the particular circumstances requires a witness's evidence to be tested, but that does not require the testing to be done by the respondent to the charge, as many of the objectives of cross-examination can be achieved without direct questioning and the testing may be done by the chair of the disciplinary panel concerned.[41]

C. Administrative Suspension and Investigation

12.21 The party may wish to suspend a member administratively (ie as part of the disciplinary process) while it carries out an investigation into allegations of wrongdoing. It is good practice for the rules to set out expressly the party's power to impose administrative suspensions on members. Both a penal suspension (ie as a punishment) and an administrative suspension amount to a denial of a member's rights under the membership contract. A party that suspends its members with no power to do so will act in breach of contract. Nevertheless, the courts have been willing to imply a power to suspend into the rules; and so it is to be presumed that the majority of parties will find a lawful way to exercise a power of administrative suspension even if there is no express provision in a party's constitution. In *Lewis v Heffer* the Court of Appeal advanced two alternative bases on which a power to suspend members could be implied into a party's rules. The first basis was that a broad, general power to take 'any action deemed necessary' to enforce the party's constitution included the particular power of suspension; the second basis was that the practice of suspending members was sufficiently established, well known and unquestioned not just in the party but in associations more generally that the power was implied by custom and practice.[42]

12.22 Where a suspension is administrative it is an adjunct of the investigative process rather than a penalty. Consequently, the party does not need to give the

[40] For example, *Choudhry v Treisman* [2003] EWHC 1203 (Comm) (a Labour Party case) in which the court held that the requirements of natural justice did not extend so far as to require that the claimants were present when a panel interviewed informants, or that the claimants be given an opportunity to question them.

[41] See by analogy the judgment of the High Court in *AB v The University of XYZ* [2020] EWHC 2978 (QB) at paras 71 and 96, which concerned the disciplinary processes of a university.

[42] *Lewis v Heffer* [1978] 1 WLR 1061 at 1072C–H and 1076F.

member concerned notice or a chance to make representations before the suspension is imposed.[43] An administrative suspension will usually be imposed before any formal charges against the member have been formulated, right at the beginning of the disciplinary process,[44] save if the rules expressly limit the power of suspension otherwise. But once the administrative suspension is in place it must be handled fairly. If the suspension is maintained too long then the delay may render the disciplinary process unfair; see, for example, the cases of *Jones v McNicol* in which a two-year administrative suspension, during which no investigation was progressed, rendered a Labour Party suspension unlawful.[45] It is not unfair for a party to impose a 'double' suspension, that is, a suspension attached to one set of allegations and a separate but concurrent or overlapping suspension in respect of different allegations; but the party must take care to ensure that each suspension is considered separately, on the evidence and particular context of the allegations in issue and imposed rationally and in good faith.[46]

12.23 The party's investigation of disciplinary complaints should be carried out fairly and honestly. The investigating officer should put his concerns to the member in the course of the investigation so that the member may have an opportunity to comment on them. Questions and requests for information should be put to members in neutral terms seeking evidence of propriety as well as impropriety.[47] In this sense the investigating officer should adopt what is necessary of investigators in the workplace and look for evidence of innocence as well as guilt; the party's investigators should not adopt the role of a prosecution service save if that is expressly set out as their role by the constitution.

D. Determination of Disciplinary Allegations

i. Bias

12.24 Actual or apparent bias are grounds for voiding a disciplinary decision. The definition of apparent bias is where a fair-minded and informed observer, having considered the facts, would conclude that there was a real possibility of bias.[48] There is great scope for allegations of bias to creep into the determination of disciplinary complaints by political parties, given the sometimes very long-standing and deeply held divisions between political factions. Party officers and committee members who determine disciplinary cases must be alive to that possibility and take steps to recuse themselves from proceedings if there is a risk of apparent bias. At the same time, however, it is important not to lose sight of the reality that political committee members will often know, and be known to, those subject to disciplinary proceedings; and the party must nonetheless function and determine complaints promptly.

[43] *Brian Green v Labour Party* (unreported, 27 March 1991) (CA).
[44] See by analogy the trade union case *Unison v Bakhsh* EAT/0375/08/RN.
[45] *Jones v McNichol* [2016] EWHC 866 (QB).
[46] ibid, approving *Hussain v McNichol* (unreported) and *Williamson v Formby* [2019] EWHC 2639 (QB).
[47] *Choudhry v Treisman* [2003] EWHC 1203 (Comm) at para 79.
[48] *Porter v Magill* [2001] UKHL 67, [2002] 2 AC 357.

12.25 Disciplinary allegations should not be determined by the same people who investigated them. The division between investigator and final decision-maker is especially important in political parties because disciplinary decisions often fall to be decided by a committee comprising several or many people; and there is often scope for some of those committee members to involve themselves in the investigation process. There is no rule that the investigating members of a committee are in all circumstances automatically barred from attending, speaking or voting in respect of the resulting disciplinary determination. But the determination of a disciplinary case by people involved in the investigation is likely to give rise to actual or apparent bias, both of which strongly risk rendering the disciplinary decision unlawful.[49]

ii. Adjudicating Political Misconduct

12.26 An important, overarching point is that the party's disciplinary system is not at all the correct forum in which to pursue political preferences about who the party leadership would like as the party's candidates for election, nor to try and manipulate the relative power of political factions. The correct place to pursue those political matters is through the party's candidate selection processes and its various internal elections for committees and other positions, which are dealt with in further detail in Chapters 5 and 6.

12.27 A difficult task for those party officers who must determine complaints judiciously is how to deal with political misconduct (ie conduct that may prejudice the party's position with the electorate because it is embarrassing or because it represents some transgression from the political imperatives of the party). It is not always easy in a judicious disciplinary process to accommodate subjective views about what best serves the political position of the party, that position being itself founded in part on the caprice of the media and public opinion.

12.28 Some party rules state that members must not do anything that brings the party into disrepute 'in the opinion' of the governing body. It has been held that the use of the word 'opinion' here does not just refer simply to the subjective view of those who determine the allegations but also to an opinion formed after due investigation and rational consideration,[50] hence party officers may not simply decide on a whim whether political misconduct has occurred. They must act in the best interests of the party[51] and not give effect merely to their own political interests or ideology.

12.29 It is not entirely settled to what extent party officers may take into account public reaction to, and opinion about, a member's conduct when determining whether that conduct has been detrimental to the party. The question was addressed to some extent in the case of *Williamson v Formby*, which was later relied on by the Equality and Human Rights Commission to make findings about unlawful political interference by

[49] *Mackay v Caley* (unreported, 16 September 1986) (CA).
[50] *Lawlor v Union of Post Office Workers* [1965] Ch 712, [1965] 2 WLR 579.
[51] *Rothery v Evans* [2021] EWHC 577 (QB).

the Labour Party in its determination of complaints about alleged antisemitism.[52] The court held that an important aspect of acting judicially is that the party should decide cases fairly and impartially in accordance with the rules and evidence and it should not be influenced by how its decisions are seen by others. Internal and press reaction to a disciplinary decision were not of themselves proper grounds for reopening the case.[53] A member must not, therefore, be tried in the court of public opinion, and a public clamour may not be well-founded, so party officers must not let media reactions affect the decisions they take.

iii. Disciplinary Sanctions

12.30 A party may impose any disciplinary sanction provided for in its rules. A power to expel members also includes a power to suspend them punitively, as suspension is a form of temporary exclusion.[54] A decision that is wholly disproportionate may well offend the rule against rationality or capriciousness (for example, an expulsion for being trivially rude to members of the public). It is not acceptable to impose a penalty on a person for holding a protected philosophical belief that is compatible with the party's fundamental aims and values, or for conduct in connection with complaining about a breach of the Equality Act 2010; doing so risks committing discrimination and victimisation, respectively. See Chapter 11 for how the Equality Act 2010 affects political parties.

E. Remedying Unfairness

i. Internal Appeals

12.31 If unfairness does arise during disciplinary proceedings there are several means by which it may be remedied. The first way is by appeal. A member will only have a right to appeal against a disciplinary decision if the party's rules provide for one. It is entirely a matter for the party whether the appeal should amount to a review of the disciplinary decision or a complete rehearing. The existence of a right of appeal does not preclude a member from challenging a disciplinary decision in the courts without first availing himself of the appeal process, unless the contrary is stated expressly in the rules.[55] Nevertheless, a member's failure to engage in a contractual appeal procedure may be a relevant factor pointing against the grant of interim relief by a court (eg an interim injunction to prevent a disciplinary decision being taken or having effect).[56]

[52] And see paras 11.29 and 11.30 for the EHRC's findings about discrimination in the Labour Party's disciplinary processes.

[53] *Williamson v Formby* [2019] EWHC 2639 (QB) at para 61.

[54] *Lewis v Heffer* [1978] 1 WLR 1061; *John v Rees* [1970] Ch 345.

[55] *Bonsor v Musicians Union* [1956] AC 104 (HL).

[56] See for example *Vachha v Hamilton* [2020] EWHC 3728 (Ch) at para 24 in which interim relief was sought by a member of UKIP in respect of a decision to suspend his membership. In that case the court acknowledged the depth of political animosity and distrust that existed between the claimant's faction of UKIP and a rival faction but found that, as the claimant relied on compliance with the constitution to establish

12.32 The courts have recognised an implied power for a political party to re-open final disciplinary decisions and to decide them afresh where it is in the interests of justice to do so. Circumstances in which the power may be exercised include where the original decision was obviously wrong, or was procedurally flawed, or where some important evidence was overlooked. The power is especially important in circumstances where there is no right of appeal against the original disciplinary decision and so fairness may require a review of that decision.[57]

ii. Intervention by the Court

12.33 Members who are expelled or suspended in breach of the party's rules or any of the implied terms of natural justice, rationality or good faith may seek the court's intervention. The court's role here is supervisory. Its function is to ensure that the party, as primary decision-maker, operated rationally and within lawful limits;[58] and it is therefore unconcerned with whether the disciplinary decision falls within a reasonable range of responses to the alleged infraction.[59] The court's essential concern will be whether the procedure adopted was fair, whether there was any error of law and whether the disciplinary decision-maker had the requisite powers to expel or suspend the member in question.[60]

12.34 The circumstances in which a court will intervene in the affairs of a political party are limited, especially if the party is an unincorporated association. The threshold for intervention is not entirely clear in the legal authorities. Nevertheless, as a general proposition, the court will intervene in three scenarios: first, where a disciplinary decision prejudices a member's contractual rights of membership; second, to protect a right to work derived from membership;[61] and third, to protect an elected politician's ability to continue to earn his living as an elected representative.[62] Essentially, therefore, the court must be willing to intervene if a member has been expelled or suspended (as both eventualities curtail a member's rights under the membership contract), or if an elected representative who receives a salary from his elected position has received some lesser sanction that renders him ineligible to stand for election again as the party's candidate. The latter scenario does not necessarily present a hard and fast rule justifying intervention, however. In *Williamson* the court observed that a suspension from

his case, he should also rely on his rights under the constitution to appeal the decision to suspend him, which could have been done quickly.

[57] See *McKenzie v National Union of Public Employees* [1991] ICR 155 and *Williamson v Formby* [2019] EWHC 2639 (QB). In *McKenzie* the claimant had been expelled in breach of the procedure set out in a union's rules and sought declarations that such disciplinary action was void and that he remained branch secretary. The union tried to rectify its mistake by holding a fresh disciplinary hearing. The court decided that the union was entitled to rehear the case and to put right the procedural shortcomings in the original decision. In *Williamson* the Labour Party attempted to re-open a final disciplinary decision but the court found it did not have proper reasons to do so and inferred that the party was instead reacting to public and media pressure.

[58] *Braganza v BP Shipping Ltd* [2015] 1 WLR 1661 at para 19 per Lady Hale.

[59] *Rothery v Evans* [2021] EWHC 577 (QB) at para 167.

[60] eg *Bradley v The Jockey Club* [2005] EWCA Civ 1056, [2006] WLR 1; *Williamson v Formby* [2019] EWHC 2639 (QB).

[61] *Lee v Showmen's Guild of Great Britain* [1952] 2 QB 329 at 343.

[62] *Williamson v Formby* [2019] EWHC 2639 (QB).

membership does not prevent an MP from standing for re-election either as an independent or for any other party. Nevertheless, 'party allegiances are deeply rooted in an MP's political beliefs. However poorly treated by their party, very few politicians would consider crossing the floor save on the basis of some philosophical or policy difference with the direction taken by their party … the reality is that very few independents succeed in general elections'. In the Court's view, there was therefore a significant risk that disqualification from selection as a party candidate would end Mr Williamson's career.[63] The same analysis is less likely to apply in the case of local councillors, who are not executive members of the local authority party group; those people receive only a modest allowance for their work as councillor and make their livelihood elsewhere.

12.35 If the threshold is met the court will see that natural justice and the contractual rules have been followed on any expulsion or suspension of rights of membership.[64] But an inconsequential or minor breach of procedure will not present a basis for the court's intervention;[65] a mere procedural irregularity is not enough.[66]

12.36 The court will intervene in *ongoing* disciplinary proceedings only in exceptional circumstances. This is the approach taken by the courts generally and not merely to political parties. The test for intervention is a high one: whether the breach is one that cannot be remedied in the ongoing proceedings themselves.[67] Nor will the court micromanage the party's disciplinary process. So, in *Williamson* the court declined to intervene to lift a suspension imposed at the early stages of an investigation; and in *Neslen* the court declined to intervene at the stage when a disciplinary investigation had been completed but the allegations had not yet been considered by the relevant disciplinary panel. Political parties, therefore, will normally be left to follow their own rules and procedures.

12.37 The essentially private nature of political parties, and their rights to autonomy under Article 11 as articulated by the European Court of Human Rights, are both likely to dissuade the courts from reaching too far into the internal workings of political parties to insert behavioural standards that are not already agreed by the party. But commonly agreed codes, like the 'Joint statement on conduct of political party members', may be documents from which the courts could imply shared basic standards into parties' contractual rules. It is for the political parties themselves to agree on a minimum standard of conduct for members; but at present such agreement appears unlikely.

[63] ibid para 22.
[64] *Lee v Showmen's Guild of Great Britain* [1952] 2 QB 329 at 343.
[65] *Neslen v Evans* [2021] EWHC 1909 (QB); *Hayes v Pack* [2022] EWHC 2508 (KB) at para 54.
[66] *Brown v Executive Committee of the Edinburgh District Labour Party* (CSOH) 1995 SLT 985.
[67] *Hendy v Ministry of Justice* [2014] EWHC 2535 (Ch); *Chakrabarty v Ipswich Hospital NHS Trust* [2014] EWHC 2735 (QB); *Williamson v Formby* [2019] EWHC 2639 (QB).

13

Conduct in Parliament

I. Introduction

13.1 The abuse of public office for personal gain is an old and persistent phenomenon and, in response, a regime of rules and standards has emerged to which politicians must adhere. For example, the Honours (Prevention of Abuses) Act 1925 followed the exposure of the sale of peerages by the prime minister to help finance his own political party.[1] In 1994 the then Prime Minister John Major established the Committee on Standards in Public Life, following the revelation that some MPs had lobbied ministers, including asking parliamentary questions, in return for undeclared payments (the 'cash for questions' affair).[2] The chairman of the Committee was a senior judge, Lord Nolan. Its First Report established the 'Seven Principles of Public Life', an enumeration of basic principles of probity to which everybody holding public office should adhere.

13.2 The Parliamentary Standards Act 2009 established the Independent Parliamentary Standards Authority to oversee, and regulate better, payments to MPs, following revelations of the abuse of a system where MPs' expenses claims were not subject to public scrutiny.[3] A new Independent Complaints and Grievance Scheme (ICGS) to investigate and resolve complaints of bullying and harassment on the parliamentary estate was a response to a report in 2018 by Dame Laura Cox DBE (a retired High Court judge), which found pervasive harassment in Parliament and inadequate processes to deal with it.[4]

13.3 This chapter sets out an overview of the rules and procedures relating to the conduct of members of both Houses of Parliament, as they stand at the time of writing.[5] The equivalent rules of the Scottish and Welsh Parliaments are referred to at

[1] 'Cash for Honours' (*Debretts*, 22 February 2022), www.debretts.com/cash-for-honours.

[2] 'Chronology – How the scandal unfolded' (*Guardian*, 22 December 1999), www.theguardian.com/uk/1999/dec/22/hamiltonvalfayed.

[3] Nick Allen, 'MPs' expenses: Sir Peter Viggers claimed for £1,600 floating duck island' (*The Telegraph*, 21 May 2009).

[4] Dame Laura Cox, 'The Bullying and Harassment of House of Commons Staff: Independent Inquiry Report' (15 October 2018).

[5] Potential changes to the rules are considered in Chris Bryant, *Code of Conduct: Why We Need to Fix Parliament – and How to Do It* (Bloomsbury, 2023), especially at Ch 7.

the end of the chapter. The Northern Ireland Assembly also has a Code of Conduct.[6] Local councillors are subject to a standards regime derived from the Localism Act 2011. Each local authority must have a code of conduct, breaches of which are a matter for the local authority. Local authorities must also promote and maintain high standards of conduct among their members. A comprehensive overview of the standards regime is set out in *Cross on Local Government Law*.[7]

II. The Seven Principles of Public Life

13.4 In 1995, Lord Nolan noted the erosion of public confidence in MPs' standards of conduct:

> The public reads extensive press reporting of cases in which Members have accepted money for asking Parliamentary Questions, are said to have stayed at expensive hotels at others' expense without declaring an interest and are employed by multi-client lobbying firms, an attitude which has become known as 'MPs for hire'. Public confidence in MPs' overall standards of conduct has been further eroded by a regular flow of sexual revelations involving politicians.[8]

The committee of which Lord Nolan was the first chairman now advises prime ministers on ethical standards, reflected in the Seven Principles of Public Life.

13.5 The Seven Principles are:

i. **Selflessness:** holders of public office should act solely in terms of the public interest.
ii. **Integrity:** holders of public office must avoid placing themselves under any obligation to people or organisations that might try inappropriately to influence them in their work. They should not act or take decisions in order to gain financial or other material benefits for themselves, their family, or their friends. They must declare and resolve any interests and relationships.
iii. **Objectivity:** holders of public office must act and take decisions impartially, fairly and on merit, using the best evidence and without discrimination or bias.
iv. **Accountability:** holders of public office are accountable to the public for their decisions and actions and must submit themselves to the scrutiny necessary to ensure this.
v. **Openness:** holders of public office should act and take decisions in an open and transparent manner. Information should not be withheld from the public unless there are clear and lawful reasons for so doing.

[6] 'The Code of Conduct and The Guide to the Rules relating to the Conduct of Members Approved by the Northern Ireland Assembly on 23 March 2021 and effective from 12 April 2021', Report No NIA 85/17-22.

[7] See SH Bailey, *Cross on Local Government Law* (Sweet & Maxwell, looseleaf).

[8] First Report of the Committee on Standards in Public Life (May 1995) 21.

vi. **Honesty:** holders of public office should be truthful.
vii. **Leadership:** holders of public office should exhibit these principles in their own behaviour and treat others with respect. They should actively promote and robustly support the principles and challenge poor behaviour wherever it occurs.[9]

13.6 The Principles themselves have no direct legal force, but the expectation is that people holding public office should act in accordance with the spirit of the Principles as much as they would with any legally binding code.[10] They are the starting point for the standards regime in Parliament, and have also been incorporated into the Ministerial Code, which sets out the conduct expected of government ministers.

III. Standards of Conduct in Parliament

A. Overview

13.7 Parliament has exclusive control over how it orders its own affairs. Each House decides the standards rules that apply to its own Members; both have approved a Code of Conduct setting out rules that Members must follow. Only the House itself can decide to suspend or expel one of its number. It would be impractical for investigations and disciplinary fact-finding to take place on the floors of the Houses themselves. Each House has a dedicated committee that oversees the Code of Conduct and the investigation of standards allegations. Officers of each House have been appointed to carry out the task of investigating breaches of the Codes and making findings of fact. These are the Commissioner for Standards (a single officer of the House of Commons) and the Lords Commissioners for Standards (two in number).

13.8 The principle of 'exclusive cognisance' is a legal doctrine that Parliament should have exclusive control over how it orders its affairs, without intervention from the courts. The standards regime is one of Parliament's internal arrangements: each House has established a Select Committee to oversee the respective Code of Conduct and to undertake enforcement action. It is not for the courts to use their supervisory powers to control what the Parliamentary Commissioner for Standards or the Lords Commissioners for Standards do in relation to standards investigations.[11]

13.9 These are the principal bodies involved in the Parliamentary Standards regime:

i. The House of Commons' Committee on Privileges and Standards is a Select Committee of the Commons. It supervises the work of the Commissioner for Standards and decides whether MPs have breached the Commons Code of

[9] 'Guidance, The Seven Principles of Public Life' (Committee on Standards in Public Life, May 1995).

[10] 'Upholding Standards in Public Life: Final report of the Standards Matter 2 Review' (Committee on Standards in Public Life, November 2021) Ch 1 at 20.

[11] *R v Parliamentary Comr for Standards, ex p Al Fayed* [1998] 1 WLR 669 at 673; *R v Chaytor* [2011] 1 AC 684 at para 77.

Conduct. It recommends serious sanctions to be imposed by the House. The principal rules approved by the Commons that apply to MPs are set out in: House of Commons Standing Orders 159, 150, 150A, 150B, 150C, 150D and 150E; the Code of Conduct together with the Guide to the Rules relating to the Conduct of Members (Commons);[12] and the Procedural Protocol in respect of the Code of Conduct (Commons).[13]

ii. The Independent Expert Panel is a body established by the House of Commons' Standing Orders. It determines sanctions and hears appeals in respect of bullying and sexual harassment cases brought under the ICGS. It also hears appeals against decisions of the Committee on Privileges and Standards relating to breaches of the Commons Code of Conduct.

iii. The Independent Parliamentary Standards Authority is an independent body established by statute that sets the financial scheme governing MPs' salaries and expenses. IPSA has a Compliance Officer who has the power to investigate MPs for breaches of the financial scheme, including the misuse of parliamentary expenses.[14] IPSA may direct MPs to repay wrongly-claimed sums and, if they do not, it has the power to deduct those sums from their salary.[15] It is a criminal offence for an MP to make an expenses claim, or to provide information for the purposes of such a claim, that the MP knows to be false or materially misleading.[16]

iv. The House of Lords' Conduct Committee is a select committee of the House of Lords. It supervises matters relating to the Lords Code of Conduct, determines the sanction to be imposed where the Lords Commissioners for Standards have found a Member in breach of the Code; and hears appeals by Members against the decisions of the Lords Commissioners for Standards.

B. The Registers of Financial Interests

13.10 Each House of Parliament operates a Register of Financial Interests. The Registers' purpose is to provide information about financial interests and benefits which one might reasonably consider to influence a parliamentarian's execution of his or her public duties.[17] The rules about financial interests are detailed and subject to amendment from time to time. In-depth guidance about the current rules can be found in publications of each House, respectively the House of Commons 'Guide to the Rules relating to the Conduct of Members' (2023)[18] and the House of Lords 'Guide to the Code of Conduct' (2023).[19] Members must also declare relevant interests. The declaration of

[12] As approved by the House of Commons on 12 December 2022.

[13] Most recently approved by the Commons on 18 October 2022 and by the Committee on Standards on 7 February 2023.

[14] Parliamentary Standards Act 2009, s 9.

[15] ibid Sch 4, para 5.

[16] ibid s 10.

[17] See 'Register of Members' Financial Interests: Introduction to the Registers for the 2019 Parliament' (House of Commons, January 2020).

[18] 'The Guide to the Rules Relating to the Conduct of Members' (House of Commons, 23 January 2023) HC 1083.

[19] 'Guide to the Code of Conduct', 13th edn (House of Lords, September 2023) HL Paper 255.

interests is a distinct requirement from registration but one which sits alongside it to ensure the transparency and integrity of parliamentary proceedings.

i. The Commons' Register

13.11 The Commons' Register was established following a Resolution of the House in 1974.[20] The Commissioner for Parliamentary Standards is responsible for maintaining the Register and for monitoring its operation.[21] MPs must register all their current financial interests, and any registrable benefits received in the 12 months before their election within one month of their election. MPs must thereafter register any change in their registrable interests within 28 days.[22] There are ten categories of registrable interest: employment and earnings; donations and other support; gifts, benefits and hospitality; visits outside the UK; gifts and benefits from outside the UK; land and property; shareholdings; miscellaneous interests; family members employed; and family members involved in lobbying. The Commons has published guidance setting out the financial thresholds for registering interests pertaining to those categories, as well as guidance on the matters that fall within them, in 'The Guide to the Rules relating to the Conduct of Members' (2023).[23]

13.12 MPs must declare interests if the interests meet a 'relevance test'. The relevance test is whether the interests in question might reasonably be thought by others to influence the MP's actions or words as a Member of the Commons.[24] Provided the relevant test is met, the general position is that MPs must declare their interests on the following occasions, which are dealt with in more detail in 'The Guide to the Rules relating to the Conduct of Members':

i. in the Commons Chamber and in general committees when they are making a speech or intervening in a debate; or during the Committee or consideration stage of a Bill;
ii. in Committee on an Opposed Private Bill;
iii. in sitting on Select Committees;
iv. when tabling any written notice;
v. when approaching others, for example, by formal or informal communication with those responsible for matters of public policy, public expenditure or the delivery of public services (including in communications with Ministers and public officials). If those communications are in writing, then the declaration should be in writing too; otherwise it should be oral.
vi. when booking facilities on the parliamentary estate, for example, private dining rooms; or function rooms on behalf of an outside organisation other than the MP's political party (but not simply for a meeting room where simple refreshments such as tea and biscuits may be available).

[20] Resolution of 22 May 1974, amended on 9 February 2009.
[21] House of Commons SO 150(2)(a) and (d).
[22] House of Commons, Code of Conduct – D Rules of Conduct (23 January 2023) HC 1083, para 5.
[23] 'The Guide to the Rules relating to the Conduct of Members' (House of Commons, 23 January 2023).
[24] ibid 'Part 2: Declaration of Members' Interests', para 6.

ii. *The Lords' Register*

13.13 Members of the House of Lords must register all relevant interests, and declare them as relevant when speaking in the House, or communicating with ministers or public servants.[25] As in the Commons, registration and declaration are two distinct (albeit related) obligations. Registration is done by making an entry in the register and its purpose is to provide continuing, public notification. The purpose of a declaration is to ensure that other Members, ministers, and members of the public are aware of any relevant interest at the point of a Member of the House of Lords' participation in legislative activity. The Lords' 'Guide to the Code of Conduct' directs that Members should declare interests briefly, usually at the beginning of their speech in a way that is unambiguous and does not require prior knowledge to be understood.[26]

13.14 The test for relevance is whether:

> the interest might be thought by a reasonable member of the public to influence the way in which a member of the House of Lords discharges his or her parliamentary duties: in the case of registration, the member's parliamentary duties in general; in the case of declaration, his or her duties in respect of the particular matter under discussion.[27]

Members of the House of Lords who fail to register a relevant interest are prohibited from undertaking any action, speech or proceeding of the House (save voting) to which the interest would be relevant until they have registered it. Where members vote in a division in which they have an unregistered relevant interest, they must register the interest within 24 hours of the division.[28]

13.15 The Lords Register of Interests is maintained by the Registrar of Lords' Interests. The categories of interest that fall for registration, slightly different to those in the Commons, are: directorships; remunerated employment; people with significant control of a company; shareholdings; land and property; sponsorship; overseas visits; gifts, benefits and hospitality; miscellaneous financial interests; and non-financial interests.

C. Behaviour Code

13.16 Parliament's Behaviour Code articulates broad principles of good behaviour governing how all members of the parliamentary community should treat each other. It is relevant in particular to allegations of bullying and harassment addressed under Parliament's ICGS (see paragraph 13.52 ff below). The Behaviour Code's principles are:

i. respect and value everyone – bullying, harassment and sexual misconduct are not tolerated;
ii. recognise your power, influence or authority and don't abuse them;

[25] Code of Conduct for Members of the House of Lords (September 2023) Rules of Conduct, para 14.
[26] 'Guide to the Code of Conduct', 13th edn (House of Lords, September 2023) HL Paper 255, paras 106 and 109.
[27] Code of Conduct for Members of the House of Lords (September 2023) Rules of Conduct, para 15.
[28] 'Guide to the Code of Conduct', 13th edn (House of Lords, September 2023) HL Paper 255, para 43.

iii. think about how your behaviour affects others and strive to understand their perspective;
iv. act professionally towards others;
v. ensure Parliament meets the highest ethical standards of integrity, courtesy and mutual respect;
vi. speak up about any unacceptable behaviour you see.

13.17 The House of Commons endorsed the Behaviour Code by a resolution of 19 July 2018 implementing aspects of the ICGS. The House of Lords' Code of Conduct provides that Members of the Lords should observe the principles of the Behaviour Code, which must be taken into consideration by the House of Lords authorities when they are investigating any allegation of bullying, harassment or sexual misconduct.[29]

D. Paid Lobbying

13.18 Paid lobbying is strictly forbidden by the rules of both Houses. It has long been a concern. In 1910 the judicial committee of the House of Lords expressed concern about people 'using capital funds to procure the subjection of members of Parliament to their commands'.[30] The cash for questions scandal of the 1990s presented an egregious modern example of paid lobbying. The Codes of Conduct of both Houses emphasise the need for legislators to undertake their parliamentary functions independently of external financial interests. The paragraphs below outline the shape and scope of the rules. Both Houses have published detailed guidance about the prohibitions on lobbying in return for financial reward.

13.19 MPs must not accept any fee, compensation or reward in connection with the promotion of, or opposition to, any Bill, motion or other matters, or intended to be submitted to the Commons or to any of its Committees.[31] The Commons has approved and adopted detailed guidance about the scope and operation of that prohibition, which is to be found in the Code of Conduct and Guide to the Rules (February 2023). The rules are qualified as follows:

i. They to not apply to financial support received from an MPs' own political party. Thus, the rules do not take into account financial support or salaries paid by the party organisation; nor do the rules prohibit sponsorship from trade unions or other party-affiliated organisations, subject to the rules on registration and declaration of interests being observed.
ii. The rules on paid lobbying do not prevent MPs from initiating or participating in proceedings or approaching Ministers and public officials because the MPs

[29] ibid 'General principles', para 13.

[30] In the context of trade unions funding salaries of Labour Party MPs which is a practice now permitted: see *Osborne v Amalgamated Society of Railway Servants (No 1)* [1910] AC 87, also cited in respect of forbidden contractual arrangements between parliamentarians and extra-parliamentary actors in para 7.32.

[31] House of Commons, Code of Conduct – D Rules of Conduct (23 January 2023) HC 1083, Rule 3.

themselves have a financial interest relevant to the matter. The rules on registration and declaration will nonetheless apply to such circumstances.

iii. The restrictions against paid lobbying last for 12 months after an MP receives a financial reward or consideration. After that period has ended, it is not against the rules for an MP to lobby on the matter in question. But MPs can free themselves immediately from restrictions imposed arising from a past benefit received within the previous 12 months by repaying the full value of any benefit to the outside person or organisation in question.

iv. Former MPs are also bound by the rules for six months after their departure from the Commons in respect of any approach they make to Ministers, other MPs or public officials. Former MPs must not use their grace and favour parliamentary pass for the purposes of lobbying on the parliamentary estate.[32]

13.20 The House of Lords' Code of Conduct forbids paid lobbying, though its scope and operation differs in some respects from that of the Commons. Detailed guidance on the Lords' rules about lobbying can be found in the 'Guide to the Code of Conduct'.[33] Members of the Lords must not seek to profit from membership of the House by accepting or agreeing to accept any payment, incentive or reward in return for providing parliamentary services or advice.[34] (That rule does not apply to the Lords Spiritual or Ministers of the Crown.[35]) Parliamentary services include, for these purposes, participation in any parliamentary proceeding, any interaction with members of either House, ministers or parliamentary officials and any ancillary services (eg setting up an All Party Parliamentary Group or sponsoring a parliamentary reception or pass).[36] Members of the Lords are permitted to work for, or to hold financial interests in, organisations involved in parliamentary lobbying on behalf of clients, so long as Members do not personally carry out parliamentary services on behalf of those clients.[37] (Such interests may need to be registered and declared in accordance with the rules.)

13.21 The House of Lords' Code of Conduct also prohibits its Members from seeking to confer, by parliamentary means, an exclusive benefit on an outside organisation or person in which the Member has a financial interest.[38] This rule is known as the 'exclusive benefit' rule; essentially, it means that Members who are paid by a particular organisation are not allowed to give a benefit exclusively to that organisation by parliamentary means. Parliamentary means here refers to the core work of the House, including all its proceedings (tabling a motion, voting, speaking in debates, asking questions, and so on). An exclusive benefit is narrowly defined as relating to a particular organisation. So, if a Member were to be paid by a pharmaceutical company, he or she

[32] 'The Guide to the Rules relating to the Conduct of Members' (House of Commons, 2023) Section 3: Lobbying for Reward or Consideration, paras 4, 8 and 16 and 17.

[33] 'Guide to the Code of Conduct', 13th edn (House of Lords, September 2023) HL Paper 255, para 26.

[34] Code of Conduct for Members of the House of Lords (September 2023) General principles, para 11(b).

[35] 'Guide to the Code of Conduct', 13th edn (House of Lords, September 2023) HL Paper 255, para 30.

[36] ibid para 26.

[37] ibid para 29.

[38] Code of Conduct for Members of the House of Lords (September 2023) General principles, para 11(a).

could not table an amendment that would confer an advantage on that company in particular; but could table an amendment that was relevant to NHS spending on drugs or the pharmaceutical sector generally.[39] Members must be cognisant of the other rules that are relevant to their activities, even if such activities do not engage the rules on lobbying set out above; for example, the rules that require them to act in the public interest and to comply with the registration of financial interests. Members need also to take care not to give the impression that they give greater weight to representations because the representation comes from paid lobbyists.[40]

13.22 The work of lobbying consultants is regulated by the Transparency of Lobbying, Non-Party Campaigning and Trade Union Administration Act 2014. Especially, a Register is kept recording the names of consultant lobbyists and their clients. The rules governing lobbying consultants are addressed in Chapter 9, Section IV.

IV. Enforcing Standards in the House of Commons

A. Committee on Standards and Privileges

13.23 The Committee on Standards and Privileges adjudicates on cases alleging a breach of Parliamentary standards. The Committee supervises the work of the Commissioner for Standards, considers his reports on alleged breaches of the rules, reports to the House of Commons and makes recommendations to the House about serious sanctions in individual cases. It is for the House to decide whether to accept the Committee's reports and recommendations by passing a motion to that effect. The Committee itself has the power to impose less serious sanctions on MPs where it determines that a breach has occurred. The Committee also has responsibility for considering policy in respect of parliamentary standards.[41]

B. Commissioner for Standards

13.24 The Parliamentary Commissioner for Standards carries out the practical tasks of monitoring MPs' compliance with the Code of Conduct and determining whether the Code has been breached. The Commissioner is an Officer of the House of Commons, appointed by the Commons.[42] He has four essential functions: maintaining the Register of Members' Financial Interests and any other registers of interests that the Commons has decided to establish;[43] providing advice to MPs and the Committee on Standards,[44] monitoring the operation of the Code of Conduct and the Registers and making

[39] 'Guide to the Code of Conduct', 13th edn (House of Lords, September 2023) HL Paper 255, paras 17–19.
[40] ibid para 32.
[41] House of Commons SO 149.
[42] House of Commons SO 150(1).
[43] House of Commons SO 150(2)(a).
[44] House of Commons SO 150(2)(b), (c).

recommendations to the Committee about the same;[45] and investigating and making findings about MPs' conduct.[46]

C. The Code of Conduct

i. Rules of Conduct

13.25 The Seven Principles of Public Life inform the Code; it is to be assumed that the Code will be interpreted concordantly with those Principles. The Code of Conduct applies to all aspects of MPs' public activities, but not to conduct purely in private or personal life with no public effect. The application of the Code is a matter for the Committee on Standards and the Parliamentary Commissioner for Standards, as set out below.[47] The process to determine a breach is inquisitorial: both the Commissioner and the Committee are directly involved in investigating and establishing the facts.[48] The standard of proof for whether an MP has broken the Code is the balance of probabilities (whether the alleged breach is more likely to have happened than not).

13.26 The current rules, reproduced below, are set out in Part D of the 2022 Code of Conduct. Rules 1–11 concern general conduct; rules 12–17 require MPs to uphold the Code of Conduct and co-operate with the standards regime.

Rules of Conduct

1. Members must treat their staff and all those visiting or working for or with Parliament with dignity, courtesy and respect.
2. Members must base their conduct on a consideration of the public interest, avoid conflict between personal interest and the public interest and resolve any conflict between the two, at once, and in favour of the public interest.
3. The acceptance by a Member of a bribe to influence his or her conduct as a Member, including any fee, compensation or reward in connection with the promotion of, or opposition to, any Bill, Motion, or other matter submitted, or intended to be submitted to the House, or to any Committee of the House, is contrary to the law of Parliament.
4. Members must rigorously follow the rules on lobbying set out in the Guide to the Rules.
5. Members must fulfil conscientiously the requirements of the House in respect of the registration of interests in the Register of Members' Financial Interests. New Members must register all their current financial interests, and any registrable benefits (other than earnings) received in the 12 months before their election within one month of their election, and Members must register any change in those registrable interests within 28 days.
6. Members must always be open and frank in declaring any relevant interest in any proceeding of the House or its Committees, and in any communications with Ministers, Members, public officials or public office holders.

[45] House of Commons SO 150(2)(d).
[46] House of Commons SO 150(2)(e), (f).
[47] Code of Conduct and Guide to the Rules (House of Commons, 2022) Part B.
[48] Procedural Protocol in respect of the Code of Conduct (House of Commons, 7 February 2023) para 5.

7. Members must only use information which they have received in confidence in the course of their parliamentary activities in connection with those activities, and never for other purposes.
8. Excepting modest and reasonable personal use, Members must ensure that the use of facilities and services provided to them by Parliament, including an office, is in support of their parliamentary activities, and is in accordance with all relevant rules.
9. Members must not provide, or agree to provide, paid parliamentary advice, including undertaking, or agreeing to undertake services as a Parliamentary strategist, adviser or consultant.
10. A Member who is the Chair and Registered Contact of an All-Party Parliamentary Group must ensure that the Group and any secretariat observe the rules set down for such Groups.
11. Members shall never undertake any action which would cause significant damage to the reputation and integrity of the House of Commons as a whole, or of its Members generally.

[*The following rules relate to upholding the Code of Conduct*]

12. Members must co-operate at all times with the Parliamentary Commissioner for Standards in the conduct of any investigation and with the Committee on Standards and the Independent Expert Panel in any subsequent consideration of a case.
13. Members must not disclose details in relation to: (i) any investigation by the Parliamentary Commissioner for Standards except when required by law to do so, or authorised by the Commissioner; nor (ii) the proceedings of the Committee on Standards or the Independent Expert Panel in relation to a complaint unless required by law to do so, or authorised by the Committee or the Panel respectively.
14. Members must not lobby a member of the Committee on Standards, the Independent Expert Panel or the Parliamentary Commissioner for Standards, or their staff, in a manner calculated or intended to influence their consideration of whether a breach of the Code of Conduct has occurred, or in relation to the imposition of a sanction.
15. Members must not seek to influence, encourage, induce or attempt to induce, a person making a complaint in an investigation to withdraw or amend their complaint, or any witness or other person participating in a complaint to withdraw or alter their evidence.
16. Members must comply with any sanction imposed by the Independent Expert Panel.
17. Members must comply with a sanction imposed by the Committee on Standards or the House relating to withdrawal of services or facilities from a Member.

ii. The Rule against Significant Damage to the Reputation and Integrity of the House of Commons

13.27 The scope of rule 11 above is broad. It covers behaviour of any nature and captures actions that have actually damaged the reputation and integrity of the Commons or its Members, as well as behaviour that might be capable of doing so. The rule may be breached by conduct that takes place at private events outside Parliament to which MPs have nevertheless been invited because of their public position. In 2022 the Commissioner investigated Mr Chris Pincher for allegedly groping two people while he was intoxicated at an event in the Carlton Club. The event was not open to the public but was, nevertheless, attended by Conservative Party politicians, staff and other guests. The Commissioner found that Mr Pincher's behaviour was deeply inappropriate and that it was witnessed by at least one other person, and probably others.

The Committee accepted the Commissioner's findings and concluded that Mr Pincher's behaviour was 'completely inappropriate, profoundly damaging to the individuals concerned, and represented an abuse of power'. The Committee therefore determined that the Mr Pincher had breached the rule. In so doing, the Committee held that the event that Mr Pincher attended had been part of his public life, and so his behaviour fell within the ambit of the Code of Conduct.[49]

13.28 The fact that behaviour has taken place purely within the bounds of an MP's personal life does not preclude it from breaching the reputation and integrity rule if the behaviour demonstrated disregard or disrespect for the law. The case of Margaret Ferrier concerned an alleged breach of Covid-19 restrictions by Ms Ferrier. The Committee concluded that Ms Ferrier's behaviour would have caused significant damage to the reputation of the House on the following bases: she knowingly and recklessly exposed members of the public and those on the parliamentary estate to the risk of contracting Covid-19; she demonstrated a disregard for the parliamentary and national guidance in place; she mislead her Chief Whip and in so doing acted dishonestly; she breached the criminal law in Scotland which had caused significant damage to the reputation of the House.[50] The first notable point here is that the Committee determined that 'disregard of or disrespect for the law by a Member cannot be considered to be part of a Member's "purely private and personal life" (which is excluded from the scope of the Code)'. The second point is the fact that an MP's behaviour has been sanctioned by a criminal court does not exempt it from being addressed as a breach of the Code of Conduct by the parliamentary standards regime.

13.29 Attempts by MPs to use their status to influence judicial decisions by lobbying or pressurising judges fall foul of the reputation rule, as the following case illustrates. Charlie Elphicke, formerly a Conservative MP, stood down at the 2019 general election, following allegations of sexual assault. He was tried and convicted in 2020. Before he was sentenced, the trial judge, Mrs Justice Whipple, was due to decide an application to release the pre-sentencing character references for Mr Elphicke (which, given the conviction, were potentially damaging to those who had provided them). Natalie Elphicke, who had been elected in 2019 to the seat previously held by her husband, together with four other Conservative MPs, sent a letter to the Senior Presiding Judge for England and Wales and to the President of the Queen's Bench Division, copied to Mrs Justice Whipple, stating

> We believe it is important for you, as senior presiding judges with relevant oversight responsibility, to consider the crucially important matters of principle which are at stake in this case, prior to any disclosure of names of any members of the public or of the references they have provided to the court. So serious a matter with significant repercussions also should be

[49] House of Commons Committee on Standards, Twelfth Report of Session 2022–23, 6 July 2023. The Committee recommended a suspension of eight weeks from the House; Mr Pincher subsequently vacated his seat in the Commons, triggering a by-election.

[50] House of Commons Committee on Standards, Ninth Report of Session 2022–23, 30 March 2023. The Committee recommended a sanction of suspension from the Commons for 30 days, which was adopted by the House, and triggered a recall petition and a by-election where she did not seek re-election.

> considered further by Parliament. We are all Parliamentarians, In order that we may freely express our serious concerns pertaining to vulnerable private individuals, we have decided to place our own references into the public domain.

The Committee found that this letter constituted an improper attempt to influence judicial proceedings, risked giving the impression that elected politicians can bring influence to bear on the judiciary out of public view, was corrosive of the rule of law, and could undermine public trust in the independence of judges. By sending the letter the MPs had caused significant damage to the reputation and integrity of the House of Commons as a whole or of its members generally.[51]

13.30 MPs should not: make private representations about proceedings which are active or are not definitively concluded to members of the judiciary, outside of the court's own processes for making representations; or make private representations about proceedings which are active or are not definitively concluded to a tribunal, such as an employment or immigration tribunal, outside of the tribunal's own processes for making representations; or otherwise attempt to pressurise members of the judiciary in the exercise of their functions.[52]

13.31 The Committee also issued the following guidance on what MPs may do in respect of legal proceedings. MPs may (subject to the other rules of the House): participate in or initiate legal proceedings; provide character references;[53] raise any case in proceedings in Parliament in terms which do not breach the *sub judice* resolution, or request that the Chair waive the *sub judice* resolution in a particular case; engage in private correspondence with members of the judiciary which does not relate to active judicial proceedings; make *private* representations to a decision-making body, mediating body (such as an Ombudsman) or regulatory body, which is not judicial in function; or make, outside of proceedings in Parliament, the same kind of public comment as any other citizen could do.

13.32 It is likely that MPs will breach the reputation rule (as well as the rules against prioritising private interests and the use of House stationary) if they seek to use their position to intimidate or influence members of the public in a private dispute. For example, Conor Burns MP wrote on House of Commons headed writing paper to a member of the public who was in a legal dispute with his (Mr Burns') father, saying 'my role in the public eye could well attract interest especially if I were to use parliamentary privilege to raise the case'. The Committee found that Mr Burns had used his parliamentary position in an attempt to intimidate a member of the public, in a dispute relating to purely private family interests which had no connection with Mr Burns' parliamentary duties. The Committee further observed the great importance of parliamentary privilege to MPs' freedom of speech in Parliament and their scrutiny of the Executive; it was

[51] House of Commons Committee on Standards, Report (21 July 2021).

[52] ibid para 75.

[53] But, where the reference is provided in relation to an MP's family member or friend, it is wise that the MP does not use House of Commons headed stationary to do so: see the House of Commons Committee on Standards, Report (Kate Osamor MP) (19 March 2020) para 27.

essential to maintaining public respect for Parliament that the protection of parliamentary privilege should not be abused by an MP in the pursuit of his purely private and personal interests. In that context a mere apology would not suffice.[54]

D. Investigations into MPs' Conduct

13.33 Investigations into a breach of the Code of Conduct are undertaken by the Commissioner for Standards under the Code of Conduct's 'Procedural Protocol'. Investigations into matters relating to harassment, sexual harassment or bullying are carried out under the ICGS, which is set out at paragraph 13.52 ff below.

i. Investigations under the Procedural Protocol in Respect of the Code of Conduct

13.34 The Procedural Protocol governs allegations about, investigations into, and determinations of, a breach of the Rules of Conduct and the Rules relating to upholding the Code of Conduct. The Protocol has been approved by the House of Commons and has the same authority as the Code of Conduct.[55]

13.35 The Commissioner for Standards may initiate investigations into MPs' conduct on his own motion, or following a complaint against an MP made by an individual, or by a self-referral by a particular MP, or into matters that arise from another investigation which the Commissioner has undertaken.[56]

ii. Words of Advice

13.36 The Commissioner has the power to instigate informal discussions with an MP to indicate concern about the MP's reported attitude, behaviour or conduct. The Commissioner may also require an MP to attend a formal meeting at which the Commissioner may indicate concern about or give words of advice on the MP's attitude, behaviour or conduct.[57] The Commissioner may decide to do this instead of initiating a formal investigation; it is his decision alone whether to give words of advice or an indication of concern to an MP.[58] Usually, the power to give an informal indication of concern is exercised in circumstances where an MP's alleged conduct does not actually engage one of the Code's rules and, therefore, is not capable of being investigated by the Commissioner under the Procedural Protocol. No formal action flows from an

[54] House of Commons Committee on Standards, Fourth Report of Session 2019–21 (4 May 2020). The Committee recommended that Mr Burns should be suspended for seven days.

[55] Procedural Protocol in respect of the Code of Conduct (House of Commons, 7 February 2023) para 4.

[56] House of Commons SO 150(e) permits the Commissioner to investigate on his own motion; see Procedural Protocol in respect of the Code of Conduct (House of Commons, 7 February 2023) para 21.

[57] House of Commons SO 150(5).

[58] Explanatory Note on the Commissioner's powers to indicate concern and issue words of advice to Members without opening an investigation (Parliamentary Commissioner for Standards, 5 June 2023) para 2.

informal indication of concern, though MPs are encouraged to consider it and to take it into account.[59]

13.37 The Commissioner normally exercises his power to give formal words of advice or indications of concern where an MP's behaviour, if repeated, would probably result in further inquiry and a case being opened by the Commissioner.[60] The issuing of formal words of advice or indications of concern is generally done in writing by letter which is retained on the Commissioner's file for six months; and the MP is informed that a formal inquiry may be opened if the conduct in question continues, or in response to new evidence or in other relevant circumstances. An MP who prefers not to receive formal words of advice or indications of concern may write to the Commissioner to that effect.[61] The content and issuing of words of advice and indications of concern, whether formal or informal, is subject to parliamentary privilege and is confidential (and will remain confidential even if an investigation into the MP is subsequently opened).[62]

iii. Making an Allegation against an MP

13.38 A complaint may be made to the Commissioner only about an allegation that an MP has breached the Code. The Commissioner has no jurisdiction to investigate an allegation of a breach of the Seven Principles of Public Life,[63] and he has no power to investigate allegations that relate to an MP's purely private and personal life, nor matters that fall in the following categories which are regulated by other authorities: an MP's conduct in the Chamber of the House of Commons (that is a matter for the Speaker); alleged breaches of the parliamentary expenses scheme (that is a matter for the Independent Parliamentary Standards Authority);[64] allegations of criminal misconduct, which are normally a matter for the police; questions about the funding of political parties and politicians or donations received by them, as that is a matter for the Electoral Commission; allegations that the Ministerial Code has been breached, which is a matter for the Cabinet Office.[65] The Commissioner may investigate policy matters, an MP's views or opinions (including those expressed on social media) and an MP's handling of their casework and correspondence, but only if those matters arise as part of an investigation into an alleged breach of the rule guarding the reputation and integrity of the House as a whole or of members generally (presently set out as rule 11 of the Code).[66]

[59] ibid paras 4 and 5.

[60] ibid para 7.

[61] ibid paras 7–9.

[62] ibid para 3.

[63] House of Commons SO 150(e); Procedural Protocol in respect of the Code of Conduct (House of Commons, 7 February 2023) para 7.

[64] The IPSA regulates and administers the business costs and decides the pay and pensions of the 650 elected MPs and their staff in the UK. It is an independent body: see www.theipsa.org.uk.

[65] Procedural Protocol in respect of the Code of Conduct (House of Commons, 7 February 2023) para 19.

[66] ibid para 18.

13.39 Anyone may submit an allegation that an MP has breached the Code. Allegations made by organisations (companies, charities, political parties etc) or made anonymously are not valid. Complaints or allegations made on behalf of someone else are invalid, except where a person raises an allegation to the Commissioner on behalf of another as part of an agreed reasonable adjustment for a disability. Allegations must be made in writing and delivered in hard copy by hand or by post, or by email. An allegation must contain the following required information: the full name and postal address of the complainant; an explanation setting out how and why the MP is said to have breached one or more of the numbered paragraphs in the Code; and any supporting evidence that is available. Where the complaint is made *by* another MP or by a Member of the House of Lords, he or she should also send a copy of the complaint to the MP against whom it is has been made.[67]

iv. Formal Investigations

13.40 The Commissioner will instigate a formal investigation if the allegations fall within his remit, if there is sufficient evidence to justify starting an investigation, and if an investigation would be proportionate. No appeal can be made against a decision not to conduct a formal investigation, though the decision may be revisited if new evidence comes to light.[68] An investigation procedure is set out in detailed provisions in the Procedural Protocol. Members will be provided with a copy of the complaint and any supporting evidence and have an opportunity to submit a response to the complaint and to any questions posed by the Commissioner. Members should usually correspond personally with the Commissioner and not through the conduit of legal advisers. The Commissioner should offer the MP an opportunity to meet him at the outset of the investigation; thereafter, the MP under investigation may request further meetings with the Commissioner and may be accompanied by a legal adviser.[69]

13.41 The scope of the investigation may be augmented if the Commissioner uncovers grounds to do so. The Commissioner has discretion to suspend the investigation in circumstances where the MP in question suffers ill health or a bereavement during the investigation; or where a related police investigation is taking place. The Commissioner will also cease an investigation upon the dissolution of Parliament or if the MP otherwise ceases to be a Member while an investigation is in progress.[70]

13.42 There are three possible outcomes of a concluded formal investigation: a decision that there has been no breach of the Code, a finding of a breach with rectification, or a finding of a breach with a referral to the Committee on Standards. We address these three potential outcomes in turn, below.

[67] House of Commons SO 150(e); Procedural Protocol in respect of the Code of Conduct (House of Commons, 7 February 2023) Part 2.

[68] Procedural Protocol in respect of the Code of Conduct (House of Commons, 7 February 2023) paras 27 and 30.

[69] ibid paras 32–36.

[70] ibid paras 39–40.

v. No Breach

13.43 The Commissioner may decide that the allegation has not been substantiated on the evidence. In that case, he will determine that there has been no breach of the Code. In those circumstances the Commissioner must notify the Committee on Standards that there has been no breach of the Code and, depending on the seriousness of the allegation, either publish a letter containing his reasoning, the evidence and the outcome of his investigation on the Commissioner's website; or, where the allegation was particularly serious or raised matters of wider public interest, the Commissioner may elect to submit a memorandum to the Committee, upon which the Committee will consider his conclusions and make its own report to the House of Commons.[71]

vi. Rectification

13.44 The rectification procedure allows the standards investigation to conclude without a referral to the Committee on Standards in circumstances where the Commissioner finds that a minor breach of the Code has occurred and the MP in question agrees with the Commissioner's findings and agrees to take (and then does undertake) remedial action specified by the Commissioner.[72] The Commissioner must notify the Committee where he concludes an investigation using the rectification procedure. The remedial action required may be words of advice to the MP, a written apology, an apology in the House on a point of order, or if relevant a correction and annotation of the Register of Members' Financial Interests, or repayment of money (where House resources have been misused or wrongly claimed). An apology will be required from the member in all cases of rectification.

vii. Referral to the Committee on Standards

13.45 The Commissioner must refer a matter to the Committee on Standards for determination in three circumstances: where the Commissioner considers that there has been a breach of the code which is unsuitable to be resolved by the rectification procedure; where the MP in question does not accept the Commissioner's view that there has been a breach; or if the Commissioner's investigation raises issues of wider importance.[73]

13.46 The referral is made by a memorandum from the Commissioner to the Committee in which the Commissioner sets out his opinion on issues of fact and whether there has been a breach of the Code. The MP against whom allegations lie must be given an opportunity to comment on the draft findings of fact or any written evidence or draft factual findings set out in the draft memorandum before the memorandum is sent to the Committee. The Commissioner must give consideration to any representations from the MP about the memorandum but has no duty to give effect to them.[74]

[71] ibid paras 44–46.
[72] House of Commons SO 150(4).
[73] Procedural Protocol in respect of the Code of Conduct (House of Commons, 7 February 2023) para 53.
[74] ibid paras 53–56.

13.47 Once the Commissioner has sent a memorandum to the Committee a copy of it will be sent confidentially to the MP to whom it relates. The MP will thereafter have an opportunity to submit written evidence. MPs are entitled to make a request to give oral evidence at the discretion of the Committee. Witnesses giving oral evidence are entitled to be treated with courtesy and respect and should be permitted to give their best evidence.[75] The Committee may also require an MP to appear before it and give oral evidence. MPs who give oral evidence are entitled to be accompanied by a legal representative, but the legal representative has no right to address the Committee and must only give private advice to the MP in question.[76]

13.48 The Committee will consider the substance of a case before it only after it has received written evidence from an MP who has indicated he wishes to provide it. The Committee must consider any procedural issues that arise before discussing whether, in its view, a breach of the Code has occurred. The Committee usually makes a provisional decision on the question of breach in order to help the chair, and those assisting the chair, to produce a draft report for the Committee's consideration. The Committee finally determines whether a breach has occurred by agreeing its report. In doing so, the Committee will normally decide whether to impose or recommend to the House a formal sanction (see paragraph 13.51 below for the Committee's power to impose sanctions). The Committee will then deliver its Report to the House of Commons alongside the Commissioner's memorandum and any written evidence.[77]

13.49 MPs have a right of appeal against the decision of the Committee to the Commons' Independent Expert Panel. All appeals must comply with the requirements of Part 6 of the Procedural Protocol in respect of the Code of Conduct (as amended). The Independent Expert Panel may dismiss or uphold an appeal; in the latter case the Panel may remit the case to the Committee or substitute its own decision for the Committee's on either the question of breach or sanction.[78]

viii. Sanctions

13.50 The Committee may decide that there has been a breach of the Code but that there should be no sanction;[79] that eventuality is rare, however, and the Committee usually imposes or recommends a penalty. The Committee itself has the power to impose the following sanctions without recourse to the House:[80]

i. an apology from the MP in writing, which would normally be published, or on the floor of the House by means of a point of order or a personal statement;
ii. requiring an MP to attend training, or to repay money;

[75] ibid para 76.
[76] ibid paras 64–67.
[77] ibid paras 68–74.
[78] ibid Part 6.
[79] ibid para 78.
[80] ibid para 79.

iii. withdrawal of services and facilities from an MP, and imposing other personal restrictions, where this will not affect the core functions of an MP;
iv. for individuals who are not MPs, subject to the approval of the Speaker, withdrawal of parliamentary passes, either indefinitely or for a fixed period.

13.51 The most serious sanctions may only be imposed by the House itself; the Committee's role is to recommend to the House the sanction it thinks should be imposed. The sanction is imposed by a vote on a motion on the Committee's Report taken on the floor of the House without debate or amendment.[81] These serious sanctions are:[82]

i. withdrawal of services and facilities from a Member, and imposing other personal restrictions, where this will affect the core functions of a Member, and where the sanction affects the nature of the offence;
ii. dismissal from a select committee;
iii. suspension from the service of the House for a specified period (during which time the Member receives no salary and must withdraw from the precincts of the House); where the Committee decides that an MP has breached the reputation and integrity rule in paragraph 11 of the Code, it should, save in exceptional circumstances, recommend that the House suspends or expels the MP in question;[83]
iv. withholding of a Member's salary or allowances even if the Member has not been suspended;
v. expulsion from the House.

E. Bullying and Harassment: The Independent Complaints and Grievance Scheme

13.52 The rules governing the ICGS are set out in the Commons' Standing Orders, Resolutions of the House and in several written policies and procedures, especially the Bullying and Harassment Policy, the Bullying and Harassment Procedure, the Sexual Harassment Policy and the Sexual Harassment Procedure. The scheme is subject to revision from time to time and the published policies should be consulted as appropriate.

i. Types of Conduct that Fall within the Scheme

13.53 The scheme captures conduct which amounts to bullying or harassment, including sexual harassment, connected with parliamentary activity.[84] Conduct will fall within the scope of the scheme if:

i. it is done by *and* against members of the 'parliamentary community', comprising MPs, peers, parliamentary officers, staff and parliamentary employees but

[81] ibid para 85.
[82] ibid para 81.
[83] ibid para 82.
[84] HC Resolution of 23 June 2020.

also employees of political parties undertaking parliamentary work, members of the press gallery, contractors and interns working in Parliament and visitors to Parliament. The scheme therefore anticipates and requires a complainant (the person at whom the conduct is targeted) and a respondent (the person who has allegedly done the conduct).

ii. the conduct takes place on the parliamentary estate or in constituency offices. Alleged bullying will fall within the remit of the scheme if it takes place somewhere else outside Parliament in the course of a person's parliamentary work; alleged sexual harassment will fall within the scheme wherever it takes place so long as it arises in circumstances related to the complainant or respondent's parliamentary work.[85]

13.54 Bullying and harassment for these purposes are defined broadly and reflect the definitions of those terms set out by Acas and in the Equality Act 2010 respectively.[86] 'Bullying' encompasses:

> offensive, intimidating, malicious or insulting behaviour involving abuse or misuse of power that can make a person feel vulnerable, upset, undermined, humiliated, denigrated or threatened. Power does not always mean being in a position of authority and can include both personal strength and the power to coerce through fear or intimidation.

As examples of bullying behaviour the Bullying and Harassment Policy for UK Parliament gives verbal abuse, abuse in writing, physical or psychological threats, practical jokes, overbearing or intimidating behaviour and ostracism. Harassment and sexual harassment are defined according to section 26 of the Equality Act 2010, which is explored further in Chapter 11. In short, harassment comprises conduct that is unwanted by its target, which is related to a protected characteristic and which has the purpose or effect of violating the target person's dignity or creating a hostile, offensive, degrading, humiliating or intimidating environment for the target. Sexual harassment is unwanted conduct of a sexual nature which has the same proscribed purpose or effect. Harassment may be committed notwithstanding that the person committing it does not intend to harass another.

ii. Outline of Procedure

13.55 Those who have suffered bullying or sexual harassment within the above definitions should call the ICGS helpline. The helpline offers two options to pursue a matter: the reporting of a concern and the provision of advice; and the submission of a formal complaint. A complaint should classify the conduct in question as either bullying or sexual harassment; the conduct cannot be investigated as both pursuant to the current regime, so a complaint must be addressed under the Bullying and Harassment Procedure or the Sexual Harassment Procedure. The complaint must be made in writing on the prescribed from, which can be found on the ICGS website.

[85] Bullying and Harassment Policy for UK Parliament (ICGS, 2022) para 4.2 and Sexual Misconduct Policy for UK Parliament (ICGS, 2022) para 4.

[86] Bullying and Harassment Policy for UK Parliament (ICGS, 2022); and Sexual Misconduct Policy for UK Parliament (ICGS, 2022).

13.56 On receipt of a complaint concerning an MP or Commons staff member, an independent investigator will undertake an initial assessment and determine whether the complaint should proceed to a formal assessment. That initial assessment will be reviewed by the Commissioner for Standards, who has oversight of all such complaints about MPs. Complainants may also ask for a review of the initial assessment. An informal resolution may be proposed before a formal assessment is made. Once an investigation is complete it falls to the relevant decision-maker to determine the complaint. Complaints against MPs are determined by the Parliamentary Commissioner for Standards and those against MPs' staff are determined by the MP who employs them; complaints against Members of the Lords or their staff are determined by the Lords' Commissioners for Standards; and complaints against staff employed by the two Houses are determined within the line management chain in question.[87]

13.57 The House of Commons' Independent Expert Panel (IEP) decides sanctions under the ICGS in respect of the scheme's operation to MPs in the Commons. The IEP also has an appellate function to hear appeals from MPs against determinations against them under the scheme, as well as to hear appeals by MPs against decisions by the Commons' Committee on Standards that a breach of the Code of Conduct has taken place. There are eight members of the IEP, including a chair. Individual cases referred to the IEP are determined by sub-panels comprising three of those members.[88] The chair of the IEP must refer to the Clerk of the House of Commons any sub-panel report which determines (or confirms on appeal) a sanction of suspension or expulsion (or any other that can only be imposed by the House itself). The Clerk must lay such a report before the House.[89]

13.58 The House itself remains in charge of deciding whether MPs should be suspended. Consequently, a rather involved procedural mechanism must be used to implement suspensions recommended by the IEP which, if imposed, could trigger a recall petition and a by-election. Where the IEP subpanel has decided to recommend a suspension as a sanction that would engage the Recall of MPs Act 2015, the chair of the IEP must send the sub-panel report to the chair, Clerk and members of the Committee on Standards. The Committee on Standards must then send a report to the House recommending a sanction equal to that recommended by the IEP.[90] The sanction decisions of the IEP may then be put to the House by a motion for implementation, in which case the MP to whom the sanction relates is unable to vote on the motion.[91]

F. Recall Petitions

13.59 If the House suspends an MP for a period of at least 10 sitting days, or 14 days in total (including non-sitting days), it will trigger a recall petition pursuant to the

[87] ICGS Bullying and Harassment Procedure (2021) and ICGS Sexual Harassment Procedure (2021).
[88] House of Commons SO 150A and 150B.
[89] House of Commons SO 150A(5)(d).
[90] House of Commons SO 150E.
[91] House of Commons SO 150D.

Recall of MPs Act 2015.[92] If the petition is signed by at least ten per cent of the eligible registered electors in the constituency to which the petition relates, the Speaker will be obliged to give notice that the MP's seat is vacated and a by-election will be triggered.[93] The outgoing MP, having lost his or her seat, is not prevented from standing again in the by-election[94] (though that eventuality will often be politically unrealistic). Note that a recall petition will also be triggered where an MP is convicted in the UK of an offence and sentenced or ordered to be imprisoned or detained, or convicted of a parliamentary expenses offence under section 10 of the Parliamentary Standards Act 2009.

13.60 The result of a recall petition may be challenged by a person who was eligible to sign it, or by the MP the petition was about, on the single ground that there was 'an undue outcome to the petition'. The challenge is made by way of a recall petition complaint in the Election Court. Where the MP brings a challenge he or she should bring the claim against the Petitions Officer. Any other person seeking to challenge the result of the recall petition should bring the claim against the MP.[95] In effect, that means that a supporter of the MP cannot challenge the petition on the MP's behalf. Any challenge must be lodged within 21 days after public notice of the outcome of the petition is given.[96] Detailed legislative provisions govern the recall procedure; in addition to the 2015 Act itself (Schedules 3–5 to which relate to financial controls), procedural rules on campaigning are set out the Recall of MPs Act 2015 (Recall Petition) Regulations 2016 and in the Political Parties, Elections and Referendums Act 2000.

V. Standards in the House of Lords

13.61 The House of Lords operates a similar standards regime to that of the Commons: there is a Code of Conduct for Members, two Commissioners for Standards (who operate independently from each other) who enforce it and a Conduct Committee, which is a committee of the Lords. Decisions about serious sanctions are taken by the House of Lords. There are nevertheless some important differences between the Commons' and Lords' regimes. First, the role of the Commissioners is not identical. The Lords' Commissioners are not usually expected to investigate matters on their own motion, but they are primary finders of fact. The Conduct Committee considers sanctions recommended by the Commissioners, but does not have the same latitude to find facts as the Parliamentary Committee on Standards. Instead, the Conduct Committee operates as an appeal committee from the findings and recommendations of the Lords Commissioners; and on appeal, may make different findings of fact to those of the Commissioners. The parameters of the sanctions that may be imposed vary slightly from those available to the Commons. Complaints of sexual harassment and bullying committed by

[92] Recall of MPs Act 2015, s 1(1) and (4)–(7).
[93] ibid ss 14(3) and 15.
[94] ibid s 1(11).
[95] Recall of MPs Act 2015 (Recall Petition) Regulations 2016, SI 2016/295, Sch 4, paras 2–4.
[96] ibid Sch 4, para 5.

Members of the Lords which are alleged to have happened when they were MPs should be dealt with by the Parliamentary Commissioner for Standards in the Commons.

A. The Lords' Code of Conduct

13.62 The Lords' Code of Conduct comprises rules relating to general principles of conduct and particular provisions regulating financial interests, as well as an obligation to comply with the Code and co-operate with the House authorities. It is, therefore, broadly similar in scope to the Commons' Code of Conduct. Members of the House of Lords are obliged to sign an undertaking to abide by the Code as part of the ceremony of taking the oath upon introduction and at the start of each Parliament.[97]

i. General Principles

13.63 The most recent iteration of the Lords' rules on conduct is set out in a document approved by the House, encompassing guidance: 'Guide to the Code of Conduct'.[98] The Lords' Code comprises General Principles and Rules of Conduct. The General Principles are especially important as they govern conduct beyond mere compliance with the rules about financial interests. The General Principles are set out, by reference to their native paragraph numbers, below:

8. By virtue of their oath, or affirmation, of allegiance, members of the House have a duty to be faithful and bear true allegiance to His Majesty The King, His heirs and successors, according to law.
9. In the performance of their parliamentary duties, members of the House shall base their actions on consideration of the public interest, and shall resolve any conflict between their personal interest and the public interest at once, and in favour of the public interest.
10. Members of the House: (a) must comply with the Code of Conduct; and (b) should act always on their personal honour in the performance of their parliamentary duties and activities.
11. Members of the House must not: (a) seek by parliamentary means to confer an exclusive benefit on an outside organisation or person in which they have a financial interest (e.g. salary, shareholding); or (b) seek to profit from membership of the House by accepting or agreeing to accept payment or other incentive or reward in return for providing parliamentary advice or services.[99]
12. Members of the House should observe the seven general principles of conduct identified by the Committee on Standards in Public Life. These principles will be taken into consideration when any allegation of breaches of the provisions in other sections of the Code is under investigation and should act as a guide to members in considering the requirement to act always on their personal honour: [the Seven Principles of Public Life set out in paragraph 13.5 above are quoted here in the native text of the Code].

[97] Code of Conduct for Members of the House of Lords (September 2023) Introduction, para 4.

[98] HL Paper 255, 18 September 2023.

[99] Note that these rules apply differently to Lords Spiritual, Ministers of the Crown and members or employees of public sector organisations. See 'Guide to the Code of Conduct', 13th edn (House of Lords, September 2023) HL Paper 255, paras 30 and 31.

13. Members of the House should observe the principles set out in the Parliamentary Behaviour Code of respect, professionalism, understanding others' perspectives, courtesy, and acceptance of responsibility. These principles will be taken into consideration when any allegation of bullying, harassment or sexual misconduct is under investigation.

ii. Rules of Conduct

13.64 The Rules of Conduct in the Lords' Code of Conduct primarily deal with the rules regulating financial interests. Members of the Lords are required to register all relevant interests in the Register of Lords' Interests and must declare any interest which is a relevant interest in respect of a matter when speaking in the House or communicating with ministers or public servants. The purpose of those obligations is to clarify the interests that might reasonably be thought to influence Members of the Lords' parliamentary actions.[100] The test to determine whether an interest is a 'relevant interest' is whether a reasonable member of the public might think that a member's actions in Parliament would be influenced by the interest. A relevant interest may be financial or non-financial.[101] Lords must also follow any rules agreed by the House in respect of financial support for Members of the House or the House's facilities.[102]

13.65 The Rules of Conduct also prohibit bullying, harassment or sexual misconduct. Members of the Lords have an obligation to treat those with whom they come into contact in the course of their parliamentary duties with respect and courtesy.[103] New Members must arrange to attend a seminar addressing bullying, harassment and sexual misconduct within three months of the Member's introduction to the House.[104]

13.66 Members of the Lords must inform the Clerk of the Parliaments within 10 working days of being notified that the Member is arrested in connection with, or charged with a criminal offence, or convicted of a criminal offence, or placed under investigation by a regulatory professional body or found to have breached that professional regulator's rules, or placed under investigation for breaching the Ministerial Code, or of being found in breach of the Ministerial Code.[105] Members who receive a sentence of imprisonment (irrespective of whether the sentence is suspended) must inform the chair of the Conduct Committee within 10 working days of the sentence being handed down. A Member is deemed to have breached the Code if he or she is sentenced to a term of imprisonment, and he or she will be referred directly to the Conduct Committee for it to recommend an appropriate sanction.[106]

[100] Code of Conduct for Members of the House of Lords (September 2023) Rules of Conduct, para 14.
[101] ibid paras 15 and 16.
[102] ibid para 14.
[103] ibid para 19.
[104] ibid para 20.
[105] ibid paras 21 and 22.
[106] ibid paras 23–26.

iii. Handling Complaints

13.67 The detailed procedure used to deal with alleged breaches of the Lords' standards rules is set out comprehensively and clearly in the 'Enforcement' section of the 'Guide to the Code of Conduct'.[107] The following sanctions may be imposed by the Conduct Committee or the House, dependent on the gravity of the breach, should the Commissioner find that a breach of the rules has taken place:[108]

i. a requirement for the member to take action to regularise his or her position;
ii. a denial of access to specific facilities or services of the House (including services that support the members' parliamentary activity) for any period of time and, if necessary, in addition to a sanction of suspension;
iii. removal from membership of select committees;
iv. a denial of access to the system of financial support for members, for any period of time and, if necessary, in addition to a suspension;
v. suspension from the House. The permitted length of the suspension depends on the date of the conduct in question. If the conduct occurred on or after 26 June 2015, or if it occurred before 26 June 2015 but was not public knowledge before then, the suspension may be for any specified period of time. However, the suspension may only be for the remainder of the Parliament if the conduct occurred before 26 June 2015 and was public knowledge before then;
vi. expulsion from the House. This sanction is available if the conduct occurred on or after 26 June 2015, or if it occurred before 26 June 2015 but was not public knowledge before then. Members cannot, therefore, be expelled from the House for historic misconduct that took place before 26 June 2015 but which was public knowledge.

VI. Standards in Scotland and Wales

13.68 The Scottish Parliament and Welsh Senedd each operate a standards regime. Many of the principles and concepts therein are common to those that govern the Westminster Parliament. The standards regimes of the devolved legislatures have the great benefit that they have not grown organically in an ad hoc way; they have a clear statutory framework that lends itself to a more straightforward navigation of the relevant rules. The relevant rules and Codes of Conduct may be accessed on the respective websites of the Scottish Parliament and the Senedd and so they are not traversed in detail here.

13.69 Standards in the Scottish Parliament are governed by various Acts of the Scottish Parliament, including the Scottish Parliamentary Standards Commissioner Act 2002, the Interests of Members of the Scottish Parliament Act 2006 and the Scottish Parliamentary Standards (Sexual Harassment and Complaints Process) Act 2021.

[107] HL Paper 255, 18 September 2023.
[108] 'Guide to the Code of Conduct', 13th edn (House of Lords, September 2023) HL Paper 255, para 190.

The Scottish Parliament operates a Code of Conduct for its MSPs[109] and Registers of financial interests. Standards in the Senedd are overseen by its Standards of Conduct Committee, which supervises the Senedd Commissioner for Standards. The role and functions of the Commissioner are set out by the National Assembly for Wales Commissioner for Standards Measure 2009. The Senedd also operates a Code of Conduct for its Members: the *Welsh Code of Conduct on the Standards of Conduct of Members of the Senedd*. The Senedd must maintain and publish a Register of Members' Interests of Members of the Senedd.[110]

VII. Concluding Comment

13.70 As noted in paragraph 13.3 above, the Codes of Conduct are subject to revision and may have been revised since this book was written. The explanations of the principles that underlie the Codes in this chapter indicate the kinds of issues MPs and other legislators should be aware of in any event. The Seven Principles of Public Life should continue to guide the behaviour of all MPs and legislators, and should interest everyone who wishes to hold them to account.

[109] The most recent of which is the 8th edn (6 May 2021).
[110] Government of Wales Act 2006, s 36 and Standing Order 2 of the Senedd.

TABLE OF CASES

ABBREVIATIONS AND ACRONYMS

Acas	Advisory, Conciliation and Arbitration Service
BUF	British Union of Fascists
CLP	Constituency Labour Party
EAT	Employment Appeal Tribunal
ECHR	European Convention on Human Rights
ECtHR	European Court of Human Rights
EHRC	Equality and Human Rights Commission
EHRR	European Human Rights Reports
EWCA	England & Wales Court of Appeal
EWHC	The High Court of Justice
GTCS	General Teaching Council for Scotland
HL	Appellate Committee of the House of Lords
HRA 1998	Human Rights Act 1998
ICGS	The Independent Complaints and Grievance Scheme (of Parliament)
ICR	Industrial Cases Reports
IEP	The Independent Expert Panel (of the House of Commons)
IRLR	Industrial Relations Law Reports
MSP	Member of the Scottish Parliament
NUS	National Union of Students
PLP	Parliamentary Labour Party
PPERA 2000	Political Parties, Elections and Referendums Act 2000
RPA 1983	Representation of the People Act 1983
TULRCA	Trade Union and Labour Relations (Consolidation) Act 1992

BIBLIOGRAPHY

Bailey, SH, *Cross on Local Government Law* (Sweet & Maxwell, looseleaf)
Bowstead and Reynolds on Agency, 23rd edn (Sweet & Maxwell, 2024)
Bryant, C, *Code of Conduct: Why We Need to Fix Parliament – and How to Do It* (Bloomsbury, 2023)
Chitty on Contracts, 33rd edn (Sweet & Maxwell, 2018)
Clayton, R and Tomlinson, H, *The Law of Human Rights* (Oxford University Press, 2009)
Erskine May: Parliamentary Practice, 25th edn (LexisNexis, 2019)
Johnston, N, 'Leadership Elections: Conservative Party' (House of Commons Library, 2019)
Kelly, R, 'Female Members of Parliament' (House of Commons Library, 7 March 2022)
Kelly, R, 'Short Money' (House of Commons Library, 8 June 2021)
Kelly, R et al, 'The Whip's Office' (House of Commons Library, 10 October 2008)
Kennerich, M, *Report on Electoral Law and Electoral Administration in Europe* (Venice Commission, 2020)
Larminie, V, '"The Parliament driver": Walter Long, party politics and the whip', *The History of Parliament online* (9 April 2019)
Lester, A et al, *Human Rights Law & Practice*, 3rd edn (LexisNexis, 2009)
Monaghan, K, *Monaghan on Equality Law*, 2nd edn (Oxford University Press, 2013)
Posner, B et al, *Schofield's Election Law* (Sweet & Maxwell, looseleaf)
Price, R and Sedgley, V, *Parker's Law and Conduct of Elections* (LexisNexis, looseleaf)
Stewart, N et al, *The Law of Unincorporated Assoications* (Oxford University Press, 2011)
Watson, C, 'House of Commons trends: How many women candidates become MPs?' (House of Commons Library, 30 October 2020)
Webb, P, *The Modern British Party System* (Sage, 2000)

INDEX

www.ingramcontent.com/pod-product-compliance
Lightning Source LLC
Chambersburg PA
CBHW061146220326
41599CB00025B/4375
* 9 7 8 1 5 0 9 9 6 9 1 5 9 *